A Spirit Wrought
By: Marie Joseph-Charles

In Dedication to:
Jessica for being the sister I always wanted
Lynne and Chrissy for being the fans I didn't know I needed
and
Adam for being a boot in my butt, a pain in my ass, and because he said he didn't understand why people dedicate books.

© 2021
ISBN: 978-1-0880-0570-5

The Book of Solomon

I then asked of the demon if there were females among them. And when he told me that there were, I said that I desired to see them. So Beelzebub went off at high speed, and brought unto me Onoskelis, that had a very pretty shape, and the skin of a fair-hued woman; and she tossed her head.

And when she was come, I said to her: "Tell me who art thou?" But she said to me: "I am called Onoskelis, a spirit wrought ..., lurking upon the earth. There is a golden cave where I lie. But I have a place that ever shifts. At one time I strangle men with a noose; at another, I creep up from the nature to the arms. But my most frequent dwelling-places are the precipices, caves, ravines. Oftentimes, however, do I consort with men in the semblance of a woman, and above all with those of a dark skin. For they share my star with me; since they it is who privily or openly worship my star, without knowing that they harm themselves, and but whet my appetite for further mischief. For they wish to provide money by means of memory, but I supply a little to those who worship me fairly."

And I, Solomon, questioned her about her birth, and she replied: "I was born of a voice untimely, the so-called echo of a man's ordure dropped in a wood."

And I said to her: "Under what star dost thou pass?" And she answered me: "Under the star of the full moon, for the reason that the moon travels over most things." Then I said to her: "And what angel is it that frustrates thee?" And she said to me: "He that in thee is reigning."

- The Testament of Solomon

Part I

Illinois

Three in the Morning

I wake up at three in the morning. I never even need to look at the clock. I always wake up at three in the morning. It has been happening since the day I was born and will continue until the day I die. It is called The Devil's Hour. At three in the morning, the wall between our world and theirs is cracked just a little and demons can reach through to caress our sleeping minds, causing a sudden wakening. I, unfortunately, am more susceptible to these attacks than others.

I am a Holy Child. My birth was graced by God himself and I resent him for it. I was born on April fifteenth, 1984. Palm Sunday. The Holiest day of the Catholic year. A dove- The Holy Spirit himself (as I'm told) - landed on the hospital room windowsill to bear witness. My mother said she knew right then that she had to raise me to do the Lord's work because I would be of vital importance to humanity. She even said the light of God shown through the stained glass window of the church when I was baptized. As I grew older, I was sure this was an exaggeration, or at least a figment of her imagination. But I am a Holy Child nonetheless.

There aren't many of us Holy Children and we prefer anonymity. It's not difficult to maintain. After all, who would believe us? Speaking out about being blessed by The Holy Trinity makes us sound like we are extremists, cult members, or that we should be locked in a padded room. So we prefer to live in the shadows. To be a Holy Child sounds like something wonderful; as if we are capable of conversing with the angels themselves. But, there is a dark side to this 'gift.' We are beacons to demons. They seek us out and torment us. They try to keep us distracted from whatever holy quest we are supposed to embark on in our lives. So we try not to draw attention to ourselves. And we wake... at three in the morning... every slumber.

Some of us grow up trying to avoid these disturbances and attempt to lead somewhat normal lives. We do things like work third shift so we can't be woken at three or resort to heavy sedatives. But, without fail, the demons tickling the backs of our brains will get our attention somehow. Most of us give up hope of normalcy after a while. What's the point in trying to be normal if the hassle is only going to drive you more mad than you already feel? I've seen snippets of others' woes spilled out on the internet in chat rooms and support groups. Those of us who do not choose to end our lives in an insomnia-induced mania move forward and accept that this is what our lives are. I don't know how many of the others understand what is happening to them or why; as I said, we prefer anonymity and I've never spoken to another like myself.

    I, on the other hand, know exactly what is happening. My mother went out of her way to make sure I understood the importance of my birth. She did name me Grace for Christ's sake (no pun or blasphemy intended). I don't really know anything about my father. He is a topic that she has refused to discuss my entire life. In truth, I think she likes to pretend that I'm the result of an immaculate conception. Sometimes I feel like the only thing preventing her from claiming I'm the next messiah is the fact that I'm female. She even tried to get me preferential treatment at school and in the church when I was little. She was a helicopter mom before that was a phrase and everyone believed she was a special kind of insane.

    I grew up in a modest ranch farmhouse on a quiet Midwestern street in Illinois. It wasn't a large farm; only about four acres were left as the original property was divvied up and sold to create our neighborhood. We had a large vegetable garden, fruit trees, and some chickens. There was usually laundry on the line out back in the summer and baskets of apples in the fall. We could see our neighbors but never really hear them. Most of them avoided us. My mother was the "crazy woman" in the yellow house who listened to too much Yanni. She was always asking the neighbors what they've done for God lately and trying to organize a neighborhood prayer group. Many of them went to our church and when she tried to organize a carpool, they changed from morning mass to afternoon. Most of all, I think they avoided us because of me. They didn't want to hear how wonderful I was and how important I was going to be to the world.

My Uncle James told me that my mother had been normal once. She wasn't always so devout or raving. When she was a teenager (not long before I was born) she was a little on the wild side. She was pretty with blonde hair and a free spirit. She would sneak out to parties and get caught with boys. Despite her devil-may-care ways, she studied hard with dreams of being a nurse someday. Then, as he puts it, one day her coin flipped and she was crazy. He said he thinks it had to do with the sudden death of their parents (the grandparents I never met) as the events occurred close together.

"She was always a few cents short of a nickel," he once told me, "but after the fire, I wasn't sure she could even find a penny."

As I got older, she became slightly less crazy when she started taking some new medication. She certainly wasn't normal, but definitely more tolerable. Since her dad was the one who intentionally started the fire that was meant to kill them all (Momma and James got out safely), I wondered how much of what was wrong with her was the PTSD and how much was genetic psychosis.

I loved my Uncle James. He was the father I didn't know I was missing and the one truly stable adult in my childhood. He was a wonderful and wise man with a heart of pure gold. When I was a little girl, I would spend every Sunday after church at his house. His wife, Aunt Catherine, would make us sandwiches and cookies for lunch. With them, I felt like I was just another kid. They never talked about my importance to the church and they let me be me. We would usually spend the day in our outdoor classroom (the picnic table on the patio) or rainy days were spent in the potting shed. He would teach me about gardening, hard work, nature, and life. He was full of wisdom and loved to share it. He and Catherine had wanted a big family with a lot of children but my cousin, Jacob, was their miracle child.

Jacob was two years older than me. Catherine and James had fawned over him when he was young and he became spoiled. Like most spoiled things, he eventually became outright rotten. He would yell at my aunt and uncle whenever he didn't get his way and after Catherine died, he became almost uncontrollable. He and I bickered constantly throughout our entire lives. He hated listening to my mom talk about how special I was and that hostility was further fueled by his jealousy over how his father doted on me. He didn't see the fact that I only got to spend one day a week- plus holidays- with his father while he had him all to himself every day, all year round. He would eventually come to live with my mother and me for a little while but that didn't make us any closer.

I wanted to get along with Jacob. I was a fairly lonely child. Unfortunately, because of my mother's persistent presence, I had very few friends. She had to approve of anyone who talked to me and the tests she put them through were typically rigorous and unnecessary. I was both alienated and humiliated. The girls at St. Teresa's saw me as a freak. While they participated in choir and volleyball after school, I had to go to the church for Latin classes with Sister Rose, Father Harold, and a boy who didn't attend my school. I ate lunch alone. I sat alone on the bus. The only reason anyone worked with me on group projects in class was that they had to.

I'm sure my appearance didn't help with the matter. I wasn't one of the "pretty" little girls. I was exceptionally small my whole life. Even as an adult, I topped out at four feet plus eleven inches tall and despite my healthy appetite, I couldn't seem to put on weight. Until I was a teenager, I had frizzy, reddish hair and thick, heavy-rimmed plastic glasses. I wasn't exactly picked on for my appearance, but I do believe it kept me further isolated at school.

When I was a little girl I went to bed night after night praying to God to make me normal. I didn't want to be special. I didn't want to be ugly. As I grew older, pleas for help turned to cursing him for making me that way.

The boy across the street, Aaron Akakios, was my one constant companion. School was miserable but I looked forward to coming home every day and spending time with him. He was the one thing that kept my life from being utterly abysmal.

Aaron

They say that God brings people into your life because you need them. I don't know if that's true, but I definitely needed Aaron in my life. He was a chubby little boy around two years older than me. He had dark hair that was never brushed. His eyes were the most unique shade of brown; almost the color of maple syrup but obscured by thick eyelashes, heavy eyebrows, and wire-rimmed glasses. The children in our neighborhood bullied him mercilessly until one of his sisters stood up for him. While it was one of the most degrading moments of his childhood, she probably saved him from further humiliation at their hands instead of hers. His parents tried to encourage him to play sports but he wasn't athletic. He was too overweight, asthmatic, and nearsighted. They tried to get him into afterschool clubs but the other kids shunned him there too. Public school children were no more accepting than those at my Catholic school.

He was the youngest of five children. All four of the girls were born within six years but he trailed behind at four years younger than the youngest sister. They were doted on by their mother and she made no effort to hide the fact that, while she loved her son, she felt no connection to him. Her daughters were her treasures.

Elizabeth Akakios was constantly buying herself, or her daughters, new clothes, shoes, and anything else that was the height of fashion. If she saw it on the home shopping channel, she had to have it. She wasn't used to the more rural life that our little town had to offer. She was from a big city in Michigan and hated that the nearest chain stores were more than twenty minutes away. Still, she and her daughters enjoyed the finer things in life.

I don't remember David Akakios very well. He was an engineer at the plant that employed most of our town's residents. He had moved the family to our sleepy little corner of the world for the work. He was gone for long hours and frequently out of town altogether. My most vivid memory is of him taking Aaron and me to get ice cream in his white 4Runner. He turned the music up loud and we laughed as we bounced around without seatbelts on.

Aaron's sisters mostly viewed him as a nuisance. They took their cues from their mother and regarded him with little less than disdain. Melanie, the oldest, believed she was a princess and was spoiled unashamedly by Elizabeth. She had started wearing makeup and finding an interest in fashion when she was around eight years old and Elizabeth made sure her daughter's wardrobe was always in vogue. She delighted in tricking Aaron into doing her chores or otherwise treating him as a servant.

Stephanie was a soccer star. She was always up before the sun and well after so she could run drills, practice, and balance her social life. Her friends were all athletic and, to their credit, had tried to get Aaron involved. They found their efforts futile, however, and turned to ignoring him.

Tiffany was a dancer. She had seen The Nutcracker when she was young and became enamored with the elegance and beauty of it. She dreamed of being the graceful ballerina on stage with all eyes on her. She and Stephanie seemed to have little in common but were almost always together. Both of their talents centered around precision, agile movements, and an athlete's diet so they could often be found helping each other exercise and eating separately from the rest of the family.

Last was Nicole. She was closest in age to Aaron but that was the extent of their commonalities. She was a snob with no real interests other than being sarcastic. Much to her parents' horror, she had pierced her eyebrow herself when she was thirteen. This act of defiance was done more for the attention and to set herself apart from the rest of the females in the pack than the desire for the piercing. Despite her snobbery, she was the one who stood up for Aaron the most, and even though she refused to admit any real emotional attachment to him, she took the best care of her little brother.

Aaron's alienation in his family was further fueled by the fact that his father worked long hours to support such a large family. There was no male influence to guide him or protect him from his sisters or give him the attention he was lacking from his mother. I remember David as a good man. He was timid at times but he had a good heart. I believe he would have been there more for his son if it had been possible.

Call it fate or whatever you will, but Aaron and I needed each other in a way that I don't believe our parents realized. I think the only reason my mother approved of our friendship was that, even though he wasn't Catholic, his family wasn't protestant or atheist and that was good enough to pass that part of her inquisition. His parents were also the only people in the neighborhood who didn't cross the street when they saw her coming. Uncle James may have been influential in her decision to let us be friends as well. He was constantly chivying her that I needed to have friends and I think she allowed me to spend time with Aaron just to placate her brother.

Whatever the reason may be, that was the most important decision she made in my childhood.

The day Aaron and I met is a memory that I have always cherished. It was after church on a hot, sunny Sunday when I was about four years old. Momma was pestering Father Harold about allowing me to take my holy sacraments early since... well... it was me. I had wandered over to the little space between the church and the school that was affectionately referred to as 'Mary's Garden.' It was a round courtyard overseen by a six-foot-tall statue of the Virgin Mother. She stood with her arms open, patiently awaiting an embrace. Her face was soft and peaceful. A host of flowering plants bloomed in all directions, spreading from her feet and cement benches stood in beds of gravel so anyone would feel welcome to bask in her presence.

It was a sweltering August day. I wore long sleeves and a long dress because I had to live as a picture of modesty. I felt like I was cooking in my skin. It was far too hot to sit on cement benches that had been baking in the sun so I squatted over the concrete walkway and picked through the gravel. As I busied myself looking for pretty pebbles, I listened to my mother grilling the other parishioners about the new family that was moving in across the street from us. Father Harold had made his excuses and managed to slip back into the church.

A boy I had never seen before squatted next to me. "Hi."

"Hi."

"I'm Aaron."

"Grace."

"What are you doing?"

"Looking for pretty rocks." I didn't even look up at him.

Looking back, I was being exceptionally rude but at the time I had all the same social abilities as the rocks I was picking through.

He was quiet and seemed to be contemplating the small collection I had piled on the bench.

He suddenly reached foreword. "You need this one. It's pretty like you."

He had pressed a smooth, clear, quartz pebble that was not quite cone-shaped into my hand. I finally looked up at him and smiled just in time for my mother to grab my arm and rip me off the ground. I dropped the pebble.

"Ladies don't squat and they certainly don't play in the dirt!" She scolded.

She dragged me towards the car. I had thought, as usual, she was keeping me from making a friend. I was so happy I was wrong. He was the new neighbor. The family my mother had been inquiring about was next door to the church at the community center and he had wandered over when he saw me playing in the rocks.

Two days later, a moving van appeared in the driveway of the house across the street from mine. I watched the family unload and direct the movers. I had never seen so many things and couldn't imagine how they could get it all to fit in such a little two-story house. I spent the better part of the day in the backyard, peaking through the fence at them. The boy from the church caught sight of me and waved. That was the beginning of it all.

So it was just us. We were united as outcasts. When we were little, we would dig up rocks in his backyard and pretend they were artifacts from a long, lost civilization. I can't recall how we came up with that game; maybe because of how we met. All I knew was that it was fun and my mother was always disappointed when I came home dirty. Her disappointment was only more reason to play the game.

When we were old enough to leave the yard, the creek behind my house presented an entirely new world. I would have never dreamt of spending so much time amongst the mud and muck if he had not introduced me to it. Coming from a house of strict rules and cleanliness, it was almost a world of defiance. My mother had, of course, protested. She would scold me and pile on chores to give me less time to spend with Aaron. Over time, I think she realized it was a fruitless endeavor and, with a little encouragement from Uncle James, let me have that one, small joy.

As Aaron and I grew older, we would do our homework in the backyard on sunny days with Momma's all-seeing eye watching through the kitchen window. We would try to study at his house but it was usually chaotic and there was the risk of a random soccer ball landing in the middle of our work. Many times we would ride our bikes up to the library to study without scrutiny or hide in the creek.

I can say with certainty that that goofy, bespectacled boy was the one thing that kept me sane.

The Holy Mother

When I was around six years old, I was given the illustrious honor of playing Mary in the church's Christmas play and live nativity scene. Thanks to my mother's aggravating persistence, I was the youngest Mary in the church's history. On December twenty-third I would go on stage in the school's auditorium and represent our Holy Mother in front of more than a hundred people at ten in the morning. The performance would be followed by a quick lunch and help move some of the props. Then at two in the afternoon I would get to spend four hours in a shack behind the church, kneeling in hay while holding a Cabbage Patch doll, surrounded by some borrowed animals from Mr. Kirkbeck's farm.

I watched the video cassette of the previous year's performance on repeat until the VCR got hot. Nancy Barnes had been thirteen when she played Mary the previous year. I felt inadequate and feared negative judgment from the community and the church. I studied every move she made and mimicked it carefully. I said the lines with her while the video played on the TV in the background. As I recited carefully, I watched my own facial expressions in the mirror. I remember failure staring back at me. I hated the idea that all eyes in the parish were going to be on me. In truth, I had very little actual stage time or lines, but as the bearer of our Lord and Savior, that play was just as much about me as it was about that doll.

Jacob's job was to sell tickets to the parishioners and people outside of the church. He took his duties far less seriously than I was taking mine. He whined constantly about going door-to-door in the chilly Illinois winter so they set him up with a table in the grocery store so he could guilt people as they were leaving with their food.

December twenty-second of nineteen-ninety was a Saturday. At six in the evening, it was T-minus sixteen hours until my big debut. Uncle James had picked up Jacob from his last attempt at ticket sales at the grocery store and dropped him off at our house so he could 'spend some time with family.' The truth was that Aunt Catherine was still at work and Uncle James had Christmas presents that still needed wrapping without worrying about Jacob trying to peek.

The sun had long gone down. It was cold enough to lose feeling in your face if you stood outside too long. Momma was inside making dinner and listening to her Christmas music on full blast. I was in the driveway with the car's headlights turned on and aiming at me as I practiced my lines for the ten-thousandth time. I was willing to withstand the cold in exchange for the impression of having spotlights on me on stage. We had had dress rehearsals in the auditorium and the only thing they accomplished was the realization that I was more terrified than I thought. Despite being bundled in thermal underwear, my heaviest coat, two pairs of gloves, a hat, scarf, and earmuffs, I couldn't feel my fingers or nose when Uncle James's beloved Crown Vic pulled into the driveway and Jacob got out.

Uncle James waved at me as he backed out of the drive. Jacob huffed as he walked towards the house.

"What are you doing out here?" he asked.

"Practicing."

"You've been practicing for a month."

"I want to be good."

He huffed again. "You only get to be in the play 'cause Aunt Janice wouldn't stop bugging Father Harold."

"Momma said Mary should be played by someone special like me. I'm glad I get to do it."

I was lying through my frozen teeth. I wasn't at all glad to be playing the Virgin Mother. I had resolved myself to the lie, however, and I would ask for forgiveness at bedtime prayers.

"You aren't special. Your mom is just nuts."

"You take that back!" I shouted in his face.

He was easily a foot taller than me and I knew I wasn't threatening, but in that moment, I didn't care.

"No. Your crazy mom is the only thing that makes you special!"

I was fuming. "You're just mad 'cause the only thing anyone thought you would be good at is sitting on your butt at the grocery store."

I didn't see it coming and I don't remember how he hit me. I think he shoved me with both hands. I know he didn't punch me. I do know my feet left the ground and I hit the cold pavement with a thud. I looked up at him with tears in my eyes.

The next thing I remember, I saw red (literal red) streaking up my driveway and slam into Jacob. He hit the front of the house with a hard thud before crumpling to the ground.

"Pick on someone your own size!" Aaron screamed at him.

The front door swung open and my mother stepped out onto the porch.

"What are you kids doing out here?" She looked around wide-eyed. "Stop playing so rough! Jacob, get off the ground and come inside. You too, Grace."

She glared at Aaron before turning and going back into the house.

Jacob pushed himself onto his feet. He straightened his coat- quite aggressively- as he scowled at Aaron and went inside.

Aaron helped me to my feet.

"Are you okay?" he asked as he looked me over.

My glasses were askew and there was a little tear in my coat but I was otherwise unscathed.

"Yeah. I'm alright," I replied.

He gave me one more look of concern before he nodded and went back across the street. I walked back into the house and started peeling off my layers. I wasn't quite sure what had happened. Where had Aaron even come from?

We ate dinner in silence. Jacob and I glowered at each other from across the table. Momma seemed oblivious to the whole incident as well as the tension in the room.

The next morning, I felt sick as I donned my blue frock backstage. Cassie Dorsey, the eighth-grader in charge of costumes, was frantically pinning and duct-taping my outfit to fit me. It was the hand-me-down that was used every year and was meant for a normal-sized teenager, not a bite-sized first grader.

I listened as Father Harold welcomed the community and gave his traditional miniature sermon. The crowd applauded and the boy playing the Archangel Gabriel stepped out on stage. My heart moved further and further into my throat as I watched the other kids go out on stage and return. I nearly jumped out of my skin when Judd Hughes, playing Joseph, put his hand on my shoulder to lead me out on stage.

"You ready?" he asked.

I shook my head. I couldn't even get the word 'no' to come out of my throat.

He laughed and half pushed, half pulled me out on stage. I almost lost the pillow they had shoved under my costume to give me a pregnant belly. As he gave his monologue, I looked out at the audience. It felt like one swelling monster with a thousand eyes that were all staring at me. I couldn't breathe.

"My dearest, Mary, it seems the stable shall be home this night." Judd motioned offstage.

That was my cue. I started shaking. He nodded at me gently. I took a deep breath. The words came out shaky and probably inaudible to most of the audience.

"Oh, Joseph. God will keep us warm and safe no matter the roof that covers us." I did it.

The curtain drew for a scenery change. Father Harold hugged me.

"You did great." He smiled.

I looked around as everyone scurried to change the stage from a desert into a barn. I had done it. No one cared how bad my performance was. There were too many other things to worry about.

I pulled the pillow out of my shirt, grabbed my doll, and went into the next act feeling far bolder. I delivered my lines with more strength and almost as well as I had practiced. I surprised myself entirely but the realization that I didn't need to be perfect gave me courage.

After the play, we moved some of the props out to the shack with the animals. The church ordered pizza for everyone. The older kids let me eat with them, though I contributed very little to the conversation. It was the first time I had actually felt like part of a group and it felt amazing. It would be years before I felt that accepted again, but I held on to the feeling for all it was worth.

After lunch, Joseph, Gabriel, the Magi, and I all went out to the shack. Gabriel lost a lot of his magic and presence after about an hour. He was allergic to the hay bales (or maybe the donkey) and kept sneezing. I giggled to myself a little.

Streams of people came through to gawk at us and feed carrots and treats to the animals. I heard Mrs. Larkin make a joke about me not being much bigger than Jesus as she walked by. Her daughter, Stacy, was supposed to be Mary until I had usurped the post. It was boring and I wanted nothing more than to go to my warm house, wrap up in a blanket, and read. My one bit of excitement was when Aaron came by with two of his sisters. He was all smiles and waved at me excitedly as they pushed him along.

At last, after it was all over, I tuned out my mother's criticisms of my performance in the car on the way home and dwelled on what a wonderful day it had turned out to be.

Communion

My first communion was not the turning point of my childhood it had been intended to be. My mother had spent my entire life pressing the importance of the sacraments on me. It almost seems funny how she had ignored her own failure to marry and the fact that her near-messiah daughter was a bastard. She had tried to convince the church to allow me to take the Eucharist early, but St. Teresa's insisted that I do it with my classmates. When that failed, she tried to persuade them to move my confirmation to immediately follow my first communion, but they dug in their heels on that too. To Father Harold's credit, he tried to help me be normal but he tired of fighting her constantly and agreed to allow my confirmation at ten years old instead of thirteen. A small victory.

As a Holy Child, the sacraments were more important for me than any other child (in my mother's eyes, at least) and she made sure to constantly impress that importance on me. I didn't fully understand what she meant but being permitted to imbibe Christ sounded like something paramount.

I had spent months leading up to the communion ceremony studying a workbook that the church had provided for each of us. I was only seven but could read much better than my peers and found the book boring. I was chided for doodling in the margins instead of using it as intended. Aaron thought it was funny. Once a week I went to confession. I didn't have much to confess as I was under the constant eye of my mother so Father Harold would tell me to keep up the good work.

I'm ashamed to admit, all of the buildup eventually started to make an impression on me. I found myself becoming more excited as the big day drew closer. I didn't enjoy the associated activities, but it was hard not to get caught up in the thrill of it all. It was all Momma would talk about at dinner and with Aunt Catherine. All of the children in my second-grade class practiced walking in procession and exactly what we were supposed to do and say. We were God's little soldiers marching in line.

The other girls excitedly chattered about their new dresses and veils and the boys talked about how big their parties were going to be. I wanted very much to be a part of all of those conversations but I was an outsider in many ways. We couldn't afford a pretty new dress and shoes for me to display and my family was small so my party would be meager in comparison. Even if I had had fancy clothes and a big family, I knew my peers would never let me join in their gossip. I only had Aaron to share my little bit of excitement with but that was enough for me.

My mother spent the day before excitedly bustling around the house. She made sure everything was spotless and even baked a cake. For reasons unknown to me, I had to weed the garden, mow the yard, and even muck out the chicken coop in preparation for guests. Uncle James wasn't going in the chicken coop but I set to the tasks with fervor and a little help from Aaron.

"So, what exactly happens for communion?" He was fighting a particularly stubborn dandelion in the back flowerbed.

"Don't you have a communion?"

"My parents do. I think. I don't know how it works. We only go to church on Christmas with grandma and grandpa."

I thought for a moment. I wasn't sure how to explain transubstantiation at seven years old.

I gave it my best try. "Father Harold is going to say a prayer over the bread and wine and turn it into the flesh and blood of Jesus. Then we eat him and thank him for giving himself up for us."

Aaron stopped fighting with the weeds and looked at me. "You *eat* Jesus?"

"Yes."

He looked thoughtful for a moment. "You *want* to do this?"

"Momma and Father Harold say it's important and all the other kids want to do it too."

"That doesn't sound right…" He seemed a little concerned.

Later that evening, after dinner, my mother took me by the hands and sat me on the couch. She was smiling wide and almost bouncing as she walked. I had never seen her look so excited.

"Grace. Tomorrow is a very important day and I want to make sure we do it right. I have a surprise for you."

She disappeared down the hall and into her bedroom. She reemerged with a white dress on a hanger. It was almost entirely floral-patterned lace with short, puffy sleeves, and pearl buttons up the back with a ribbon around the middle. Presented with the dress was a pair of little white gloves and a lacy veil. This was the type of dress that all the other girls were so excited about and now I could share in the excitement. She could read my face and welled with pride. I cried a little.

I lay awake for most of the night while staring at the dress hanging on the back of my door. Everything would be different after tomorrow. I didn't know how, but everything would be different.

My alarm woke me with a start the next morning. I jumped out of bed and put on my chore clothes. My mother had started seeing a new doctor when I was around five years old and had relaxed some of her more stringent rules; this meant I could finally wear pants for things like chores and I loved it. I bounded out the back door to feed the chickens and check for eggs. When I returned to the house, my mother stood in the kitchen with her mouth agape.

"Grace! We don't have time for you to be playing with the chickens! You have to get ready for the ceremony! Go get cleaned up immediately."

I was confused. I had tried to abscond from my chores in the past and been berated for it. I did as I was told, however, and went to shower.

After I was sufficiently clean, I stood in my underwear and admired the dress on the back of the door for a few more minutes. I couldn't believe something so pretty was mine. I was painfully careful when putting it on. I didn't want to wrinkle it or tear the lace. Momma came in and wrangled my frizzy hair into a braid and tucked the veil into my head. My chunky glasses pushed it out away from my ears a little but I didn't pay very much attention to it. I gently slid the gloves over my hands and stood looking at myself in the mirror. My mother stood behind me with her hands on my shoulders. She was practically glowing. I took it all in and smiled. Looking back on it, I looked much like an over-frosted cupcake, but back then, it was the most beautiful thing I had ever worn.

We were the first ones to the church and I couldn't sit still. I kept fidgeting and twisting as the other children and congregates filed in. I sat alone in the pew, twiddling my thumbs, and kicking my legs as my classmates greeted their friends and showed off their new clothes before finding their assigned order in the first two rows. I didn't have anyone to share the excitement with, but it was in the air all around me and I couldn't help but feel it.

Father Harold's sermon was particularly longwinded. It was a special day, after all, and it seemed to be an eternity before our moment arrived. When given our cue, we stood and filed out in a row. We had practiced this a dozen times in the weeks leading up to now and I felt positively electrified. I don't know what I expected to happen.

I cupped my hands in front of me and held them up.

Father Harold held up the wafer. "The body of Christ."

"Amen." I could hardly contain myself.

This was it. Everything for the last seven years had been leading up to this point. My mother had so much honor and expectation riding on this very moment. He placed the wafer in my hand and when I placed it on my tongue… nothing happened. I knew the skies weren't going to part or angels appear as my mother believed but I felt absolutely nothing. I stepped over to Mrs. Anders with the wine and took my sip. It was one of the most vile things I had ever tasted. Yet still, nothing happened. I blessed myself as I took my seat back in the pew. Nothing at all had happened. I didn't feel the light of God. I didn't gain a new Holy Sight. I was just me even though I had just eaten a cracker and had my first taste of alcohol. I was devastated.

At the end of mass, Father Harold had us all stand and turn to the congregation to present us. I looked back a few rows and saw my mother overflowing with pride. Next to her stood Uncle James and Aunt Catherine with Jacob between them; presumably to keep him out of trouble. They were both smiling wide. I felt a sudden shame as if I had disappointed them somehow. Next to Catherine, in a clean white shirt and red tie, stood Aaron. I still remember how messy his hair was and that his glasses were crooked, but he had cleaned his face and come to be there for me.

When we were dismissed, the other kids all ran to their parents as I held my head down in chagrin and walked to my family. Uncle James gave me a big bear hug that lifted me off the ground. It made me feel a little better. Aunt Catherine hugged me and kissed the top of my head and Jacob gave me a thumbs up out of pure obligation.

I turned to Aaron. "You came?"

He smiled. "You said it's important. My mom brought me. You look like a bride."

I think I blushed a little.

"Come on, Aaron. You're riding with us." Uncle James put his hand on Aaron's shoulder and escorted him out to the car.

We all returned home to a roast beef lunch and cake my mother had prepared. She presented me with a little figurine to commemorate the special day. James and Catherine officially gave me a necklace but Uncle James slipped me a twenty-dollar bill when no one was looking. Jacob spent most of the afternoon pouting in the corner because all attention was on me instead of him.

I still couldn't understand what all of the fuss was over. I didn't know *what* was supposed to happen that day; only that *something* was supposed to happen but nothing did. The nagging, empty feeling would stick with me.

After Aaron had been called to come home, I sat on the edge of the patio in the backyard. Uncle James came out to join me.

"What's wrong, Kiddo?" He asked. "This party is for you, you know."

My lower lip started to shake. "I'm sorry Uncle James." I couldn't stop the tears.

"Whoa. What's all this about? Sorry for what?"

"I'm not really special. I ate the bread and drank the wine and said the prayers but I'm still just me."

He seemed stunned for a minute.

"What did you think was going to happen?" He rubbed my back to try to calm me.

"I don't know. Momma said I'm special and today was important. I thought something was supposed to happen."

"Grace, you are special. And never mind your mother and how she feels about all this. She's just… passionate. Today was a ceremony made up by men. A rite of passage. That's all church is. It's a building with ceremony and tradition. It can't change you and you can't let it define you."

I leaned my head into his chest and calmed my tears. "But I'm a Holy Child."

"You and a thousand different other kids. You aren't the only one born on Palm Sunday or any other holy day. You are you, Grace. And you can't let anyone or anything tell you who or what you are. The church is a place to go to seek direction if you feel lost. But God and Lucifer and even angels and demons are all around us. We may not see them, but they are there. They aren't just confined to brick walls. God doesn't care where you are on Sunday; he cares who you are every day. All the holy water and cheap wine in the world won't change who you are."

    I sat there feeling safe with his arm around me. The church was just a building. The ceremony was just a ritual. There would be more sacraments. More rituals. But they were just motions to go through as my ancestors had done for almost two-thousand years. I am me. I am Grace Nightingale and nothing was going to change that.

    I mulled Uncle James's words around in my head for days. It was a lot for a seven-year-old to comprehend. My first communion had changed me; just not in the way anyone had intended.

Catherine's Ascent

Childhood wasn't a blissful time, but I was content. I had a strict routine of schoolwork and church. My best friend broke the monotony of it all with silly games and a listening ear. Sundays after church were family time with Uncle James and Aunt Catherine. Life was tranquil for the most part. All sense of comfort and ease came to a grinding halt when I was around eight years old. A part of my childhood ended the night Aunt Catherine made her ascent to Heaven.

It was about six or seven in the evening on a Wednesday. My mother was in a tizzy about something as she cooked and I was working on my schoolwork at the kitchen table. Nothing seemed to be out of the ordinary. The phone rang and she answered as usual. I remember hearing a frantic voice coming through the other end of the phone and watching her face turn from consternation to horror. She turned off supper without putting any of the food away. She ushered me into the car while muttering incoherently. I realized something was horribly wrong as we pulled into the parking lot of the emergency room.

I was uncomfortable at the hospital. I wasn't disturbed by being surrounded by sick or injured people and their families in the waiting room. My problem was the walls. They were white. Not off-white or a little grey. They were pure white. It was the kind of white you envision when you think of heaven. I felt like the hospital was just a place to prepare people to be ushered into the afterlife by preparing them for the blinding white at the end of the tunnel before they reach the gates of paradise. The more I thought about it, the more it upset me.

I sat in the putrid pink chair in the waiting area and tried to focus on something other than the walls. A little girl with blonde curls sat on her mother's lap. She was pale and looked clammy. Her mother held her lips against the girl's febrile head as she gently tried to rock her and comfort her. A man sat with an ice pack against a knot on his forehead while his companion repeatedly apologized and looked like he might cry. The big tube TV on a chest of drawers was snowy but I could just make out a new episode of *Empty Nest*.

Uncle James paced anxiously. He and Catherine had just picked up Jacob from baseball practice when she lost consciousness on the front porch. As he paced, he would regularly pause and cast a watchful eye down the hall where they had taken her. I listened as his words swung wildly between prayer and blaming himself.

Jacob seemed completely oblivious to the seriousness of the situation. He played on the floor with a deck of cards and raided the vending machine for dinner. He would periodically flick my ear or kick his empty soda can at me. Whenever he got bored, he became exceedingly annoying and I was a welcome target whenever available.

Momma stayed by the pay-phone to field calls to Catherine's family. They were mostly in Indiana and Tennessee and trying to find out if they needed to come to see her.

I remember hearing her repeatedly say, "I don't know. It's bad. I don't know."

Her face was drawn, and tired. She had long forgotten about being hungry and I didn't want to disrupt her with complaints of pangs in my stomach. She had more important things to tend to.

At a little after ten in the evening, the doctor emerged from the hallway. His face was long and his eyes were sad. I knew what he was going to say before the words even came out of his mouth. He announced a bleed in her brain had killed her. My Aunt Catherine was gone.

Uncle James fell to the ground in tears. My heart broke with his. I think the whole hospital heard his sobs. The image of him on his knees in the hospital begging God to give her back left a permanent scar on my soul. My mother tried to settle him but he was inconsolable. I sat in a chair hugging my knees and crying into my skirt. Jacob just stared blankly at his father. I'm not sure if he was shocked at the news of his mother, the reaction of his father, or completely numb to the situation.

Aunt Catherine's funeral was beautiful. Relatives from all over and half of our town came to pay their respects. Our tiny church was bursting at the seams but all were welcome. She had left such a positive permanent mark on everyone who met her and now she was gone. When I'd taken my turn to pay my respects, I remember thinking how plastic she looked. The funeral home had done their best with her but it still wasn't quite her. Despite her doll-like appearance, she seemed at peace. Jacob didn't speak a word throughout the church sermon. I don't believe he truly grasped the gravity of what had happened until he saw his mother in a box.

After that night in the hospital, Uncle James wasn't the fun, smiling, or jovial man he had been. He started to drink more and I was allowed to spend fewer and fewer Sundays with him. He stopped attending church and had taken to denouncing God in anger. He frequently left Jacob unattended while he sat with a bottle to ease the pain. By my eleventh birthday, my mother decided he was only partially welcome on holidays; he was still family after all.

Jacob handled his mother's death the only way he knew how; by becoming completely out of control. His temper tantrums and defiance of his father became more unmanageable. He started stealing and acting out at school. I hadn't truly realized just how much Catherine's loving touch had kept him under control all those years. Eventually, several years after her death, his behavior and unruliness would become more than Uncle James could handle and Jacob would come to live with my mother and me. The move should have brought us closer. We should have been more like siblings. That was not to be. He resented staying with us and I hated how he treated Momma and me.

Just Breathe

"Gracie, you have to see what I found!"

Aaron was always a little excitable, even at eleven years old. That Saturday, he was eagerly tugging on my arm and pulling me towards the woods. I was tired. I had stayed up late reading a forbidden book that I had checked out of the school library and hidden in my closet. I was grateful that St. Teresa's librarian didn't feel the same way about fantasy books that my mother did. I had gotten up early to feed chickens, check the tomato plants, tidied my room, and made lunch. By the time momma had released me from my duties, it was early afternoon and I wanted a nap. Aaron had found me dozing off with my back against a tree in the backyard while pretending to read the church newsletter.

"I'm tired, Aaron. What's so important?"

I grumbled as he pulled me along the creek bed, through the sticker bushes, and into a meadow. He was almost bouncing as he parted some tall weeds and revealed a tiny spotted fawn laying in a patch of tamped-down grass.

"It's just like Bambi." He smiled.

"What's 'Bambi?'" I asked.

He looked at me and blinked as if a foreign language had just come out of my mouth before he returned his focus back to the deer.

"I wonder where the mom is," He finally said.

"I don't know but we should probably leave it alone," I advised.

"What if a bobcat finds it? It can't protect itself."

His brow wrinkled like it always did when he was worried.

"Well, you can't take it home to protect it. You don't know how to take care of it," I pointed out.

He sighed. "I know."

He didn't leave it alone, just as I knew he wouldn't. Every day we would meet at the fireplug after chores or Sunday school. We would sneak into the meadow to check and make sure she was secure. He even brought her a bowl of water so she wouldn't have to venture down to the creek where it wasn't safe. I'd never seen him so concerned for another living thing. I think he secretly pretended it was the pet he was never allowed to have. I didn't have the heart to tell him that the last few times we looked at her, I didn't think she looked well. Then again, I was only nine years old and had never been that close to a baby deer before.

This went on for almost a week. The following Friday, I waited by the fireplug but he never came. I felt a twinge of dread and made my way to the meadow without him. I could see him next to the fawn's nest, crouched in the tall weeds. I approached them cautiously and looked over his shoulder.

The little fawn was laying on her side. Her abdomen was caved in and she was being buzzed by flies. Her purple tongue poked out a little from her lips but I will never forget her eyes. They were gone. I don't know if they were plucked out by crows or eaten by insects, but the sockets were barren. It was a horrific and saddening sight.

I looked at Aaron's face. He was trying not to cry. His round cheeks were turning purple from holding his breath in an attempt to hold back the tears. I knelt beside him and put my arms around him.

"It's okay Aaron. Breathe. Just breathe," I whispered.

He took a deep breath in and let it all go. He turned to face me and we held each other while he mourned. My heart cracked a little; not for the deer, but for my best friend. He was in so much pain and there was very little I could do.

"Just breathe. It's okay. Just breathe," I kept repeating as I hugged him.

He eventually regained his composure and we walked silently hand-in-hand out of the woods. He squeezed my hand and headed towards his house. He was sullen for a few days after that and I'm sure his sister's teasing him for being in a 'bad mood' didn't help.

Losing that little deer had hit him hard. I think he blamed himself. Aaron was a sensitive soul with a big heart. Unfortunately, that heart was easily broken. Melanie told him that if a momma animal smells humans, they will abandon the babies. It was a cruel thing to say, but I didn't expect much sympathy from her. After that, he always made sure to give the wildlife a wide birth when we roamed the woods. He even gave up looking for salamanders in the creek with me. I didn't understand his grief. She was a deer. When she was older, she was likely to have ended up on the dinner plate of one of our neighbors. But, I did understand that he needed me and I had to be there for him.

The City

One day, when I was ten years old, Aaron and I were laying in the grass in my backyard reading. It was one of those perfect summer days when the sun was warm and the grass was cool. Birds and bugs sang their happiest melodies from high in the trees. The air was sweet from the feral honeysuckle bushes. We had come to savor these times. Momma was forcing more of my involvement in the church but I had already begun disconnecting myself from it. Uncle James had stopped attending altogether; refusing to pay homage to a god who would take the mother of his child away from him. The more custom and ceremony Momma forced me into, the more I thought about what he had said about church being a bunch of traditions made up by men. God didn't care where I was on Sunday as long as I was a good person every day. I didn't dare tell my mother that.

Aaron closed his book and looked at me. "What's yours about?"

"Same stuff as always." I closed the book I was reading about Joan of Arc.

"Too bad your mom won't let you read fantasy books."

"Fantasia is work of the devil. Books about magic will only lead me into Satan's arms. Reading books that aren't based on truth is a waste of time that could be spent serving our Lord. I am far too important to the faith to spend my time on such frivolity. Blah. Blah. Blah."

"Think she'll ever realize that's what you read when we're at the library?" He raised an eyebrow at me.

"Not as long as I keep bringing home this stuff." I rolled my eyes at the book.

"She is right about one thing."

"What's that?"

"You are special."

I felt my face flush. "How's that?"

"I don't know. But I know you are." We smiled at each other. "My mom is taking my sisters shopping in Chicago this weekend and says I have to go too since I can't be trusted home alone. Do you want to come?"

I had never been outside of our little town before; let alone to a big city. I couldn't imagine all of the tall buildings, traffic, and people who didn't know me. I had seen pictures of Chicago and it seemed like such a far-away and exotic land. I wanted so desperately to try some food that wasn't home-cooked.

I looked back at the house. "She'll never let me go."

I felt a little ache in my chest.

Aaron immediately picked up on my sadness. "Let me talk to my mom. Maybe she can convince her."

I half chuckled. "Fat chance."

"It's worth a try. We both need to get out of this town for a little while."

I giggled. He was only two years older than me but I could tell when he was trying to sound more grown-up (as if I didn't know about his Ninja Turtle collection).

The sliding door to the kitchen opened with a thud. "Grace. Come get ready for seven o'clock mass."

I looked at my mother. Her arms were crossed over her chest and the look on her face was stern. I could see the wall clock past her head. It was only five-thirty.

Aaron and I stood up and brushed the grass off of our clothes.

"Yes ma'am," I replied half-heartedly.

Aaron handed me my library book.

"See you tomorrow, Gracie." He was the only person on Earth who called me that.

I entered the kitchen and she slammed the door behind me.

I could hear my stomach grumbling all through mass. Wednesday services were the worst. They were right at supper time and my mother would never allow us to eat before we left. She said she didn't want to risk my dawdling at the table and making us late. To her credit, I probably would have found some way to make us late but I still resented the implication. I was so grateful for the Eucharist not only because it meant that mass was coming to an end, but because that little flavorless piece of cardboard and sip of grape-flavored gasoline would at least tame my stomach enough to stop the embarrassing noises. I had long accepted that this was a meaningless tradition and even felt silly about my expectations when I had taken it the first time.

It was eight-thirty before we finally pulled into the driveway. My mother had insisted on staying after mass to chat with Father Harold. He made every effort to get away from her and eventually one of the altar boys had to come to his rescue.

As she shut off the car and got out, Elizabeth Akakios came running across the street. She was wearing baggy sweatpants and a sweatshirt. Her frosty-highlighted hair was pulled back with a clip and her feathered bangs were a mess. I envied the ability to dress in such a manner and still look like a queen.

"Janice! May I speak with you for a moment?" she called.

My mother turned to her. "Of course, Elizabeth. What can I do for you?"

"I am taking my girls shopping in Chicago for the weekend. We are leaving Saturday morning and returning Sunday night. Can I leave Aaron with you for the weekend?"

My mother guffawed at the idea of babysitting. I was confused. Elizabeth could tolerate my mother but she certainly didn't like her so I couldn't figure out why she would want Aaron to stay with us.

"I hardly think that would work. I have a busy weekend of activities planned with our church." At least she wasn't lying.

"Oh, he'll be on his best behavior," Elizabeth assured her. "He really is a good boy. I just don't think I can take him with us. The girls are all so much older than him and I really don't think he will behave without someone to play with."

She spoke about Aaron as if he were still only eight years old. I wasn't sure if she still viewed him as a helpless little boy or if this was part of her ploy to convince my mother to allow him to stay with us for the weekend. I listened intently and tried to figure out Elizabeth's game.

"As I said, I don't think I will be able to help you," Momma said through gritted teeth.

My mother crossed her arms and set her jaw. I knew that look. I received it whenever I tried to get out completing my chores correctly.

Elizabeth glanced at me and then back to my mother. "What about her?"

"Grace is younger than Aaron. While she may be mature for her age, I don't think she would be an appropriate babysitter."

"Oh! You misunderstand. I mean to bring her with us."

"With you? To Chicago? Absolutely not!" Momma's voice elevated to an octave I had never heard before.

"As you said, she is mature for her age. She can keep Aaron entertained while keeping him out of trouble."

"A big, lawless city is no place for Grace."

"You do understand that Chicago has some of the most beautiful historic cathedrals in the country right?" Elizabeth stepped towards my mother.

"Yes-"

"And an art museum full of beautiful renaissance Christian artwork?" Aaron's mother crossed her arms to match my own mother's stance.

"Yes, but-"

"Don't you think Grace should be exposed to such things to gain a better understanding of Christianity in this world?" She set her jaw.

"Of course but-"

"Then it's settled!" Elizabeth turned to me. "Grace, be at my house at six-thirty Saturday morning." She turned back to my mother (whose jaw was still agape). "And don't worry; I'll make sure she goes to church Sunday morning."

With that, Elizabeth winked at me and turned back to her house.

I smiled. That was pure genius. The only way she could have played that game more beautifully was if she had somehow tricked Momma into believing it was her idea. I expected nothing but protestation and a change of mind, but it never came. She did not like the idea of my going to Chicago but, after two nights of prayer, she allowed me to go.

That Friday night I strategically made sure my mother had seen me pack church clothes with my pajamas into my school bag. I had never been away from home for a night except for a few times I had stayed with Uncle James and Aunt Catherine. I had laid everything out on the bed. I had one-hundred and thirty-six dollars and forty-two cents from birthday, chore, and Christmas money I had saved. Toothbrush, toothpaste, underwear, socks, church dress, day clothes, pajamas, hairbrush… I went over the checklist in my head again and again before I carefully packed my bag.

The three a.m. tickling in my brain came, but I was already awake. The excitement kept my eyes wide and my mind reeling. I couldn't stop imagining what a big city would be like or the food I would get to try. I was out of bed before the sun was up. I dressed, ate a bowl of cereal, and rushed to take care of the chickens. At six-thirty Saturday morning, I eagerly stood on the Akakios front porch. I lifted my hand to knock when the front door swung open and Aaron's youngest sister, Nicole, looked at me.

She huffed. "I knew you'd somehow be tagging along."

She left the door open and turned away. I stepped into the entryway. It wasn't often that I entered their home. Aaron and I preferred to spend our time outside and cold winters were usually spent in the library. Aaron came down the stairs and set a little black duffle bag at my feet. He was grinning ear to ear.

"Are you ready?" He was so excited he could barely contain himself.

"Yes!" I tried hard not to squeal.

"Are you two love birds going to be noisy the entire trip?" Melanie was coming down the stairs with a cloth suitcase. I couldn't imagine what all she had packed for an overnight trip in a bag that big. But then, she was also twenty-two years old and I hadn't thought about my own existence at that age.

"Shut up," Aaron snapped at her.

"Aaron and Grace are sitting in a tree-" Stephanie was cut short as she was coming out of the kitchen with a toaster pastry.

"Okay, Ladies. We have a long drive. Everybody in." Elizabeth looked tired but her hair and makeup were flawless.

"Hey. I'm not a lady!" Aaron puffed up his chest.

"I stand by my statement." She cackled. She turned to me. "I meant what I said to your mom. Your job is to keep Aaron busy and out of our way, understand?"

I nodded. "Yes ma'am."

"Good!" She clapped her hands together. "I said it once and I'm saying it again. In the van!"

We stacked and tucked bags wherever they would fit in the brand new forest green Mercury Villager. Aaron and I were stuffed amongst the cargo in the very back seats, but we didn't mind. We kept ourselves entertained with games of hangman, war, and I-spy. Nicole, who was stuck in the back row with us, tried to pretend we weren't there. The familiar streets of our small town steadily turned into rolling farmland.

Despite the frequent bathroom breaks and a car full of whiny girls, the five-hour-long drive seemed to pass quickly. We stopped for lunch at a burger joint before checking into the hotel. At home, a burger and fries were a rare treat and I had never seen a burger that big before. Aaron's sisters and Elizabeth were stunned and a little disgusted by how much I could eat. I used a bit of my money to buy ice cream for everyone which seemed to ease their revulsion. I purchased a disposable camera at a shop in the strip mall before we were back on the road.

I couldn't believe my eyes as we entered the city. I marveled at the tall buildings and busy streets as we made our way to the hotel. Everything I had imagined it would be was real. We looped up and around and I caught a glimpse of Lake Michigan. The pond back home was nothing by comparison. There were people and busses and a train! Aaron laughed at me as I kept my face pressed against the window. It was all so surreal.

Our hotel was a cheap hideout. Elizabeth obtained the key from the front desk and we all brought our bags inside. There were two king-sized beds and two little cots on the floor. The walls were covered in brown striped wallpaper and heavy drapes framed the window. The television was seated on a big wooden dresser and a small refrigerator was set next to that. There was a single chair in the corner and lamps EVERYWHERE. There was barely enough space for all of us to maneuver around the room, but I didn't care. It was a palace. Melanie quickly laid claim to the bed with Elizabeth while Stephanie, Tiffany, and Nicole jumped on the other one leaving Aaron and me with the cots against the wall. When sleeping arrangements were settled and luggage was stowed, we left to explore.

We set off through the city on foot. Elizabeth and the girls stayed ahead of us walking at a quick pace and in a close group while Aaron and I fell behind. I realized very quickly that the people there were not like back home. On the sidewalks in town, people gave you space to walk and apologized if they bumped into you. In the city, people just ran into me or bumped me. Because I was so small, some people even tripped over me. At one point, I lost sight of Elizabeth and began to panic. Aaron took my hand to keep from losing me and smiled. It was one of the most comforting gestures anyone had ever given me.

We followed the cluster of girls from store to store. Melanie and Tiffany tried on beautiful dresses while Nicole was more interested in visiting the makeup counter and Stephanie tackled the shoes. They pulled Elizabeth in a dozen different directions with Aaron and me in tow.

We feasted on street food at the edge of Lake Michigan. Elizabeth took a picture of Aaron and me sitting against each other eating corndogs and drinking pop. We sat there, watching the boats on the water, and eating all the junk food my mother would have never let me have. I couldn't get over the openness and expanse of the lake. The creek back home had been the largest body of water I had ever seen up to that point and this was the whole ocean by comparison. Aaron and I leaned on each other and watched the people until Elizabeth finally said we had to go back to the hotel. I didn't want to leave. The whole day had been the kind of experience I had only dreamt of.

It was with a great deal of effort that I eventually fell asleep. I'd like to think it was due to the adrenaline that was coursing through me from the day but, in reality, I'm certain it had more to do with all of the caffeine I had been allowed to drink. Either way, at the devil's hour, I bolted awake. I could hear Aaron's sisters snoring peacefully but he was lying on his cot and staring at me.

"Did you have fun today?" He asked.

"Of course!" I was grinning so hard, my face hurt.

He smiled at me. "Good. I'm glad your mom let you come."

"I'm glad your mom talked her into it."

"Tomorrow we get to go to the museum."

My eyes lit up. "Really? I thought that was just something she said so my mom would let me come."

He laughed a little. "She did. But then I said you've never been to a museum so she said she would drop us off while they were shopping."

"For God's sake. Go to sleep you two." Melanie threw a pillow at us.

We both giggled before rolling over and going back to sleep.

The Start of My Path

The next morning, I awoke before everyone else. I was so used to getting up at dawn to care for the chickens that my internal alarm clock was more reliable than a traditional one. I looked out the window and smiled. The sky was an ombre mesh of purple, to blue, to orange behind tall buildings. We didn't have any views like this back home. Our tallest building was the hospital and even that was only two stories. I brushed my teeth, washed my face, and combed my hair. I sat on the floor in front of the big window and watched the sun come up over the city. It was absolutely amazing. Right now momma would be getting up to take care of the chickens for me and getting ready for church. Uncle James and Jacob were probably asleep in the family room in front of the television. I mused at how a five-hour drive felt a million miles away.

I heard a buzzing behind me. Elizabeth rolled over and hit the top of the alarm clock. Nicole covered her head with a pillow. Aaron rolled over and noticed my empty cot. I saw a sudden look of panic cross his face as he sat upright. He grabbed his glasses and put them on to scan the room. The fear faded as quickly as it came when he saw me sitting in front of the window. He stretched and came to sit beside me.

He yawned. "You woke up early."

"Yeah."

We sat in silence and watched the city rouse for the day. Meanwhile, behind us, little by little his sisters came to life. They immediately started complaining about who was hogging the bed or blankets and who snored too loud. There was never any such complaining at my house, lest my mother give me something to complain about. They took turns in the only bathroom, helped each other put on makeup and fix their hair.

It was very entertaining to watch. "Is it like this every morning?"

"No." Aaron mused. "In my house, we have more than one bathroom."

"Grace, dear, get your church clothes on." Elizabeth was piling her hair on top of her head.

I grabbed my bag and looked at the little bathroom. It was full of half-dressed girls fighting over the mirror. I turned and looked at the closet. Sometimes it was good to be small. I turned on the closet light and used it as my private dressing room. Aaron was highly amused.

When everything was settled and all the bags were re-packed, Elizabeth checked us out of the hotel and we headed out for a day that would change my life forever.

We pulled up in front of a beautiful brick and stone cathedral called Saint Stanislaus Kostka Catholic Church. Elizabeth carefully positioned me on the steps in front of the building and took a picture with my disposable camera.

"Ok, Grace. Run in and get a few pictures for your mom so we can head to breakfast." She handed the camera back to me.

"You aren't going to make me stay for mass?"

"Oh, Dear. I told your mom I would take you to church on Sunday morning. I didn't say anything about making you stay for mass. I can keep a secret if you can."

I had never deceived my mother like this before but it wasn't *really* a lie. Looking back, that woman taught me a lot about the art of deception and manipulation. I smiled and ran into the church with Aaron right behind me.

Inside the church was massive. The huge archways and columns accented the elegant stained glass windows and murals both above the windows and on the ceilings. The pews looked like they were original to the church when it was built in the eighteen-hundreds. I took enough pictures to fill up the rest of my camera before I genuflected at the altar and left.

That morning, I decided that Belgian waffles were the most amazing food ever created. I loaded them with butter, syrup, and powdered sugar. I ate four of them with a mountain of bacon and orange juice. My mother would never have let me eat this much sugar in one meal and I reveled in the freedom. Aaron's sisters looked at me with fascination and disgust as they strategized how to make the most of the day. I ducked into the convenience store next door to the restaurant and bought two more disposable cameras. I had a feeling I was going to need them.

Elizabeth swore me to secrecy once again as she left Aaron and me at the art museum alone. We all knew my mother would never forgive her and I would have to do some kind of Penance if our secret was discovered.

After she and Aaron's sisters drove off, he turned to me and smiled.

"She's really okay with leaving us here by ourselves?" I asked.

"Of course. Why wouldn't she be? She says this way I can't get in the way. Plus, I get to spend the day with you instead of watching Melanie trying on dresses and Nicole making fun of us."

I nodded. Not only was I in a huge new city, I had never been to an art museum before or had any kind of exposure to culture for that matter. I was a small-town Illinois girl, born and raised. I had only read about such beautiful architecture, paintings, and sculptures. The idea of being left to explore this new world with my best friend had me completely buzzing.

Before we even entered, I was blown away by the sheer scale of the building. The exterior was a fairly drab-colored stone, but its many archways gave it a very autocratic feel. The stairs were guarded by two green lions that were frozen in time and further added to the majesty. Near the top of the building, beautiful carvings of men and horses depicted seemingly ancient scenes while the names of famous artists scrolled around the top. I was in complete awe.

    I could have died in that museum and I would have died happy. I stood in reverence at the beauty and grandeur of things I had only ever seen in textbooks. Gothic and Renaissance paintings the size of my bedroom wall, elaborate tapestries and intricate furniture with gold adornments, and marble statues so soft you could have sworn it was real flesh and fabric. Hindu, Daoist, Muslim, Egyptian, Native American, and a whole host of religions I truthfully hadn't realized until that day were laid out before me. I listened to guides discuss color and brush strokes and depth. I listened to other guests give their own interpretations of the artwork. I read every plaque next to every piece.

    Aaron followed along with me, musing at my wonder. I took pictures of the Madonna and Child and statues of the saints, but I spent very little time contemplating them. Momma would appreciate them more than me. The building was a whole new world of possibilities and understanding at my fingertips. I had every intention of making the most of the experience.

    I was truly saddened when the van pulled in front of the museum and we were forced to leave. We had true Chicago-style pizza for dinner and I vowed I would never look at Angelino's pizza when Uncle James had treated me on occasional Friday nights the same way again. The girls all gaggled about what their mother had bought them and what they wanted to do for the next visit. Meanwhile, Aaron and I sat at the far end of the long table away from their noise. He stuffed his face with meat and cheese and listened to me chatter uncontrollably about all of the things we had seen and how open my eyes had become.

    In the back of the van on the way home that night, surrounded by a multitude of shopping bags, I played the day over and over in my mind. In all my time at the library reading about and looking at pictures of artifacts and artwork, I had never realized what an impact actually *experiencing* them would make. I can truthfully say that that single day opened my eyes to just how big the world really is, and it eventually became the framework for my entire adult life and the start of my own path.

Welcome Home, Jacob

When I was twelve, Jacob came to stay with my mother and me while Uncle James explored sobriety. Jacob was fourteen, lashing out, and getting into a great deal of trouble and poor James couldn't handle straightening them both out simultaneously. The final straw was when he 'borrowed' Mr. Nelson's truck and took all of his friends to the movies one town over. They all returned unscathed and without police involvement after Uncle James stood guard and made Jacob muck out all of Mr. Nelson's stables and paint the paddock fence.

I stood in Aaron's front yard the day Jacob moved in. I watched them unload his things from a borrowed van while he argued with his father. He didn't want to live in our house any more than I wanted him there. Aaron stood next to me and watched the spectacle.

"This is going to be bad. Isn't it?" he asked.

"Yup." Was all could I respond with.

"Why is he moving in?"

"Because Uncle James needs to take care of himself and Jacob is a selfish brat."

"Why doesn't he stay with his mom's family?"

I felt a little pang in my heart at the thought of Aunt Catherine. It had been four years, but the pain was still there.

"They don't want him either," I replied.

"Oh." We stood in silence for a minute. "They think your mom can straighten him out?" He asked as he watched Jacob punch the white van.

"I don't know. I think she's just the only one who didn't say 'no.'"

"Oh." He nodded solemnly.

It was painful to share a house with Jacob. He and Aaron were roughly the same age, but worlds apart in maturity. Jacob never helped with any of the chores. He tormented the chickens for fun until a mean rooster we had named Leviathan spurred him so badly that he needed stitches. There was only one bathroom in that little house and he would miss the toilet when he peed. I honestly wasn't sure if he was doing it out of spite or simply because he didn't care. He rigged the mudroom door so it could open from the outside, even if it was locked. This was how he would sneak away in the middle of the night to get high with his friends. I didn't know how much I would appreciate that he did that until later.

We had constant screaming matches when he would take my things or make fun of my hair or glasses. My mother tried to discipline him but she didn't know what she was doing with such an unruly teenager. Counseling with Father Harold didn't work. Grounding him was a joke. When she took away his bike, he obtained another one from thin air. I would hear her at night saying her payers and asking Saint Pancras and Saint Dominic Savio for guidance, but none ever come.

As far as I was concerned, Jacob was a lost cause. He knew what he was doing was wrong but he couldn't have cared less. He only cared about himself. When Momma would take us to visit Uncle James to support his sobriety, Jacob belittled him, ignored him, or would shout accusations about how he had ruined his life. I hated seeing Uncle James cry and I hated Jacob for making him do it.

This went on for years. He would periodically disappear for a day or two; the longest being six. When he returned, he accused Momma and Uncle James of not loving him because they didn't call the police or report him missing. He didn't realize that they didn't have to. I was only two years younger than him and everyone in town knew we were related. Someone always had a friend-of-a-friend who knew where he was hiding. It would somehow be relayed to me directly or via gossip and I would deliver the information back to the adults. We always knew where he was and worrying about him was nothing less than exhausting.

After his accusations of un-love, he would often pout or further lash out. He wasn't physical but the pain he caused was real. I remember watching this spectacle play out over and over and thinking to myself that Jacob was not human. He was a monster and back then I didn't believe he had any hope for redemption.

The Spirit Board

"Tell me again. Why are we doing this?" I couldn't see Aaron's face in the dark, but I knew what it looked like. He always got wrinkles on his forehead above his glasses when he was worried.

"Because I need to. I need to try."

"But why in the woods?"

"It's clean ground. There are no people to disturb it. It's not consecrated by any religion. I just have to see if it will work. You didn't have to come."

"I'm not going to let you go running around in the dark by yourself." He huffed slightly. "Besides, I'm the one with the board."

We were fumbling around by the light of the full moon. It was shortly after midnight and even most of the bullfrogs and crickets were sleeping. I had slipped out the kitchen door and made sure to leave it unlocked for my return. Aaron had met me by the fire plug on our street and we headed into the woods with a few light supplies in our book bags.

"You know I think your mom is crazy and filled your head with nonsense, but what if it does work?"

I paused. "We'll cross that bridge when we come to it."

"I don't like that answer."

"Well, it's the only answer I've got," I replied as I caught my foot while trying to step over a fallen branch.

He caught me by my book bag and kept me from hitting the ground.

"Thanks," I said.

We finally stepped out of the trees and into the meadow. The grass was low and wavy. The air was sweet and cool. We had gone there a hundred times but that time it was different.

We tamped down the grass and spread out our blankets. Aaron pulled a spirit board out of his backpack and set it up between us. It was an old-style wooden one, unlike the cheap cardboard ones I'd seen in the toy aisle at the store. I ran my hands over the warm wood grain.

"Where did you get this, again?" I looked at him.

He pushed his glasses back up on his nose. "My dad had it. I don't know where he got it from."

"Looks old."

His brow furrowed again. "Gracie, wouldn't you have better luck finding answers at a church if you're a Holy Child?"

"I've been in church for thirteen years. I've never had any answers. Remember my communion? And my confirmation? Nothing happened. I have woken up at three in the morning, every morning, for thousands of mornings. Momma says I'm special and different but no one can tell me why or what I'm supposed to be doing. This is the only other option I've got." I felt like I might cry as I spoke.

"What if you wake up an angry ghost and get yourself haunted or something?"

"You don't really believe that, do you?" I looked him in the eye.

He shook his head.

"Besides, it's not likely someone died here, so there shouldn't be any ghosts around here to disturb. The only thing to attract any ghosts would be us. Maybe I'll get to talk to my Aunt Catherine."

"What would you say to her?" he asked.

"I don't know. Tell her I miss her. Tell her about Uncle James's drinking, but I'm sure she knows from watching him from heaven. Maybe ask her for some advice for Momma on how to get Jacob under control." My mind started racing with possible things I may say to my aunt if her specter should appear.

Aaron looked back at the board. "You did a lot of research before you decided to try this, didn't you?"

"Of course. I've read the bible cover to cover and there is nothing helpful in it for me. And Momma can never know about any of this."

"My lips are sealed." We lay on our backs and stared at the stars. "Gracie?" He turned to face me.

"Yeah?"

"What if you don't fall asleep?"

"I will," I promised him.

After about half an hour of listening to the wind, I heard the gentle droning of snoring next to me. The melodic sound almost blended into the night. I'm not sure how much longer it was before I fell asleep too.

I may not know what time I fell asleep, but I knew what time it was when I woke up. I felt the familiar tickle in the back of my brain. I sat up and stretched.

I reached over and shook Aaron awake. "It's time."

He yawned and stretched. "Okay."

He started to drift back to sleep. I flicked his ear.

"Ow! Okay!" He sat up.

We each put our hands on the round glass disk on the board. It was smooth and cool to the touch. I felt a shiver run down my spine as I prepared for what we had come to do.

I took a deep breath. "My name is Grace Gertrude Nightingale. I am a Holy Child. I wish to speak to any spirits who may listen."

I watched the glass with bated breath. It didn't move.

"See," Aaron stated excitedly. "Nothing. Can we go home?"

"Wait a minute." I scolded him. "My name is Grace Nightingale. I am here with Aaron Akakios. Is anyone here with us?"

I held my breath. Ever so gently, the glass began to slide. I felt suddenly sick and my heart was in my throat.

Yes.

I looked at Aaron. By the light of the moon, I could see that his face was as white as a sheet.

"Are- are you a ghost?" He stammered.

It slid. *No.*

I swallowed my heart back down. "I am a Holy Child. Are you an angel come to guide me?"

No.

"Not a ghost and not an angel?" Aaron was completely confused.

I wasn't. I think I always knew. Three in the morning is the Devil's Hour.

"Are you a demon?"

It slid again. *Yes.*

My heart returned to my throat. "Are you the one who always wakes me up?"

Yes.

"Why?" I was trying not to become emotional.

The glass didn't move.

"Do you want to hurt her?" Aaron sounded genuinely concerned.

No.

"Will you leave me alone?"

No.

I felt a welling of anger. All I wanted was to be normal. I didn't want to have a destiny with the church. I wanted to know what it felt like to sleep through a night and this thing was telling me it wouldn't let me have that.

"Why? What did I do to deserve this?"

The glass didn't move.

"What do you want from me?" I shouted.

The glass still didn't move. I started to cry. I picked up the board and threw it.

Aaron knelt on the ground and held me as I sat and sobbed for what felt like hours. I just wanted to be normal. I didn't want to be special. I didn't want to be a Holy Child. I didn't want demons toying with my brain. The more I thought about it, the harder I cried.

Eventually, Aaron pulled me back so he could look me in the eye. "Gracie. Let's go home."

I swallowed down as much of the pain and tears as I could and slightly nodded my head. I allowed him to pull me back to my feet. We made our way back through the sticker bushes, across the creek bed, and home. We stood in the street between our houses. He wanted to say something, but I don't think he knew what to say. He opened his mouth but shook his head and went home.

As I crept in through the kitchen door, I realized I wasn't alone. I turned and saw Jacob sitting on the couch. The smug look on his face as he stood to face me with his arms crossed was unforgettable.

"You going to tell Momma?" I shut the door behind me.

"Not unless you give me a reason." He turned and headed down the hallway towards his room. "By the way; next time, use the mudroom door. It squeaks less," he called over his shoulder.

As I undressed and crawled into bed, my mind was muddled and whirling. I was born to be a tool of God but I couldn't talk to angels. I had never seen an angel nor did I have any idea what my purpose was. But, I could communicate with a demon. I didn't know which one he was or why he had chosen me, but I supposed there was nothing I could do about it. God wasn't going to take away this 'gift' or give my responsibility to someone else; so I was just going to have to finally accept that I was what I was. The more I thought about it, the more I realized that acceptance didn't mean submission. I didn't have to follow whatever *his* plan was. God had done nothing for me except cause suffering. He made me different from everyone else. He broke apart my family. He offered me no guidance; my only answers had come from a demon. He was clearly the God of the Old Testament; a God who only cared when it was convenient.

Aaron and I went about life as if that night had never happened. The next day, after school, he seemed to want to talk about anything else. I wasn't sure if it was because he was scared or maybe he didn't believe it actually happened. I was accepting of his avoidance of the subject. It was a lot to take in and, to be perfectly honest, he was a quite cowardly teenager. I was sure the thought of his best friend communicating with a hand of the Devil did nothing to help that.

Best Friends

It was June; around three months or so since I had conversed with the demon in the woods behind my house. That night was dark and my entire young world was turned on its head. I had no warning or inclination that anything was wrong. I certainly didn't understand the lasting impact these events would have on my life.

I was lying in bed with a book and a flashlight. I could hear my mother's snoring through the wall. I had seen Jacob tiptoeing through the backyard hours before. It was peaceful. The only sounds were the cracks and creaks of the old house settling for the night. I had a sudden, strange feeling that I wasn't alone and dropped my book. I looked at the window and there was a pudgy face in glasses looking back at me.

I opened the window and almost hit Aaron's head. "What are you doing here?"

His brown was wrinkled and his face was puffy. His bloodshot eyes were sad and his lip was quivering. I could tell he had been crying for quite some time.

"My parents just told me and I have to tell you," he choked out.

"What?" I sucked in my breath as I asked.

I was panicking. The only time I had ever seen him in such a state was when the baby deer had died all those years ago. I couldn't imagine what could move him to tears again.

"We are moving this weekend. My grandma is very sick. We are moving to Boston to take care of her."

"What?" I almost shouted. I paused a moment to make sure I hadn't woken my mother. "You can't move! Why can't she come here to be with you?" My eyes started to burn.

He sniffled a little. "Something about needing the right doctors."

"You can't move!" I said louder and no longer caring if my mother heard. "You're my best friend!"

My vision began to blur as the tears moved up into my eyes.

"I don't want to go. I have to go."

I heard myself whimper and the tears started to roll down my cheek. He squeezed my hand. I looked into those beautiful brown eyes. They were red from fighting the tears that came so freely to mine.

"I don't know what I'm going to do without you." He said quietly.

"Will you ever come back?" I choked a little.

"I don't know when, but we will see each other again. Even if you move too, I will find you. You are my best friend. You are the most important person in the world to me." He looked me straight in the eye.

"Promise," I told him.

He squeezed both of my hands through the window and pushed his forehead against mine. "I promise."

We stayed that way for a long time before he gave me one more squeeze and ran back to his house. Looking back on it, I think even at the tender ages of thirteen and fifteen, there was something more than friendship between us.

That weekend was one of the most devastating in my life. I stood leaning against the fence as the moving truck pulled in front of their house. Nine years before I had been peering through that same part of the fence as I watched them carry boxes into the house. This time I watched boxes and furniture being carried away with yet more tears in my eyes. This was truly happening.

When the last case was loaded and the back of the truck was closed, Aaron came and put a little box in my hand. He held it there and squeezed it before running back to the car. That was it. No words. No hugs. We had said our goodbyes days ago. To do it again would be too painful. I watched his dad's 4Runner turn the corner out of my neighborhood, carrying my best friend out of my life for good. I looked at the little box he had given me. Inside, there was a little smooth quartz crystal strung on a chain. I've only cried harder than that one time in my life.

My world was a dark place after Aaron left. I wouldn't go outside except to feed the chickens and even then, I would return to the solitude of my room. I would lay on the floor or in my bed in silence. When I was awake, I would relive my favorite memories of Aaron and inevitably end up falling asleep in a puddle of my own tears. Jacob didn't even dare disturb me. Every time I heard the phone ring, my heart held a little hope that it was Aaron calling so I could tell him how much I missed him. But the call never came. My mother berated me daily for staying in bed and refusing to eat before she decided I needed help. She took me to church every day for a week so that God could heal my heart and make me realized that he was all I needed. I only felt worse. She finally decided I need a change of scenery and sent me to a two-week Bible camp. I hated that too.

I shared a cabin with three other girls who had obviously been through this together before and had no interest in allowing me to join their clique. They pushed their beds together and left mine in the far back corner against the wall. Every night, they would sneak out and do... I don't even know what or talk loudly in their little area with their backs to me. In the mornings the camp forced us up at dawn to "welcome God's light" and then shoved us all into a dimly lit mess hall at overcrowded picnic tables for oatmeal and fruit. We listened to our morning sermon followed by the activities that were preplanned for the day. Activities included discussing the wonder of God's gifts on nature hikes, making candles to light at mass, singing lessons, and a whole host of other brainwashing that was compounded by the rigorous schedule and lack of real food.

On the fifth night there, I managed to escape the mess hall with a dinner roll wrapped in a napkin and creep back to my cabin.

I just wanted to be alone. There were close to a hundred boisterous kids and teenagers in that mess hall and I was feeling suffocated.

When I got back, I opened the door and flipped the light switch. I hadn't even stepped all of the way inside yet when I heard a funny noise. I assumed a rat had made its way in and was looking for food and shelter. We occasionally would get rodents in the chicken coup back home and I decided I needed to find it and release it where it would be safe. I braced myself for what I might find and followed the noise. It wasn't a rat. A little black ball of fur was huddled in the corner under my bunk. Her glowing yellow eyes were wide with fear.

"Come on out. I won't hurt you." I lay on my belly and wiggled my fingers at her.

The terrified kitten backed further away from me and hissed as it trembled. I remembered the dinner roll and tore a little piece off. I threw it towards her. She sniffed it, looked at me, and devoured it. I tossed more to her. I knew cats shouldn't eat bread but she was clearly starving and needed my help. I managed to lure her close enough to pick her up and hold her against me. She was so tiny she fit in one of my hands.

She became my only friend in that abysmal place. I named her Hope because she was the one thing I looked forward to every day. I kept her hidden away in my bunk and stole table scraps to feed her. She loved to playfully bat at the quartz around my neck and I told her about the boy who gave it to me and how I couldn't wait to see him again. She slept with me every night and her purring eased the pain in my heart. When one of the other girls discovered her, she threatened to tell our group leader if I didn't let her play with her. I told her if she told my secret, I would tell about her and the other girls sneaking out. It was the first time I had ever stood up for myself and it was successful.

When my mother came to pick me up, I had almost made it into the car before my satchel meowed and moved.

"What is that?!" My mother almost screamed.

I sighed. I had been caught. I set the bag on the ground and I opened the top. Hope leaped into my arms and nuzzled under my neck.

"Where did you get that thing?!"

"She is not a thing. Her name is Hope and she's my friend."

Emboldened by my earlier bout with my cabin mate, I faced off with my mother for the first time in my life.

"Cats do the devil's work." She scolded me.

"She's a kitten, Momma. She is not an agent of Satan."

"You are not bringing that thing home." She crossed her arms.

Surprised by how bold I still felt, I sat down on the ground in defiance. "Then I'm not going home."

It may have been a juvenile act for a thirteen-year-old, but it was a move I had seen Jacob use many times when we were young. Since he was the only frame of reference for insubordination, I did the only thing I could think to do.

"What is the matter with you? This placed was supposed to help put you on the right path."

"It did! It helped me find her!" I squeezed the little kitten closer.

"Grace Gertrude! Put that thing down and get in the car!"

On hearing my middle name, I was struck with a beautiful epiphany. I would beat my mother at her own game.

"Momma she's meant to be mine. My Saint is Gertrude. You gave her to me. Gertrude is the saint of cats. I'm meant to have this kitten. There wouldn't even be a saint of cats if all cats are evil."

My mother's face reddened. She opened her mouth to yell and then closed it several times. She could not dispute my logic and it enraged her. My middle name was Gertrude because it had been my grandmother's middle name. But, your middle name is meant to be your guiding saint and while Gertrude is the saint of mental health, she is also the saint of cats. My mother was stuck. She took a deep breath and exhaled carefully.

"You will be responsible for it. I am not spending a dime on that thing. You will pay for its food, its litter, and its medical expenses. If it harms a single one of the chickens, it goes!"

I smiled for the first time in weeks. "Yes ma'am!"

I couldn't believe she had given in. I had never been defiant like that before. I felt a whole new sense of self open up. I was empowered. I saw part of the huge cloud that had been hanging over my heart float away.

I mowed lawns, raked leaves, shoveled driveways, and tutored my classmates. Eventually, I got a job at the library re-shelving books. Every spare penny I earned went to make sure Hope was happy and healthy. When the demon woke me at three in the morning, she would be on the pillow beside my head. Her purrs reminded me that I was not alone. Just when I needed her, she was my best friend.

The Predator

    The Catholic school I attended had a community garden where we grew vegetables and made them available to the public. Of course, because of my 'important' religious standing, my mother felt I should be an example to the rest of the students and somehow got me put in charge of taking care of it. I hated it. She had made me give up my job at the library because the garden was for the church. I just wanted to be a normal fifteen-year-old but I did as I was told. The only thing I genuinely enjoyed about working in the vegetable garden was the privilege of wearing shorts. When she had allowed me to start wearing pants, my life had gained a small sense of normalcy, but she still didn't want me to show my legs. I needed to retain some sense of purity and modesty. After a mild case of heatstroke, she permitted shorts. Tank tops were still forbidden as I had grown more endowed than many of my peers. Still, the freedom of shorts was incredibly liberating.

    The community garden had a shed that remained locked throughout the week and on the weekends it was carefully monitored. The school- and subsequently the church- were afraid that tools and things would be stolen. I think it had more to do with the fact that when they were leaving it unlocked, kids would go in and have make-out sessions in between classes. The only people who had keys were me, Father Harold, a handful of teachers, the groundskeeper, and Brett.

    Brett was a stereotypical jock. He had peroxide blonde hair, blue eyes, big muscles, and the ability to make all the girls swoon with one look. He was our star football player and completely infallible to the teachers' eyes. He was sent to Saint Teresa's because he couldn't stop getting into trouble at his old school. He was caught out late, drinking alcohol, and pulling pranks with his friends so his parents felt a Catholic school should be able to straighten him out. Their hope was sorely misplaced. It just made him better at hiding his misdeeds. One of the things he hid best was his fondness for that tool shed. There were several times I caught him sneaking girls in and out of it. I also knew he liked to go in it on the weekends (long after the adults were gone) to drink or get high or both. He had stolen a key from Sister Jane and would come and go as he pleased. He didn't bother me so I left him alone. I wish our arrangement had stayed that way.

One Sunday after my help had left, I was finishing tidying up some things in the garden. The younger students never put away the tools properly but I didn't mind. I didn't like being in charge of the garden, but that was time that I didn't have to spend with Momma or the church. I was bent over a small patch of Earth but I don't remember exactly what I was doing. What I do remember is feeling a warm hand on my buttocks. I stood up quickly and turned around. Brett was looking down and smiling at me. My barely five-foot-tall and hundred-and-ten-pound frame was dwarfed to his six-foot-two-inch height and two-hundred-and-thirty pounds of muscle. He was three years older than me and so we never had direct contact before that. I looked him in the eye.

"Hello, Grace."

I didn't even know he actually knew my name. I was just the vegetable garden warden. I opened my mouth but no words came out.

"Cat that your tongue?" He smiled. "It's okay. I have that effect on women."

Still no words.

"You know," he stepped a little closer to me, "I never really noticed just how cute you are. Probably still a virgin too. What are you doing later on tonight?"

Nothing but silence from me. To this day, I'm not sure why I froze. I wasn't particularly attracted to him. Maybe it was the shock of actual interaction. Maybe it was the shock from the sexual connotation. Whatever it was, I wished I had said *something*.

He reached his arm around me pulled me up against him. "Me and some of the guys are going to be back here later tonight for a little Sunday fun if you're interested."

I felt his hand slide inside my shorts and between my legs. I may not have been able to say anything but I pushed hard enough to get away from him.

His smile was crooked and a little... sinister is the best word I have for it.

"I know you don't mean that. Don't worry, you'll be mine eventually. I always get what I want." His voice was slimy and I felt my skin crawl.

"Hey, Brett!" A boy's voice came over the hill. "Brett, we gotta go."

He turned and waved at the voice and turned back to me. "Catch you later, Grace."

Looking back on it now, it is almost funny. I was so confused and so disgusted and maybe a little scared and I had no idea what was going on. I had been raised in such a sheltered life in such a sheltered world. Girls would have given anything to trade places with me in that moment and I didn't know what to do. I may have been innocent, but I wasn't stupid. I knew exactly what he wanted. My mother always told me to maintain my purity and to save myself. I guess even with as much rebellion against her that was forming in my body, some things just kind of stuck. I felt the need to wash. I picked up the tools in the shed and walked towards the church to cleanse myself. No boy had ever shown interest in me before, let alone propositioned me. I felt dirty at having been touched but also curious; I was a teenage girl, after all.

When I got home, Momma was still at work. I could hear Jacob's music playing from his room. He was the last person I wanted to talk to, but he was all I had. I walked in without knocking. He was sitting on his bed with a magazine he undoubtedly had stolen from the general store up the road. He looked at me and turned off the radio.

"What do you want?" He narrowed his eyes at me.

"You've had sex, right?"

"Whoa!" He sat upright in the bed. "What is this about?"

I looked at him. "Does it make you different?"

He looked at me harder. "I don't think this is a conversation we should be having."

I looked at the floor. "Please, Jacob."

He sighed. "No. It didn't make me different. But I'm not you. If you aren't ready for something, don't do it or it *will* change you."

I stood in silence for a moment and thought about what he was saying.

He continued. "But don't let all that churchy stuff your mom puts in your head get in the way of anything. It's your life. You live it how you want. Ask for forgiveness later if you do something really stupid."

I stood a moment more in quiet contemplation. "Thanks, Jacob."

I turned to walk out of his room.

"Grace," he called quietly.

I turned back to look at him. I had never seen anything that resembled worry on his face before.

"Be careful," he said.

I nodded before going back to my room.

That night, we had supper at the table in uncomfortable silence. I'm not sure if Momma realized something had transpired, but I was grateful that Jacob never mentioned our conversation again.

I lay in bed afterward and rolled the events of the day around in my head. I was angry at Brett for putting me in such a position. I had never before had to consider sex as a teenager and I was outraged that he had put this on me. He was a predator. How dare he just assume I would give in to him? But, to the same point, wasn't that normal? I had always wanted to be normal. It was late when I finally fell asleep but, when I woke at three, everything was different. It started with Hope hissing in the dark.

I am Onoskelis

She appeared in the corner of my room. The light of the full moon illuminated her clearly. Her raven hair touched the back of her knees and her dark eyes looked like two glass marbles set in alabaster. Her pale skin appeared almost as white as the moon itself. She was long and slender and wrapped in brown furs.

She looked up from her hands and into my eyes. "Have I come to you?"

I sat gawking at her. "Who? Who are you?"

The woman giggled a little and looked at herself in the mirror before turning to me. "I am called Onoskelis."

I laughed. This was ridiculous. Onoskelis was a demon I remembered learning about in my theology classes.

"That's impossible. This is a weird dream," I chortled.

"Lack of apperception does not equal impossibility," she replied flatly.

"You don't look like you have the legs of a mule," I pushed.

She huffed. "I have appeared in many forms to many different beings but none of those forms have had the legs of a mule. I appeared before Solomon in a form not unlike that which you see before you. My hope had been that he would take pity on a beautiful woman but, alas, all he saw was a demon. My imprisonment was a lie to better his ego. And the legs of a mule were concocted out of spite and pride when I denied him my body. He dared not tell of Persephone coming to my aid."

I laughed again. "You don't sound like a four-thousand-year-old demon," I pushed further.

"I live in caves on Earth. I can hear humans. We all can. We can even see you but you cannot see into our world or interact with us. Only rare individuals like *you* have such privilege and you are difficult to encounter."

I couldn't believe this nonsense. "Okay. Explain who you really are and why you are in my room."

"I must alter my attire. What clothing is considered fashionable?"

She ignored my demand for an explanation and looked into my eyes. I suddenly felt like fingers were probing into the corners of my brain. It was as if I was being explored from the inside. It didn't hurt. It was, in fact, an oddly familiar feeling.

"Yes!" She smiled.

Her eyelashes grew fuller and thicker. Her lips darkened to a deep maroon. Her hair moved up into a long ponytail seated on top of her head. Her furs melted together into a black silk slip dress with a celestial print and her feet sprouted perfect black chunky platform sandals. It was the exact outfit I had seen the other girls my age wearing and on the covers of the magazines in the checkout lane at the store. It was what I had daydreamed of wearing a thousand times, knowing Momma would never allow something so scandalous.

"Whoa." I sat upright.

When she was satisfied with what she saw in the mirror, she turned to face me.

"I've traveled from cave to cave on the full moon for more millennia than many others like me. The last time I was able to cross over into this world was three thousand years ago when Solomon managed to summon me by happenstance. But you have made it possible to do so again."

It suddenly made sense. "That was you in the woods two years ago. You spoke to me and Aaron on that spirit board."

"Yes. You and I have always been connected. That night you called to me on a full moon and I was able to make myself known. We are not all so lucky to be able to reach through the veil between our worlds and many of us gave up trying long ago."

"What do you mean?"

"Demons, angels, and Gods all live on a different plane from humans. We can see you and hear you but conditions have to be perfect for us to interact with you. I was banished to live in caves for eternity for my seductions but Persephone made it possible for me to travel when the moon is full."

"Persephone is Greek mythology."

"You humans have thousands of faiths and they all have elements that are right and even more elements that are wrong. None have been wholly correct. Take example the names for your primary god- Zeus, Iehova, Allah, Jupiter, Ra… all different names for the same being but you all fight as if whatever you call him means something. In reality, you are all so convoluted by lies and written words of men that we abandoned all efforts of trying to help you figure it out an eternity ago."

"Why are you here?" I was enthralled and confused.

"Persephone is the wife of Abezethibou. You know of him?"

"Yes. He left heaven with Satan. He's the demon who helped the pharaoh fight Moses."

"Yes. Your church is not completely leading you to lies."

"Don't tell my mom. She says the bible is the final word of God and I shouldn't be reading any other scriptures. I have read them at the library."

"Such unwillingness to educate yourselves is exactly what is wrong with you humans. There are a thousand gospels written by hundreds of men. You blindly chose which to believe and have chosen to kill for those words. There is no proof the books you selected tell the correct story. They even contradict each other." She sighed. "To continue, Persephone took pity on me because of her own imprisonment. She made my travels possible. Tonight is a full moon, so I was able to leave my cave. You are my gateway and the moon was my key. I do not know what conditions prevented it the many times I have tried before, but I am here to help you now."

"What do you mean?"

"You are not like others. You are a conduit; a direct portal between our worlds. Do you not ever wonder why you have woken up at three in the morning for as long as you can remember?"

"Yes."

"This is why! This is what you were meant for! To bridge the two worlds."

"Is that what my mom means when she says I was chosen by God?"

"Believe that if you so choose. Your mother is not of a completely sound mind, but she is right about you being special."

"Does that mean other demons can use me to come here?"

"I do not know of any who have succeeded but some have tried. That's why you and people like you wake up at three. It's when the gap between our worlds is shortest and we wake you when we try to cross it. We cannot do it when you are awake; your conscious mind is like a stone wall that keeps us out."

"So what are you going to do here?"

"I must return to my cave before the full moon is gone. I do not know what will happen to me if I do not return and I fear it could prevent me from ever revisiting. I wish to have a little fun while I am here but I wish to help you, too. There is a man who has wronged you. I must help you confront him. He must learn from his mistake."

"How do you know-?"

"I hear your thoughts and see through your eyes. I know everything there is to know about you. Do you wish this Brett to see his errors?"

I thought for a moment. I was standing in my bedroom having a conversation with a demon from another plane of existence. The thought that I was having a nervous breakdown crossed my mind. Maybe I was schizophrenic. I looked at the succubus impatiently waiting for my response.

"Yes." I stood up.

"You will have to do exactly as I tell you."

I knew Onoskelis was known for seduction. Seducing men and strangling them was the reason she had been imprisoned. I thought about what Jacob had said about not doing anything I wasn't ready to do. But he also reminded me that I could ask for forgiveness. I didn't know the first thing about tempting a man but I knew that would be part of Onoskelis's plan. I didn't know the rest of it until it was too late.

Good Night, Brett

She somehow managed to tame my curls into something that didn't quite look like a nest on my head. She used olive oil from the kitchen to smooth them and pulled them straight so that instead of a tangled mess, I had beautiful waves of red. She tore through my closet and found a skirt she deemed suitable and then cut it impressively short with a pair of sewing scissors. When I put it on it was almost as short as the cheerleaders' uniforms at school. I giggled as I pictured my mother fainting if she ever saw me wearing something so salacious. She used a black pen to create something that looked like eyeliner for me and mixed the contents of a magic marker and some petroleum jelly to stain my lips red.

She touched the quartz around my neck.

"That stays," I insisted.

She nodded without questioning before examining my modest shoe collection and shaking her head.

"We will need to find shoes that make you taller on my next visit. We have very little time tonight and much work to do."

After she'd shown me how to walk, how to lean, fixed my posture, and exactly how to manipulate my eyes, she stood back and looked at me. She smiled a wicked and satisfied smile.

"You are my masterpiece. I challenge Michelangelo to hang his head in shame."

I beamed at her. I was uncomfortable and scared, but excited.

"Tonight, you must do as I have taught you. You must make him believe he is wanted. I will do the rest."

I looked in the mirror. I was really going to do this. I, Grace Gertrude Nightingale, was going to seduce a man. The Grace that looked back at me was almost unrecognizable. Her hair was satin. Her eyes were bright. She was poised and confident. I didn't believe she was me.

"We are running out of time," Onoskelis urged.

I quietly made my way out through the mudroom door. Riding my bike in a skirt that short was horribly uncomfortable but I managed to make it to the church grounds without incident. It was after four in the morning, but he was exactly where I knew he would be. He was tucked in the corner of the tool shed, nearly passed out. I slipped in and closed the door behind me. His eyes were watery and his nose was red. There were several beer cans on the ground around him but we were otherwise alone. He stood up unsteadily and put his hand against the wall to stabilize himself and failing in his attempt to not appear to be an inebriated slob.

"I knew you would come." He smiled a crooked, drunken smile.

I took a deep breath and remembered what Onoskelis had just taught me. It was my turn to be the predator. This intoxicated cretin was my prey. I smiled and walked up to him coyly. My heart was pounding in my ears. I was really doing this.

"How could I say 'no'?" I put my hand around the back of his neck. "You are every girl's dream." I pushed down and he sat on the ground. I bent over and looked him in the eye. "And tonight you're mine."

I knelt with my legs on either side of him. I could feel the bulge in his denim between my legs. I pushed my lips against his. I felt his tongue in my mouth. It was awkward and gross. I then knew what beer and marijuana tasted like. I pulled back, trying not to make my disgust obvious, and he smiled.

After that, I'm not sure what happened. As I looked at him, the edges of my vision became blurred and blackened before I lost consciousness. When I awoke, I was still straddling him but his eyes were bloodshot and his face was blue and expressionless. His belt was secured tightly around his neck. I realized he was dead.

"Oh, my God. Oh, my God. Oh, my God." I felt panic welling up inside of me as I leaped to my feet.

I heard a laugh and turned around. Onoskelis was standing in the shadows cackling at me.

"What is wrong?" She asked.

She was beaming brightly. She seemed almost proud.

"He's dead!" I screamed.

I was standing now. I'm not sure how my feet were staying under me. My legs felt like rope and I was shaking uncontrollably.

"Of course he is. I told you he would pay," she said matter-of-factly.

"You killed him?" I felt like my eyes would bulge from my skull as I screamed in disbelief.

"That is what I do. I strangle men. You know this. He was not a very worthwhile one. His intoxication prevented him from mounting an adequate defense." She poked at him with her toe.

"I'm going to go to be arrested!" Everything was starting to spin.

"Why would you be arrested?"

"He's dead and I'm here! My fingerprints are all over. His friends saw him touch me earlier. No one's going to believe that a demon that travels on the beams of the full moon did it. They're going to think I'm fucking crazy!" That was the first time in my life I had ever used a swear word. "I'll be locked in a padded room!"

"Who is to suspect a girl half his size was able to do this alone? There are no witnesses and everyone knows you are always in this shed. Of course, your fingerprints are going to be everywhere. Nothing will happen to you. If you keep this secret, it will be near a week before he is found. It is Monday morning and the shed will be sealed all week."

Monday morning. I opened the door to the shed and looked at the horizon. The sun wasn't quite coming up yet but the sky was obviously lighter. I turned back to Onoskelis.

"Tell no one and everything will be fine," she reassured me. "I must leave now. I hope to see you on the next full moon."

I blinked and she was gone. I closed the shed door behind me and slipped the padlock into place. I needed to get home. My mother would be waking up for work soon and I had morning chores. I couldn't be caught out like this. I rode my bike home as fast as I could but I was still terrified and unsteady.

Onoskelis was right. There was no reason to suspect that I had ever done anything wrong. I repeated this over and over as I feverishly pedaled my bike. When I got to my little farmhouse, I slipped back in through the mudroom door. I scrubbed and scrubbed until I was able to get the ink off my face. I lay down and covered myself with the blanket and pretended to be asleep as my mother came to wake me for breakfast and chores.

"Stop being so lazy and get up." She shut the door behind her without ever having looked at me.

All day I felt as if I was in a dream. A combination of exhaustion from being awake and adrenalin for fear of my crime being discovered kept me from being able to focus. Little Hope stayed at my feet and tried to keep me grounded in reality as I went about my day and did my chores but I don't remember actually doing any of them. I remember getting supper ready and setting the table as my mother came home. She sat down at the table and looked me in the eye.

"Do you know where Brett Thomas is?" She asked.

I felt a burst of terror and I stared back at her with my mouth wide open.

I stammered a little, "N-no. Not really. Why?"

"His parents said he never came home last night. Half the town is looking for him."

I saw the blue, expressionless face waiting to be found in the tool shed.

"Be sure to say a prayer for him." She cut into her chicken.

I nodded solemnly.

As the week went by, I started to relax. Every day my secret went undiscovered, a weight lifted from my shoulder.

Just as Onoskelis had predicted, they didn't find the body until Saturday morning when Father Harold went to unlock the shed. By that point, Brett was a partially decayed and bloated lump. By all rights, he should have been found sooner. No one from the school spoke up and told the police about his little hiding place even though we all knew about it. I don't know why no one confessed about the shed and I didn't care.

The community garden was roped off as a crime scene so I got the weekend off from gardening duty. I spent that Saturday leaning against the sorghum tree in my backyard with a library book. The whole town was abuzz with theories about what had happened to him. Not a single one of those theories had anything to do with me. The police never even came to talk to me. The more time that passed, the more I had become complacent with what had happened. Brett was a garbage human being. How many other innocent girls would he have corrupted had I not helped Onoskelis seduce him?

That Sunday, the church said a prayer for his soul and his family. I looked down at the floor.

"I'll see you down there later," I whispered.

Confession

"Forgive me father for I have sinned."

"I doubt that, Grace." Father Harold's voice came through the wooden screen between us. "Is this a real sin or something your mother told you you did wrong?"

I smiled a little. "I have done something evil. And I fear I may do it again. I think I'm glad I did it but I don't want it to keep happening."

"Whatever you have done, God will forgive. As long as you truly repent, you have nothing to fear. But be cautious. Remember Romans twelve: twenty-one."

"Do not be overcome by evil, but overcome evil with good. I understand, Father. And I will fight."

"Good girl, Grace. What did you do anyway? Steal a pack of gum?"

I pictured the blank stare on Brett's lifeless face. "No sir. A little worse than that. But I promise I will make my peace with it and move on. Thank you."

The Gamer

    Brett's unsolved murder weighed heavily on the town. For months, it was all anyone talked about at church or the grocery store. Only I had known the truth and the more I thought about it, the more absurd it felt. I was sure I had been there when he died but a demon to help me? That must have been some strange dream that my mind had confused for reality. Regardless, I wanted to feel guilty about what had happened, but I couldn't. Once the fear of being caught had subsided, I felt almost nothing. I had even continued to try to style my hair as Onoskelis had done (with minimal success) and started wearing lip gloss from the drug store, despite my mother's insistence that I looked like a harlot. I should have wanted to repress any memory of that night, but I liked the way I looked when I did those things. I was sixteen years old and I liked feeling like I had some semblance of control in my life. Brett was dead. There was nothing I could do to change that but I could move forward with my life.

    I would spend hours in the woods behind our house or at the library just to get away from all the gossip and my obligations. With no friends and Jacob the Tormentor still in my house, I needed a safe place to sit and meditate on life. Aaron and I had spent so much time in those woods that they still held a bit of magic, even without him. I had a special hideaway next to the creek where I couldn't hear the droning of cars, barking dogs, or other people. It was a place of quiet contemplation that I believed no one else knew about and I didn't think anyone would ever find me there. That's how Toby came into my life.

    It was my junior year of high school on a sweet-scented October afternoon. After church, I changed into my day clothes and snuck out the back door and into the trees. The air was clean and there was just enough chill to keep me bundled in my jacket. The leaves were noisy underfoot but not quite crunchy. This was my most treasured time of year. I shuffled down to the creek to sit on my favorite boulder. Peace and quiet at last.

I sat in solitude for about twenty minutes before I heard sticks crunching and a thud behind me. I turned to see a teenager falling out of the woods about ten feet away.

"Oh. Hey. I didn't know anyone else knew about this place." He smiled a crooked smile at me.

I was familiar with Toby but I didn't really know him. He was older than me but in the same grade. He had failed his freshman classes and was forced to repeat them. We had a few CP classes together but didn't associate very much. I was in more honors classes and I think he was just barely passing. He was an archetype of the clichéd brooding Goth-ish teenage male. He only wore black and always had a wallet chain running along the side of his pants. He wore a spiked dog collar around his neck and a studded leather watch. He sometimes had a fire engine red streak in his shoulder-length black hair and his blue eyes were usually rimmed with dark eyeliner.

I was startled and didn't know what to say. I think I smiled back.

"You're in my study period, right? Grace?"

He knew my name. I recalled an image of him using his trapper keeper as a pillow in the back corner of the classroom.

"Y-yeah. Toby?" I stammered.

I felt a little awkward. I still didn't have very much practice at social interaction with peers.

"That's me. You mind some company?"

"Uh. Sure." I scooted over on the rock.

He sat down and pulled a joint from behind his ear. He lit it and took a draw.

"You want a hit?" He passed the joint towards me.

I had never done any type of drug in my life. I didn't even take aspirin if I could help it. Mom insisted that "God would heal what ailed me."

"Um. No thanks." I tried to be polite.

"It's cool." He took another draw. "I like it here. It's so quiet, ya know?"

He looked out over the water.

"Me too. It can get pretty chaotic in my house," I agreed.

He took another draw. "You got any siblings?"

"No, but my older cousin, Jacob, lives with me. We don't get along," I said, choosing my wording carefully.

"Damn. That's rough."

I smiled. No one had ever seemed to sympathize with me before.

"What about you?" I asked.

"None from my dad but my mom and her husband just had a baby. It's always screaming. That's why I come down here."

"Where's your dad?" I suddenly realized I may be getting too personal.

"He lives about an hour from here. I go see him every other weekend. I hate going but Mom makes me. Your folks together?"

"I don't know my dad." I had never felt ashamed by saying those words before.

"You like it at home?"

"I'm down here, aren't I?" I turned my head and looked at him.

He smiled. "Fair enough." He pointed at the quartz around my neck. "Cool rock."

I instinctively touched it. "My best friend gave it to me before he moved away."

"That's cool. Like having a piece of him with you all the time."

"Exactly." I felt myself smiling.

We sat together and talked about school and what we liked to do in our spare time. He was particularly animated when he talked about his video games. I had never played a video game before and I found his enthusiasm amusing. He was the only person besides Uncle James who supported my desire to study anything outside of the church. He wasn't at all like I had stereotyped him to be. He talked to me about his art and offered to show it to me sometime. I thoroughly enjoyed his company. It was nice to just sit with him and be myself. I hadn't felt like that since Aaron had left.

As the sun was setting, I excused myself to go home for supper.

He stood and offered me his hand to help me down off the boulder. I was very surprised by the gesture and I felt a little flutter in my stomach as I took his hand.

"Maybe I'll see you down here again sometime?" He raised his eyebrows at me.

I smiled. "No doubt."

I had a ridiculous grin on my face the whole walk home. I had spent an entire afternoon with a *boy* my own age and had fun. Momma would have lost her mind if she had known; especially Toby. She would have sworn he was a devil-worshipper and agent of Satan simply because of the way he dressed. I giggled at the thought. Hope would be my only confidant about that afternoon. She could keep a secret.

The next day in study hall, I was working on my algebra when a folded triangle paper football landed on my desk. I looked around. No one seemed to have seen it. I unfolded it. It was a beautiful colored pencil sketch of a peace lily against a background of blue and green. I had told Toby the day before that those were my favorite flowers. I looked over my shoulder. He was looking up at the ceiling and pretending to try not to make eye contact. I smiled.

After class, we met back at the boulder. That's how it all started. We met in the creek almost every day. If it was too cold or too wet, we would meet at the library or get pop and fries at the only fast-food restaurant in town. Often, we wouldn't even really talk. I would study while he worked on his sketches or napped. Sometimes he even brought his hand-held video games with him. He would escort me to the edge of the woods, making sure to stay out of view of my house as to not draw the attention of my mother's all-seeing eye. She would never have approved of my dating in school and certainly not someone like him. Our budding romance had to remain a secret. I had my first real, honest kiss in those woods and my cat was the only one who knew.

One day, after Christmas, Jacob almost ruined everything. I was taking notes from my history book while Toby was sketching a battle scene I was reading about.

"So, Grace, who's your friend?"

I looked up. Jacob was grinning at me with his arms crossed on his chest. He looked extremely smug and I felt myself sinking into my chair.

Toby stood up and reached across the table with his hand out. "I'm Toby. Grace is my tutor."

I was surprised at how easily Toby had lied. Jacob looked skeptical. He shook his hand.

"Doesn't look like you're taking very good notes." He indicated Toby's sketch pad.

"Dude. I'm failing for a reason. Got that ADD thing. Mom thinks tutoring is going to fix it."

I was hit with a sudden thought. Did his mom know about our time together?

Jacob smirked. "Yeah. Right." He turned and looked at me. "How long have you guys been... tutoring?"

"Jacob, don't be a jerk." I rolled my eyes at him.

"Fine. Fine." I didn't like the look on his face. "You going to be home in time for dinner?"

"Probably."

"Okay, then. Nice to meet you, Toby." He turned and walked away.

Toby sat back down. "He's going to tell your mom, isn't he?"

I sighed. "Yup."

"You going to be okay?"

"Depends on the mood she's in when he tells her."

I tried to go back to studying but I found it hard to focus after Jacob's intrusion. Toby affectionately rubbed my back. He could feel the tension radiating off of me. Eventually, I decided to give up and head home to face whatever was waiting for me.

I walked in and set my book bag by the front door. I could smell the pot roast and potatoes. I took a deep breath and walked into the kitchen. Jacob was already sitting at the table and smirking at me.

"Grace!" My mom smiled at me. "You're just in time for dinner. Jacob said he saw you at the library."

I swallowed hard. Why was she smiling?

"Yeah." My voice was unsteady.

"You didn't tell me you were tutoring again."

He told her I was tutoring. What was he playing at?

"Yeah. I thought it might be a good way to help me study and something I can put on my college applications."

"College. Of course." My mother still didn't see why I wanted a career. "Are you tutoring someone from the church? I don't want you around any bad influences."

Toby was a long-haired, heavy-metal, an atheist, and a pothead but he was far from a bad influence.

Before I could say anything, Jacob spoke up. "You should bring your students here. There's plenty of space at the table and then you won't have to be worried about coming home in time for dinner." He was using all of his strength not to laugh as he said it.

"Yes. You should bring them here to study." Momma didn't care if I was home for dinner; she wanted to scrutinize the people I was spending time with.

I wish I could have shot arrows out of my eyes. I would have loved to kill my cousin on the spot.

"I'll make the offer but their parents might not like them coming to a stranger's house," I explained.

"Nonsense," Momma said. "We aren't strangers and there's no safer house in town."

Jacob was bouncing in his seat from stifling laughter. I wanted nothing more than to grab a knife out of the butcher block and run it across his neck.

The next day at school, I told Toby what happened.

He smiled. "All right. I'll be over at four."

I was suddenly terrified. What was going on? I didn't pay any attention at school. I was running scenarios that included my uncle strangling Toby, my mother disowning me, and my cousin poisoning his chicken pot pie. I felt sick.

I was home before three-thirty. I set out my books and papers at the kitchen table for our 'study session.' Promptly at four, the doorbell rang. I could see the door from the living room. Jacob ran past me to open it. I couldn't believe what I saw on the other side.

Toby had his long hair pulled back into a ponytail. His eyeliner and dog collar were gone. He had traded in his black band t-shirt and baggy jeans for a blue polo shirt and khaki pants. I almost didn't recognize him.

"Good afternoon." He gave Jacob a smug smile. "I'm here to see Miss Grace."

I almost couldn't contain my laughter. He entered the house and walked straight up to my mom as she came out of the laundry room.

She looked him up and down but didn't have her normal look of disgust.

"You must be Toby," she finally said.

"Yes, ma'am." He shook her hand. "Thank you for letting me come into your home."

"So polite!" She seemed genuinely shocked. "You are very welcome. We are having chicken and broccoli for dinner if you would like to stay."

"Thank you, ma'am. That would be wonderful."

I managed to turn my outburst of laughter into a cough.

"Are you ready?" I gestured to the chair next to me.

As he sat down, he winked at Jacob who was still standing next to the front door. He pulled out a spiral-bound notebook full of algebra and opened his textbook. I looked over the notes quickly. They were correct.

As if he could read my thoughts, he smiled at me. "I do listen when you talk, you know." He lowered his voice and moved closer to my ear. "And now I have a reason to graduate."

He made sure my mom wasn't looking before he squeezed my hand.

That night couldn't have gone any smoother. Jacob kept picking at him and trying to get him to slip up and admit we were seeing each other but he so gracefully navigated his questions, that he even impressed my mother. When Jacob mentioned his long hair, Toby motioned towards the crucifix and asked if he would fault our Lord and Savior for his haircut. Jacob turned red. Momma beamed bright and asked Toby if he went to church. Toby explained that he attended St. Teresa's with me but skillfully dodged having to lie about attending church. Momma was surprisingly sated.

At the end of the evening, I walked him out to the front porch.

"How did I do?" He held his books to his chest.

"That was perfect!" I exclaimed. "But I think I prefer you in your normal clothes."

He smiled. "Me too."

I felt a wave of nervousness sneak into my stomach. "I've never really lied to my mother before. I've hidden a few things, but never lied."

"It wasn't a lie." A cold, January wind kicked up and we stood closer together. "Just a little misdirection."

I smiled. We made sure the coast was clear before he kissed my cheek and left.

Our 'little misdirection' went on for over a year. We preferred to spend warm days on our boulder in the woods or hide at the library. He would come over, dressed in his disguise, every few months to keep my mother's suspicion at bay. He could drive before me and we would often find secret places to park or drive to places where no one knew us so we could be together in public. When he turned eighteen, his parents moved to Nevada and left him alone in the apartment while he finished high school. That opened up a whole new world for us. We would spend hours laying on the couch together while he played his beloved video games. His living room became a gallery for his art; much of which he claimed I had inspired. There were always dirty dishes, takeaway containers, and soda cans strewn around, but we didn't care. Life was good and I was happy.

Early in my senior year of high school, Uncle James fell off the wagon for the hundredth time. This time it resulted in a DUI and a suspended driver's license. Without the ability to drive, I inherited his treasured Crown Victoria. That car felt like driving a tank, but it had wheels that rolled and I could legally drive it. I had been saving all of my money to put into a secret college fund and not having to designate a portion of that to purchase my own vehicle made me feel closer to my goals.

I felt like my whole world was coming together. Unbeknownst to my mother, Pennsylvania State had already accepted my application. I had a plan to escape that little one-horse town and hopefully never have to look back. To top it all off, I had a wonderful man whom I couldn't imagine my life without who supported my ambitions. I wish I could have kept those rose-colored glasses on forever.

After class one Friday while Momma was at work, I used my newfound freedom to hop two towns over to go to the big chain stores and look for a new pair of shoes. We had shoe stores, of course, but a twenty-minute drive could save me twenty or thirty dollars by buying from one of the superstores and it was worth the trip. I parked next to a meter on Main Street and started walking towards the store. As I passed by the smaller shops, a little boutique that was decked out in pink grabbed my attention. I don't know what exactly drew me to it, but I walked in and my jaw dropped at all of the different lingerie. There were corsets and bras and things made of lace that I didn't even know how to describe.

"Looking for something special for someone special?" A cheerful brunette stepped out of a back room.

"Oh. Um." I thought for a quick second. "My boyfriend's birthday is in a few days and was just kind of browsing."

"We can make sure it's a birthday he won't soon forget!"

Before I knew what was happening, she was asking me a barrage of questions about Toby's likes and dislikes and what kind of impression I wanted to make. She took out a tape measure and started making notes on my 'unique shape.' She grabbed a few things off of hooks and shoved me into a small fitting room.

I tried on a black lace thing and stood looking at myself in the mirror. I was really wearing *that*. I blushed at my own reflection. I had never worn so little with the intent of someone seeing it. That was when the realization hit me. I was still a virgin. The closest I had come was Brett and that hadn't ended well. Was I really ready to do this? Giving myself to Toby seemed like such a natural next step. He had been so respectful of my boundaries throughout our whole relationship. Jacob had once told me not to do anything I wasn't ready for, but the more I thought about it, the more ready I felt. It was a *normal* thing for teenagers to do and, no, Toby and I weren't married but we were planning our lives together and that was pretty close.

"Everything all right in there?" The brunette called.

I snapped out of my trance. I changed out of the black lace and into my normal clothes. I stepped out of the fitting room and handed it to the brunette.

"I'll take this one."

That night, Toby asked me to meet him for dinner. I was practically vibrating with excitement over his birthday present. I'd hoped I wouldn't ruin the surprise. All happiness instantly dissipated, however, when I saw his face. I had never seen him look so sullen. His eyeliner and hair pulled over his face could not hide the dark circles around his eyes. He didn't say anything as we ordered our food and took our trays to a table in the corner.

"What's wrong?" I finally asked.

"We have to talk."

My heart moved towards my throat. "Okay."

"I applied to an art school in Nevada. I didn't think I'd get in. I really just did it to show my mom I was planning something after high school. Well, they liked my stuff. They liked it a lot. Mom and John said I can move in with them."

"But... but what about Penn State?"

"Penn State is your dream. And you should follow it. I didn't really expect this to happen but I don't think it's an opportunity I can pass up."

I started feeling my chest cave in.

He continued. "I'm sorry, Grace. I didn't mean for this to happen. But I never really thought I had a future. Not until I met you, anyway. And I love you, but I love my art, too."

My head started spinning. His voice sounded like it was fading into the distance. I couldn't listen to anymore. I left my uneaten tray of food and ran to my car before the tears started.

I ignored his calls the next day and the day after that. I understood what he meant. And I understood that this was a wonderful opportunity for him. But I'd had a plan. We were going to find an apartment together in Pennsylvania. He was going to work while I was in school. We were going to have a normal, happy, adult life together. I couldn't afford housing on my own. And what about our long-term future? What about all the times we had talked about growing old together on a porch swing far away? All of that was meaningless prattle between two love-blind teenagers now.

Three nights after Toby brought my world crashing down, I woke from a dead sleep. Three a.m. I rolled over to pet Hope. She hissed and darted off the bed. As I watched her flee to the closet, a motion in the opposite corner of the room caught my eye.

There she stood in a black leather skirt and black blouse. Her long hair was pulled up in a high and tight ponytail but it still almost touched her buttocks.

"Hello, Grace." Onoskelis smiled.

"Y-you! I thought I made you up." I sat up and stared at her in disbelief.

"No. I am very real. Persephone chided me over our last adventure. She said I brought too much unwanted attention so I had to stay away. Else I am wrought when you need me and you have not needed me."

"I need you now?"

"Yes." I felt her probing around in my brain again. "His name is Toby."

"No. I won't let you hurt him."

"He hurt you."

"Yes, but I'll heal."

"Would you not like a little revenge?" Her smile was beautifully wicked.

"Well-"

"I see you in black lace and him writhing over his mistake."

I glanced at the pink bag that was tucked away in the closet. "Well-"

"We do not have to cause him physical harm. Only make him regret his decision."

I should have known not to trust her, but the thought of Toby regretting our breakup made me smile. I thought about how beautiful it would be to see him upset; to make him realized what he was giving up. I retrieved the bag from the closet where Hope was still tucked away.

"Yes, my girl." Onoskelis smiled wide; her teeth were almost the same color as her porcelain skin.

I put the lingerie on and covered myself with my long dress coat. As I passed Jacob's room, I peaked in the door. He was gone. No doubt he had snuck out the same way I intend to. I quietly crept out of the mudroom door. With no Jacob and a mother who could sleep through anything when she was on her medication, I started my car on the street without fear of waking anyone. Onoskelis was giggling in the passenger seat as we pulled into Toby's apartment complex. I could hear my heart pounding in my ears. I felt a little faint as I took a deep breath and knocked on the door. My heart and breath all came to a dead stop as the door swung open.

"Grace?" Toby stood in his boxers and a t-shirt. "I didn't think I would ever see you again."

I looked up into his eyes. I used every ounce of will in me to steady my voice. "Can we talk?"

"Yeah. Of course." He turned into the apartment and I followed.

I shut the door behind me and turned. The apartment was barely recognizable. There were no dirty dishes or pop cans left all over. There were not strips of flypaper hanging from the ceiling. The carpet had just been vacuumed and the air smelled of cleaner. And there he was, standing in the middle of it all.

"Sit, please," I instructed.

He sat on the couch. I bit my lip in fear and anticipation of his reaction. Then I unbuttoned and dropped the coat.

His eyes lit up. "Wow."

I laughed a little in relief. "This was supposed to be your birthday present."

"Well, happy birthday to me!"

He reached for me and I forgot all about my revenge. He stood up and pulled me close to him. I put my hand on his cheek and looked into his eyes before pressing my lips hard against his. It was one of the most passionate kisses in all of my memories. As we separated, I glanced into the bedroom. I could see the open plastic suitcase he had been packing on the bed. He was leaving for Nevada the day after graduation. All of the feelings of hurt and anger I had felt over the previous three days flooded back in a massive tidal wave. It didn't matter what happened that night. He was still going to leave me. I could see Onoskelis grinning brightly through the kitchen window.

"Grace?" He looked into my eyes.

I looked up at his face just as the edges of my sight went blurry and the room went dark.

When I awoke, Toby lay dead on the couch. His marble eyes were speckled with red from the burst blood vessels. The cord from his video game controller was wound tightly around his neck.

"Oh, my God." I stood up quickly.

"Do not worry. He will take care of him." Onoskelis was sitting calmly at the kitchen table.

"You said-"

"Shh. Thin walls." She pressed a finger to her lips.

I was suddenly panicked. I didn't know how much noise Toby had made as he was dying. I was going to prison this time.

"You said we weren't going to hurt him!" I whispered harshly.

"We had not intended to. Then you became angry and I knew our plan was not going to work, so I helped."

"Helped?!"

"Of course. You would never forgive yourself if you let him leave without repercussions," she stated bluntly.

"What about the repercussions of what we just did?" I felt numb but sick.

"No one will know. I will see to that. Just as I did last time."

Last time. Brett. I had killed more than once. I was a serial killer before I had even turned eighteen.

"They will not write books or films about you. You will not be caught," Onoskelis reassured me while rolling her eyes.

I had momentarily forgotten that she could see into my mind.

"What are we going to do? We can't just leave him here. What if his parents try to visit to help him move?"

Onoskelis looked towards the bedroom.

After we hid Toby's body, I took us home shortly before dawn. I was careful to park my car in the exact same place it had been and cautiously ensured the mudroom door didn't slam behind me. Once back in the familiar safety of my bedroom, I stripped down. I put the lingerie in the garbage under the crumpled homework. I put on a t-shirt and sat on the edge of the bed, trying not to cry. Toby was gone. My first real love. All of the sweet things he had said to me and done for me came back in single-file memories. Each one was more painful than the last.

"You will recover," Onoskelis said in an attempt to be comforting.

"I don't want to just get over it. I don't want to just get over him!" My eyes stung with more tears. "And I don't want your help ever again."

Her eyes narrowed at me. "You do not mean that."

"Yes, I do!"

My bedroom door flung open and Jacob rushed in. "Who are you talking to?"

I swore he looked right at her just before she dematerialized.

"Hope." I gestured towards the cat in the closet. "She's acting weird."

He crossed his arms. "Do you think I'm stupid?"

"Yes," I said flatly. "There is no one else in here and do you see a phone in my hand? Who else could it be?"

He looked skeptical. "The voices in your head; just like Aunt Janice when she's off her meds."

I threw a pillow at him as he shut the door.

Toby's family reported him missing after he hadn't contacted them and he hadn't made it to Nevada. It was over a week before the police knocked on my door. Jacob and I were the only ones home. They said someone identified my car at the apartment but no one had reported seeing or hearing anything out of the ordinary. I told them Toby and I had broken up because he was leaving for Nevada and I had gone over for one last kiss before he left. I technically didn't lie. After I had satisfactorily answered their questions, the officers nodded and left. I closed the door behind them and turned to see Jacob staring at me. It was almost as if he knew but he wasn't sure what he knew.

Part II

Pennsylvania

Chetna

I took the first chance I could to flee home. I was beginning to feel like suspicious eyes were watching me everywhere and I wanted to disappear. There was also, of course, getting out from under my mother's pressing thumb. She protested my ambitions until the day I left. I didn't know what I was going to major in when I got to college and truthfully, it was the last of my concerns. I was a nineteen-hour ride from everything I knew and anyone who knew me. I could not control my excitement as I rode those Greyhound buses to freedom at Pennsylvania State. I didn't even know they were carrying me to my soul mate, Chetna.

My freshman roommate was a girl who was so seemingly normal, I thought she was only pretending to be nice when she asked me to go out in public with her. She was a beautiful first-generation Indian-American. She was just over five feet tall. Her hair was long, black, and shiny like Onoskelis's. Her skin was a smooth, beautiful shade of old copper and her face was carefully composed with makeup. She looked like a work of art.

"Do you want the right side or the left?" Her voice was surprisingly melodic.

We were both standing in the doorway, having arrived at our room almost simultaneously.

"Oh. Um." I didn't want to answer wrong.

"It really doesn't matter to me." She smiled.

"Um. The left? Is that okay?"

"Totally! Like I said, doesn't really matter to me. I'm Chetna, by the way." She held out her hand.

"Grace." I shook it.

"Nice to meet you, Grace. What's your major?"

I felt a little embarrassed to answer. "General studies." I set my bag on the cot they called a bed.

"Couldn't decide, huh?"

"Not really." I suddenly felt a little deflated. "What about you?"

"Plant biology. This was the furthest botany program from home that I could get into. I had to get away from my crazy parents. They just didn't understand why I want a career before marriage or to work at the family store. I want my own life, you know?"

"I can relate to that." I smiled. "My mom has had my life planned out for me since the day I was born. I guess that's why I couldn't pick a major. I've never really been given a chance to think about it."

"Totally get it! Just do what I did; find what you're passionate about and run with it. I love ferns and aromatic plants. So here I am." She plopped on her cot. "What do you enjoy?"

I thought about all of my trips to the library to read forbidden books. "History. Culture. Those kinds of things."

"So like anthropology or archeology?"

"I don't know about all the digging. I did it a lot when I was a kid but the travel would be nice."

"Sounds like you're an anthropologist in the making, then."

I smiled. This was probably the most positive peer interaction I had had in my entire life, aside from Aaron and Toby.

There was a gentle knock on the still-open door.

"Where do you want your crap?" A tall Indian man with a scruffy beard stood in the hall.

"The mini-fridge next to the bed. The vanity over there and just put the rest of my bags anywhere. Here. I'll help." She hopped off the bed.

He nodded and they left me to unpack. I had one, large duffle bag that held virtually all of my worldly possessions. The bed, desk, light, and closet were provided by the school but I had no sheets for the bed, papers or books for the desk, and only clothes I hated to hang in the closet. I sat on the bed. The happy, excited feeling I'd had on the bus was gone. I started to wonder what I was really doing there. I unzipped the bag and saw the crucifix my mother had packed laying on top of my clothes. I shoved it deeper into the bag. This was my chance at a new life and a new identity. The one welcome piece was a koala bear lamp that Uncle James had bought when I was a baby. I gingerly placed it on the nightstand. He was the one person who was proud of me and I welcomed him in spirit.

It wasn't long before Chetna and the stranger returned. She was rolling two suitcases with her while he steered a hand truck with a small refrigerator, a little chest of drawers, and something that looked like a cross between a folding TV tray and a wood suitcase. He couldn't see over it all and was skillfully navigating backward. He undid the straps and, as instructed, put the drawers, TV tray, and a little folding stool I hadn't noticed near the desk and the mini-fridge next to the bed.

He stood back and stretched. "Anything else, Your Majesty?"

She laughed and hugged him.

He turned to me. "Is there anything I can help you with, miss?"

Being called 'miss' when not by a teacher felt strange. "No thank you. I don't have much."

"Oh, my God!" Chetna threw her hands to her face. "I am so rude! Ishwar, this is my new friend, Grace. Grace, this is my brother, Ishwar. He is the only one in my family who supports me in starting a new life and I love him for it!" She hugged him again.

He broke free and shook my hand. I felt a smile come back. I had never been around people so welcoming, let alone been called a friend by anyone but Aaron. I touched the quartz around my neck. It had become such a habit that I rarely noticed I was doing it anymore.

The siblings said their goodbyes and Chetna turned to the TV tray against the wall. "My baby!" She cried and ran up to it.

She unfolded the legs and propped it up. She lifted the lid to reveal a wide mirror. She unfolded two flaps to extend the length and snapped some kind of insert into place to complete the table. The TV tray unfolded like a puzzle box into a vanity table complete with lights around the mirror. I was further in awe as I watched her open the smaller of her two suitcases that was completely full of makeup, brushes, stands, and everything else. She carefully arranged the jars, palettes, and brushes as an artist would prepare a workspace. She caught my gaping expression in the mirror and smiled at me.

"Call it a minor addiction. I just love to feel pretty!" She exclaimed. "What's your favorite makeup brand?"

"I've never really worn makeup." What Onoskelis had done wasn't technically makeup and my drug store lip gloss could hardly compare to Chetna's collection. "My mother forbade it."

"Oh, Honey!" She put her hand over her heart. "I have so much to teach you!"

My duffle bag started to shake. My eyes widened. I'd almost forgotten.

Chetna pointed to it. "What's in your bag?"

I sighed and opened the cat carrier that was tucked under my clothes. Hope leaped out of the top and started to survey her new surroundings.

"Her name is Hope," I said sheepishly.

"You smuggled a cat into the dorm?" Chetna's eyes widened. "Do you have any idea how much trouble you could get into?"

I looked at the floor. I was already going to be homeless in a new city. I just knew it. Chetna picked Hope up and pressed her forehead to the cat's.

"We'd best be careful that no one finds out about you little Missy."

She kissed the cat and set her back on the floor. That was it. She became the best friend I could have ever asked for.

I envied Chet. She was beautiful even without her makeup. She could walk up to almost anyone and make them feel as if they had been friends for ages. She seamlessly blended in with everyone from nerd to sorority sister. I, however, stayed in the comfort and solitude of the shadows at parties and even more so in class. One of my professors once asked me why I never spoke up and shared my obvious grasp of concept with the class. Some days I considered it but I feared the same judgmental glares I received back home.

I had never been to a party. I had no idea what to do or how to behave. That first weekend after we'd moved in, Chetna insisted that I accompany her to one.

"You're not wearing *that*!" She looked at me with her eyes wide.

I stood in front of her in a long plaid skirt, a white blouse, and my nice black church shoes. My messy hair was tamed in a bun at the back of my head and, of course, I wore the quartz around my neck. I looked at myself in the mirror. I had worked hard to make myself presentable.

"What's wrong with it?" I asked.

"Nothing if you want everyone to think you are studying to be a nun."

I turned to her. "What should I change?"

"Everything."

Chet went to her closet and pulled out a long, red skirt.

"I'm way too short for that," I laughed.

"Put it on like a sleeveless dress." She tossed it to me.

"I've never worn a sleeveless dress," I said as I looked at the skirt in my arms.

"College is about new things and it seems to me like you have a lot of them coming." She raised her eyebrows at me.

I took the skirt. I stripped down and put it on with the waistline under my arms. My breasts held it out in front of me. I looked in the mirror again.

"I look like a parachute," I stated.

"That's because we haven't finished the look!"

She put a black belt around my waist and cinched it tight. She then sat me in front of her vanity and set to work. She sprayed and oiled my hair before pulling out all of the tangles and frizz. She worked some magic with a curling iron and created a beautiful cascade of corkscrews. She had a little more trouble with my makeup.

"We need to take you shopping." She frowned. "Our skin tones just aren't even close."

She did the best she could with what she had. Honestly, it was amazing. As I looked at the finished product staring back in the mirror, I was briefly reminded of the sorcery Onoskelis had performed years ago.

Chet smiled and nodded approvingly. "Much better."

That night, she kept me close to her as she mingled and made new friends. She introduced me to anyone who would listen and several men tried to steer me away from her, but she kept them at bay. She knew I couldn't fend for myself in an environment like that and kept me safe. It was several hours before I could relax enough to realize I was having fun.

Over the year, we bonded further as she taught me how to care for my hair, convinced me to switch from glasses to contacts, and instructed me on basic makeup application and techniques. By the end of my freshman year in college, I hardly resembled the messy-haired weirdo in glasses who had first stepped foot on campus. She gave me the confidence to pick a major, too.

Anthropology definitely wasn't a good fit for me but, after remembering the feeling I'd gotten from the Art Institute in Chicago, I pursued that passion. I excelled at art history and she and I helped each other with our homework. I would wake at three in the morning and find her sobbing over one of her romance novels or furiously scribbling notes at her desk and we would stay up together until dawn.

I never told her about Onoskelis but I did eventually become comfortable enough to explain to her that I was a Holy Child and what that meant to my mother.

It was winter quarter and I woke at three as always. She was sitting up in her bed with one of her paperbacks. She looked over at me. The light from her bedside lamp was casting soft shadows across her face and over her side of the room.

"Can I ask you something?" She looked concerned.

I sat up. "Sure."

I was drowsy and just wanted to go back to sleep.

"How come you always wake up at three? It's kind of weird."

I lay back down. How do I explain this without sounding like a lunatic? "Promise you won't judge me?" I asked.

"Promise."

I inhaled deep. "Remember how I told you my mom is really religious and controlling and planned my life out for me?"

"Yeah."

"It's because I'm a Holy Child." The words were painful as I said them.

Being known as a Holy Child was an identity I'd left in Illinois. Here, I was just Grace. I was an art history major, not a beacon to demons. I had no great future laid out in front of me.

"A what?" I could hear the judgment in her voice.

I sighed. "I was born on a holy day. My mom has spent my whole life preparing me to do something great for all mankind in the name of God."

"What does that have to do with waking up at three in the morning?" She sounded confused.

"It's the Devil's Hour. Demons can interact with humans at three and because I'm a Holy Child, they pick on me. It wakes me up."

"Grace?"

I flinched. "Yeah?"

"That's crazy. You know that, right?"

I half-heartedly laughed. "I know. But that doesn't make it less true."

She was quiet.

"What do you think about my little secret?" I turned to face her.

"I think it's insane and you should probably seek professional help. But you're a good person and a good friend and I think that's what's important."

"Thank you."

"Good night." She turned off her bedside light.

That's when I knew she was my soul mate. I had told her the most utterly insane-sounding thing possible and she just accepted me for who I was.

At the end of freshman year, I cried as we said goodbye. Ishwar came to take her home and I could hardly stop hugging her. While she was back in San Jose, I would be staying behind with Hope. We promised to e-mail and text each other every day over the summer and we'd try to get our own little apartment together when she returned in the fall.

Over the summer quarter, I took a part-time job at a warehouse. I was good at organizing and it taught me good cataloging skills. While working, I continued to take a few classes so Hope and I could stay in campus housing. I could have gone home and returned for the fall semester, but I couldn't bring myself to do it. I was far from the point of desperation that would make me want to return to that town. I had gone home for Christmas but only managed to stay for a few days before the discomfort became too much to bear. It wasn't the college experience I had envisioned for myself, but I was happy to have this life that was my own.

The Pilot

True to our word, the following year Chetna and I found half of a duplex to rent not far from campus since I had left my uncle's car in Illinois. It was far from lavish. There were cracks in the walls and stains on the ceiling above the stove from a previous fire. The old floorboards creaked with every footfall and the steep stairs felt like one wrong step could send you to your death. The second floor was a narrow hall with a door on either side. I claimed the room on the left. We furnished most of the small space with a truckload of hand-me-down furniture that had been gifted by Chet's family and driven across the country by Ishwar.

I could have sent for my bedroom things back home. I could have rented a truck or had Ishwar detour in Illinois. But, the truth was, I didn't want it. That was my old life. I felt like bringing it to this new place would be an intrusion. Those things belonged to a different Grace Nightingale. I was becoming far less embarrassed by the face that looked back at me from the mirror. I was somebody else now and I couldn't let *her* where she wasn't welcome. Instead, I found a bed frame and dresser at a thrift store and bought an inflatable mattress. I made a desk and bookshelf out of cinder blocks and plywood that I had spray painted and borrowed one of the extra kitchen chairs from the set Chetna's mom had sent. It wasn't much, but it was home.

Chetna was still the glorious woman I had met the previous fall. She was incredibly driven at school. She studied hard, often long into the night. Almost every weeknight, when I would come home from the warehouse, I could see the light from under her bedroom door and hear her playing her study music. The weekends, however, were for relaxation and fun.

I'm not sure why I agreed to join her at that party. School had only started back two months prior and I was already buried in books and work. The little room we stood in was extremely crowded and I'm sure everyone was drunk. In the center of the room, some men were playing cards and making stupid bets. Some people were drunkenly dancing while others lay passed out on various pieces of furniture or even the floor. I saw one man with his arm around the waist of a barely-conscious girl as he escorted her towards the stairs. Another girl, seemingly one of her friends, interjected and suggested she'd better get her home. The man was visibly angry, but handed the girl over and went to seek out more prey.

I was not comfortable and I definitely did not fit in. I was standing near a wall with a plastic cup of pop and watching Chet flirt with a skater named Kevin.

"Hi. I'm Christian," a voice made me nearly jump out of my skin.

I hadn't even heard him approach me. He was lanky and lean. He had sandy-colored hair and deep, chocolate eyes that sat close to his nose.

I smiled and shook his extended hand. "Grace."

"Nice to meet you, Grace. I don't normally do this but I had to come up and say that you are one of the most beautiful women I've ever met."

I felt my blood rush to my face.

"I bet you say that to all the girls." The cliché rolled out of my mouth and I instantly regretted saying it.

A smile. "Hardly."

"Are you a student at Penn State or just here for the party?" I tried to change the subject.

"Student."

"What are you in school for?"

"Architecture." He stood a little straighter. "But really, I'm a pilot and I'd rather do that."

"Really?" I felt myself tugging the quartz crystal and returned my hand to my cup.

"I fly my dad's Cessna on the weekends but I really want to build one of my own. I could take you up in it some time," he offered.

"I'm not really about getting in a vehicle with someone I just met, let alone an airplane." I smiled politely.

"Okay. How about meeting someone you just met for dinner?" he asked smoothly.

I was a bit taken with this light-haired stranger and agreed to dinner the following weekend. I pulled a pen out of my handbag and scribbled my phone number on the back of a receipt.

Chetna insisted on helping me prepare for the date. We went to the mall and she dragged me through several stores before selecting a skirt that was slightly shorter than I was comfortable with and a spaghetti strapped top. She then took me on the hunt for makeup. She had gone over the bare basics with me the previous year but this year was the advanced course. There were so many shades and layers and brushes to look at. I was in a completely foreign land. She showed me how to match things to my skin tone, selected powder pallets, and other 'necessities.' It was all a bit much more than I had wanted to spend and I was secretly calculating how many extra hours I would need to pick up at the warehouse to make up for it. When we returned, she made me shower and shave. She then held me down while attacking my face with a pair of tweezers, insisting that the caterpillars on my forehead were unacceptable. When she was satisfied, she sat next to me in the mirror and applied the various creams, pastes, and powders along with me so I could get a feel for how it was done. In the end, she smiled wide.

"My masterpiece!" She exclaimed. I remembered being called that before.

The following night, we went to a little bar off-campus. Our table was about fifty feet from where a live band played loudly on stage. We sat on the same side of the table so we could hear each other talk. He repeatedly pressed his bare arm against mine and leaned in towards my neck to talk into my ear. The only drinking I had ever really done was during Eucharist at church. Whenever I had attended a party or gone out with Chetna, I had always drunk pop or water. During dinner that night, however, I realized I had a taste for raspberry daiquiris. I had never felt so free of inhibition before. I told him about my classes and my cat and he smiled while keeping the drinks coming. Everything about that night made the hair on my arms stand on end and I kept getting chicken skin. The food was terrible but I had never had so much to drink. I had to take off my shoes and tiptoe barefoot when we got back to his fraternity house. There was a strict 'no women after eleven' policy and breaking the rules was thrilling.

Losing my virginity was far more physically painful and messy than I had expected it to be. As we lay in his bed together afterward, a small, anxious piece of me was waiting for the floor to open and swallow me into the fires of Hell for having premarital sex. Of course, no such thing happened. We lay with me wrapped in his arms and I steadily calmed down. It was done and I had never felt so close to someone.

Looking back, I'm not sure why I fell so hard and fast for Christian. In truth, I think it was the fact that he was the first person to show interest in me since Toby. We had virtually nothing in common. We only went out to dinner once a week or so. After dinner, we typically ended up back at his fraternity house. We would end the nights wrapped in each other's arms until just before dawn when I would shimmy down vines that grew up the side of the building, along the tree line, and away before I was discovered. I wish I had given my virginity to anyone but him but, at the time, I thought I had been in love.

We spoke on the phone almost daily but he practically never text messaged me back if I reached out first. I was young and naïve. I lived for those phone calls. I attributed our infrequent communication to our busy schedules. When he did call, I would spend hours listening to him complain about his classes and fellow students. Whenever I would try to talk about my day, he would listen for about two minutes before shifting the conversation back to himself. I assumed it was because he didn't have a good relationship with his parents so no one in his life cared enough to be as attentive as I was, so I didn't fuss.

For months, this was our routine. Once a week dinner, sex, and cuddling. He would go flying on the weekends but I usually had to work. I wanted more, but we were such busy people. I should have known better but love (or whatever I was in) was truly blind. In March of 2005, the proverbial blinders came off. It was almost his birthday and I wanted to do something amazing to subtly show him that I saw a future for us.

I took off of work to prepare him a good, home-cooked meal. I made a pork roast, mashed potato casserole, broccoli, and I even baked him a chocolate cake. His fraternity brothers let me into his room and I set up a table and candlelit dinner for two. I waited with bated breath for him to come home from his evening class. And waited. And waited.

At a little after eight, the candle had burned out, the food was cold, and I felt like an idiot. I was ready to pack up and admit defeat when his door swung open and he and a blonde woman I may have seen on campus before came in laughing and holding hands.

He stopped just inside the doorway and froze. "Grace?"

"Late class, huh?" I tried to ignore the tears welling up in my eyes.

"I'd better go. Call me." The blonde kissed his cheek and left.

"What are you doing here, Grace?" He looked confused and angry.

"I was trying to surprise you for your birthday," I said through swallowed tears.

"What? Why?"

"What do you mean 'why'?" I was somewhat taken aback by his question.

"It's not like we're dating or anything." He was almost yelling and threw his hands in the air.

With that, all of the pieces of the puzzle fell into place. That's why our interaction was so limited. That's why he rarely answered when I called. He wasn't in classes. He was with other women. I was just casual sex to him; a friend with benefits at best. I felt sick. Our daily conversations meant nothing to him. I was such a fool.

A wave of realization came over him. I could see it in his eyes.

"Wait." He held up his hand. "You thought we were a thing?"

"No." I suddenly felt calm but angry. "Call it a fool's hope."

I stormed past him and down the stairs. I ignored the awkward stares and snickers from his friends. I was completely humiliated. I fell asleep that night in an utter rage over my stupidity. All of the signs had been there. Had I really been so desperate for human affection?

At three a.m. I woke. I knew I shouldn't have done it. I knew what she was capable of; what she would want to do. But I didn't care. When I had come home weeping, Chetna made me tell her what had happened. She told me kindly to forget him and move on, but I couldn't. I didn't want to move on. I wanted him to pay.

"Onoskelis? Are you near? I need you," I called.

I went to the window, but the night was cloudy and I couldn't see the moon.

For the next few days on campus, all eyes were on me. I could feel their giggles and hear their whispers. It was as if the entire college knew what had happened and couldn't contain its ridicule.

On the Friday night after it happened, I was bolted in my room, attempting to study, but finding it impossible to focus. I wasted several hours on the fruitless attempt before giving up and going to bed. As I fell asleep, I was seething. How dare he use me like that? How dare I be so blind? How many other women was he using? Was I really so disposable?

"Of course not. He is a man. Just because he treats you as refuse, that does not make you so." A familiar, slivery whisper woke me at my appointed hour.

I turned and Onoskelis was standing by the window, the light of the full moon illuminating her.

"*He* is the garbage," I said through narrowed eyes.

"Yes. We must, as you say, take him out."

I didn't want to admit it. I didn't want it to be true, but she was right. We picked out the shortest black dress I owned. I left my hair long and down and put Chet's makeup tips to use. Onoskelis grinned with satisfaction, her teeth almost appearing as fangs as we looked at my reflection in the mirror. I set out on my thirty-minute walk to the frat house and carefully stayed in the shadows to avoid being seen.

The men frequently broke curfew or drunkenly lost their keys so they had rigged the front door to open if you knew how to wrench the handle just right. I had been taught how to open it so I could visit Christian late at night. That night I found the common room and halls abandoned. It was nearing four a.m. and most of the men were passed out or somewhere else for the weekend. Fortunately, I found him alone when I slipped into his room. I hadn't actually made a plan in case the blonde or some other courtesan was there.

As I stood over him, I couldn't help but see how peaceful he looked. Those nagging feelings of affection started to return. I glanced to the corner where Onoskelis was waiting. She slightly shook her head. She knew exactly what I was thinking and she did not approve.

I gently ran my finger from his forehead, down his nose, and to his lips. He slowly opened his eyes and when he focused, He shot awake fully.

"Grace? What the fuck?"

I held my finger to his lips. "Shh. I couldn't take it anymore." I pulled the blankets back and threw my legs on either side of him. "Just one more time?"

He smiled, grabbed me, and rolled so he was on his knees, his hands on the pillow on either side of my head. He kissed me hard and passionately. I had him. I could see Onoskelis moving in behind him. I brought my legs up on his shoulders and, as I began to squeeze them around his neck, the corners of my eyes went dark.

When I woke, his arms were around me as we had done so many times after we had 'made love.' I wanted to feel remorse but I only felt satisfaction. I carefully positioned him as if he was just sleeping. I collected every one of my long, strawberry hairs from his pillowcase before slipping out the window, down the vines, and along the tree line. I could make this escape with my eyes closed.

The next morning at breakfast, I was tired but feeling vindicated. I sat in a chair at the kitchen table with my knees pulled up to my chest and my feet on the seat. I was munching on a bowl of cereal with my textbook open (though it was difficult to study) when Chetna came to join me.

"Were you on the phone last night?" she asked as she reached into a cabinet to get a bowl out for herself.

I froze. "No. Why do you ask?"

"I thought I heard you talking but I didn't hear someone else and then it sounded like you left."

"Oh!" I pretended to laugh. "Yeah. I was talking to myself and then I went for a walk. I think stress is starting to crack me."

"Oh." She looked thoughtful for a moment. "Okay. I thought you had Christian in your room at first. Maybe you guys had made up but I didn't hear him talking back."

"No." I looked down at my bowl. "I don't think I'll be seeing him again."

I expected his frat brothers to point the police directly to me once the body was found, but they didn't. It turned out that not only did they believe me to be too small and weak to have hurt him, but none of them had bothered to even learn my name. His womanizing antics had been known to everyone but me. Suspicions were abounding that the boyfriend of one of his lovers had taken revenge. But, no one ever looked at me. Chetna and I talked about how I felt about it when we first heard the news, but even she didn't believe I had it in me.

When classes resumed after spring break, everything seemed to return to normal. The fraternity put up a small memorial but otherwise, no one really spoke of the incident. Stress from impending finals took over and Christian was virtually forgotten.

The One Who Got Away

For years I thought Xander was my one who got away. He was wonderfully handsome and always well dressed. He could charm anyone he met with his wit and perfect smile. He knew what he wanted in life and wasn't afraid to work hard for it. I was so blinded by all of these things.

It was May of 2005. We met during semester finals week; one of the most stressful weeks of the year. I had given up on eating right, brushing my hair, paying attention at work... everything except my grades. Chetna was in a tizzy back in the duplex so I tried to escape to the campus library. Dressed in sweat pants, a school pride hooded sweatshirt, flip-flops, and no attempt made at styling my hair, you would have thought I looked ridiculous and out of place. Not during finals week. There were students all over school grounds walking like zombies, asleep in the computer labs, and even the stereotype sorority girls had given up on makeup for the week.

The library was packed with students. They had flashcards and books spread everywhere, including the floor. Most of them had headphones on with mp3 players trying to drown out any distractions from the real world or audio recordings of lectures. A girl in the corner was even sobbing softly to herself.

Amidst all of this, he and I found each other. There were literally sparks when we first met. We were reaching for the same book in the library and there was a static shock between us.

"I'm so sorry." I drew my hand back.

"My apologies." He smiled.

Wow. That smile. He wasn't particularly tall; but then, most anyone is tall compared to me. His chestnut hair was neatly cut and swept to the right. Heavy eyebrows hung over captivating green eyes. His build was slight, but he was well dressed in a maroon sweater and khaki pants.

"I didn't see you there," he said.

I returned the smile.

"At my height, I'm easy to miss. My cousin always said he could find me in a crowd by looking for the gap."

He laughed. Even his laugh was magical.

"Ladies first." He handed me the book.

I attempted to act demure. "And who should I return it to when I'm finished?"

"My name is Xander." He took my hand and nodded like a gentleman from a Brontë novel. "I'm in the pod of tables under the window. Who shall be returning the book?"

I did a curtsy type of maneuver. "Grace."

"Yes, you are. In every sense of the word. I will see you later this evening." He released my hand turned towards the large windows on the far wall.

I felt all of the blood rush to my face. I had never so freely flirted before. I had no idea what had come over me but I was glad it had happened. I found an empty chair behind a wall of bookshelves and set to work studying. It was a miserable attempt. My mind kept wandering back to the debonair stranger. Was he actually interested? Was he mocking me? After a few hours of this woolgathering interlaced with studying, I gave in and went to deliver the book.

He smiled as I approached. He stood and the whole table of men stood with him.

"Gentlemen, this is Grace."

They all smiled and nodded at me. They invited me to sit and join their group. Every one of them was a political science or pre-law major. I felt very out of place but Xander kept welcoming me back to the conversation with that amazing smile. As the library closed, he helped me gather my things.

"May I be bold?" He asked.

I was a little taken aback. "You may," I replied.

"I enjoyed your company this evening and I would like to spend some time as just the two of us."

I felt my face get hot. "That sounds acceptable," I said, trying not to giggle.

"Excellent!" He smiled wide. "May I have your phone number?"

I scribbled my number on a three-by-five and handed it to him. He folded it and tucked it carefully into his wallet. We parted ways and I raced back to the duplex to tell Chetna. I banged on her door without even waiting for a reply.

"Chet!" I was almost yelling. "You'll never believe what happened at the library!"

Chetna was sitting at her desk with several open books. She looked annoyed by the intrusion but her mood lightened as I explained the evening's events. I knew she would be happy for me.

That weekend, after the stress of preparing for exams was over, my suave stranger from the library and I went for a stroll at the arboretum on campus. He asked me about where I was from, why I had chosen my major, and how my classes were going. Not normally one to talk about myself, I freely opened up to this man.

Chetna had recommended the arboretum and I was glad she had. The fresh air after exams and studying in my small room was a welcome refreshment. There weren't very many flowers in bloom so early in the year, but bulbs were ready to explode with color any day now. The trees and grass were bright green with new growth. The air was damp from the recent rain but the world smelled clean.

I'd hardly noticed his annoyance with having gotten his shoes muddy as he told me about his family's greenhouse. He said his mother liked to have fresh flowers around the house throughout the year so a greenhouse on the estate just seemed practical. Having grown up in farm country, the idea of an estate was a foreign concept to me and it made me feel a little inadequate. He told me about his parents and how he had aspirations of going into politics instead of continuing in the family business. I didn't really feel like we had very much in common, yet the conversation never ceased and I relished being in his presence.

Eventually, the air turned chilly and we decided to warm ourselves with coffee and scones at the café nearby. It was far more posh than any coffee shop I had ever been in before. Our server was friendly as she brought out our drinks. I had never seen such a delicate coffee cup nor had I ever drank coffee with a heart drawn in cream. I preferred my coffee black but I didn't exactly understand the menu, either. I was a little uncomfortable there but his smile quickly put me at ease. We continued our conversation over the hot beverages while soft jazz music played in the background.

When he took me back to campus where we had met for the day, he kissed the back of my hand gently and said he would call me soon. As I walked home, I thought about our day and interaction. The more I thought about it, the more convinced I became that he had seen me as just a bumpkin and he was being polite. Chetna, of course, wanted all of the details of the date as soon as I walked in the door. She assured me it didn't sound like my concerns were founded at all. She was right. He called me that night and asked if he could take me to dinner the following weekend. Of course, I said yes.

He was just so charming in the beginning that I thought there was no way it was real. He constantly had something nice to say about the way I looked. He had flowers sent to me after my exams. He insisted on opening doors and escorting me arm and arm everywhere we went. I hadn't been treated so well since Toby and it felt wonderful.

The Bonaventures

I was absolutely terrified the first time I met his parents. He kept reassuring me that they were good people but they were the type of people I was not used to socializing with. His family was fairly well off in Philadelphia. They weren't billionaires, but they certainly did not need to worry about anything. His father was just as chivalrous and affectionate towards his mother as Xander was to me. They welcomed me with open arms that first Thanksgiving when I went home with him. They didn't question the motive of a poor girl from Illinois dating their son and I took a small amount of comfort in that. Prior to meeting them, I had half expected to be accused of being a gold digger and that wasn't the case at all. I found out later that I was exactly what they were looking for in a daughter-in-law, just not for the reasons I had hoped.

Hope had watched as I packed my duffle bag for the weekend away.

"Don't worry," I reassured her, "I won't be away for long and Chetna will make sure you get plenty of treats and attention."

She meowed indignantly and sauntered to my pillow to lie down and sulk. When Xander came to pick me up, I kissed her on the head before I left. I had never gone away without her before and I felt a twinge of guilt.

It was a little over three-hour drive from the duplex to Philadelphia but they were worlds apart. The duplex was small and dark but homey. The Bonaventure Estate was immense. The house stood three stories high and was made of beautiful grey stone. The white pillars rested atop a stone staircase and guarded the carved front door. The flowerbeds were perfectly manicured and old trees stood watch as they had since the house was built in the nineteen-thirties. As we drove around the fountain in the circular driveway and pulled up to the stairs, I felt smaller than I had ever felt in my life.

He squeezed my hand before we exited the car.

"Don't worry. They're going to love you." He smiled.

I tried to smile back. I let myself out of the car and walked back towards the trunk.

"What are you doing?" He looked genuinely confused.

"Our bags?" I was just as confused.

"Don't worry about those." He motioned for me to follow.

As we walked up to the house, I felt a surge of panic. He took my hand in his and held it tightly.

"I promise they will love you," he repeated.

I took a deep breath in as we climbed the last of the steps to the front door. I exhaled slowly as he opened it.

"Knock knock!" he called.

A beautiful brunette but slightly-graying woman in a blue blouse and skirt came rushing down the hall crying, "My baby boy!"

She ran up and hugged him and kissed him on the cheek.

"Mom!" He blushed slightly.

"Oh, tosh." She smiled. "And you must be Grace!" She smiled at me.

"Yes, ma'am," I replied.

"Only the help calls me ma'am." She smiled wider.

I tried to smile back but I didn't like that comment. She shook my hand vigorously.

A balding man in khakis and a pink button-down shirt came down the hall as well. "Happy Thanksgiving!"

"Happy thanksgiving," Xander and I replied.

He shook my hand as well. "It's nice to finally meet you, Grace."

"The feeling is mutual," I smiled.

I felt like I had never had to smile so hard for people in my life.

"Formal introductions," Xander stated. "Grace this is my mother, Beverly."

"Call me Bev," she interrupted.

Xander rolled his eyes. "And my dad, Paul."

"No need to call me anything special." He winked at his wife.

"It's very nice to finally meet you both," I said.

"Shall we start with drinks in the study? I will send Marcus out for your bags." Paul motioned for us to follow him.

We followed his parents down the hall to a large open area. The room had bookshelves that reached up to the ceiling and a large sitting area in the center. A wall of sliding glass looked out into a lovely flower garden and I could see part of the greenhouse Xander had mentioned on our first date. The room we stood in was probably about the same size as the entire house I grew up in. I felt very small again.

From a chair in a corner, a thin man about the same age as Xander stood up.

"I didn't think you were coming!" He shook Xander's hand.

"Grace, this is my brother Collin. Collin, meet Grace."

"Wow," he said as he shook my hand. "No offense, but I thought the bean boy was lying about you. It's nice to meet you and see that you are real."

"Um. Thank you. Nice to meet you too."

Xander had never mentioned that he had a brother.

I turned to him. "Bean boy?"

"Not my favorite nickname. It's because when I was a kid I was skinny and they called me 'string bean.' No special story but he still calls me that just to get under my skin."

An older, portly man in black pants and a black button-down shirt came in. His face was very straight and stern. He set a tray with a snifter and a tea kettle on it on the coffee table in the center of the room.

"Thank you, Marcus." Paul looked at me. "What's your poison?"

"Um. Tea, please."

"Well I did ask if you wanted poison," he laughed.

He handed me the tea in the daintiest china cup I had ever touched. I was terrified of breaking it. He poured tea for his wife as well but refused to hand it to her until she kissed him on the cheek. I thought that was sweet. The men helped themselves to the cognac.

As we all sat and sipped, Xander and Collin bantered back and forth, trying to one-up each other as they talked about school. Paul subtly refereed them while Bev and I talked about my classes and my major. She did seem genuinely interesting in what I had to say but despite that, it all felt very surreal. It felt very much like something out of a movie that played on stereotypes of wealthy people. I was not comfortable at all.

At around five-thirty, Marcus stepped into the room.

"Dinner is prepared," he announced.

Paul clapped his hands together loudly. "Excellent! I'm starving."

We exited the study and further down the hall to a dining area. It was massive. The room was outlined with dark wood carvings that accented taupe walls with a beautiful dark wood table and enough chairs to seat at least twenty people. Laid out was a beautiful turkey with all of the fixin's you could possibly want. Your standard green beans and mashed potatoes that I grew up with were there but there were several dishes that I couldn't identify.

"Oh, Marcus!" Bev exclaimed. "You certainly outdid yourself this year."

"Thank you, ma'am," he said before he left the room.

Paul grabbed a bottle of wine and poured it for everyone.

"Grace," Collin snickered, "seeing as how you are the guest, would you like to say the prayer before we eat?"

Everyone turned to me.

"Sure." I made the signum crucis and bowed my head.

They all looked at me a little odd but bowed their heads as well.

"Bless us, O Lord, and these thy gifts which we are about to receive through thy bounty, through Christ our Lord. Amen."

"Amen," they all followed.

"Just out of curiosity, what denomination was that?" Bev asked.

I was suddenly scared. "I was raised Catholic, ma'am."

"Catholic. Oh. Well, it's lovely, dear. And no need to call me ma'am."

I looked down at my lap. I was feeling a little ashamed but I didn't know why. As everyone tucked into the meal, Xander leaned over to me.

"You did great." He had read me like a book and was trying to be reassuring.

"Is being Catholic wrong?" I whispered.

"Nothing about you is wrong," he stated flatly. He put his hand on top of mine as a gesture of reassurance. "They are just Presbyterian. There is a little bad blood with Catholics but there is nothing wrong with you."

The food was absolutely wonderful but I spent most of the meal in silence. I felt like an alien on a strange planet. Xander kept his parents and family talking about his classes and plans after school and Paul prattled on about his company. I was glad the focus wasn't on me.

After dinner, we went back to the study for coffee before bed. I did not partake. Too much caffeine before bed and there was no way I was going to fall asleep so I quietly sipped my glass of water. They looked at me as if I was the exact alien that I thought myself to be. Around eleven, yawns started to circulate through the group and we all decided to turn in. Xander escorted me up the stairs to his bedroom. Collin was across the hall. He winked.

"Try not to be too loud," he goaded

"You can be so vulgar sometimes." Xander rolled his eyes.

The bedroom was impressive and overly embellished and I had never seen a bed that big before, either. I sat down on the edge and tried not to cry."

"Are you okay?" he asked.

"I'm fine. I just feel very out of place," I confessed

"Well, I can tell you that they adore you!" He assured me.

I smiled a little. "Even Collin?"

"Even Collin. Just don't take anything he says too seriously. He has always been the problem in the family."

I thought about Jacob. "We have one of those in my family too."

He smiled.

"What about Marcus?" I continued.

"What about him?" he asked as he took off his shirt and got ready for bed.

I slipped off my shoes and dug through my duffel bag. "What exactly is he? A butler?"

Xander laughed a little. "I don't think that term is really used anymore. He is more like the house manager. He makes sure my parents' schedules are taken care of and the house is clean and the gardeners are paid. He basically takes care of everything that Mom and Dad are too busy to worry about."

"He doesn't get to spend Thanksgiving with his family?" I felt kind of sorry for the man.

"You are so sweet," he said and he kissed my forehead. It felt very condescending. He continued, "this year he works Thanksgiving so he will have Christmas off while my parents are in Europe. He alternates holidays every year."

He climbed into the bed next to me.

I finished stripping down and put on an old T-shirt to sleep in. That didn't make me feel any better about the poor man.

The next morning we came down to a bountiful breakfast of eggs, French toast, bacon, and fruit. Both Paul and Bev were already that the table when we descended the stairs. Collin was standing near a sideboard table pouring orange juice.

"So lazy!" Paul chided.

"Oh!" Bev playfully slapped him on the shoulder. "They had a long day yesterday."

"Well, eat fast you two. We have golf in an hour," Paul announced.

That nagging voice telling me that this was a stereotype kept whispering in my ear and I was nothing short of horrified. I had never played golf before. What if I hit someone? What if I lost my grip on the club and sent it sailing across the green? If I lost my ball in a pond, did I have to go after it?

We took separate cars to the Country Club. Paul was all too eager to show off his new Mercedes but we didn't all fit in it so Xander and I rode in his car. While the men headed out to the course, Bev and I went to the driving range and she graciously introduced me to the sport. Considering I had never even touched a golf club, I did fairly well I think. I missed almost as many times as I make contact with the ball, but I never hit the ground or made what she called a divot.

The entire day was spent at the club. We had lunch together and afterward, Bev and Paul went to play tennis while Xander and I circulated around for introductions. Everyone we met had smiles that felt forced as if they recognized I was a Martian on Neptune. That evening's dinner was far more modest but very good and the next day, we headed home. I cannot say I was unhappy to leave the Bonaventure Estate, but I knew that if Xander and I were to have a future together, I would have to work hard to make myself comfortable there.

I Love You

The more time we spent together, the more heedlessly I fell in love. Whatever he said, I agreed with. He changed subtle little things about me so gradually that I barely even noticed. Whenever I mentioned hiking or doing anything outdoors, it was always too cold or wet or there was something that sounded more fun to do and I blindly went along with it. Eventually, I stopped venturing out into the wilderness altogether. He bought me lots of pretty skirts and dresses to wear when we would go out. I didn't mind wearing dresses but getting away from home and my mother had meant I was able to wear anything that I wanted and jeans and sweatpants were my new preferred wardrobe.

He bought me beautiful jewelry to wear when we went out. He insisted that I deserved better than "a random rock on an ugly chain." I wore everything he bought me but the next day that quartz crystal would be back around my neck, much to his consternation. I explained to him that it was a gift from a best friend who was lost to me and hoped he would understand but he just couldn't. I honestly was reaching the point that I wasn't sure why I wore it either; I just knew the comfort that it gave me was not something I was willing to surrender.

At Christmas, he asked if he could go home with me and meet my family. I didn't mind him meeting Uncle James despite his drinking and honestly, I would have loved to have had his approval, but I just couldn't bring myself to introduce him to my mother. He never questioned why I woke up at three in the morning and I never told. Being a holy child was something I truly wanted to ignore. It was a part of my life that I didn't want to acknowledge and I knew if I told him or if he met my insane mother, I would very likely lose him forever. I didn't dare risk that.

When he asked the third time, I told him 'no' but it was no longer enough of an answer.

"Are you ashamed of me?" he asked.

"What? No? How could you think that?" I was sincerely taken aback by the accusation.

"Why won't you let me meet your family?"

I took a deep breath. I needed to word it carefully. "You know how you have pictures of your family in your room?"

"Yes." He sounded puzzled.

"Have you seen pictures of mine in my room?"

"Now that you mention it, no."

"That's because my family isn't like yours." I took his hands. "My mother is very religious, my uncle is an alcoholic, and my cousin is a criminal. I avoid them personally. I don't want to take you home to meet them because I don't even want to see them myself."

That was the first time I had admitted out loud that I didn't want to be around my family. I loved them despite everything, but I had never really admitted that I had moved on from them.

I continued. "Three days with them will be hard and, as much as I would love to have you with me, it's something I have to do alone."

"I don't agree with this at all, but I respect you and your decision." He kissed my cheek.

"Thank you."

In the summer he went back home to Philadelphia to work at his father's media center. It wasn't that far of a drive but he was busy working and with social and family obligations and I was busy at the warehouse and taking classes so that I could keep my housing. We hardly saw each other but we spoke on the phone at length for hours every night.

One night, as we were getting off the phone, I went to hang up and one of the most beautiful moments in my life happened.

He said, "good night."

"Goodnight," I responded.

"I love you."

"I love you, too," I yawned and hung up the phone.

Then it clicked. We had just admitted our feelings for each other for the first time. I was completely over the moon. I sat on my bed and smiled giddily.

Less than two minutes later, I received a text message.

Did that just happen? He had asked.

I smiled. *Yes.*

Are you OK with that?

Very. Are you? I suddenly became aware that he had not expected me to say it back.

I have wanted to say that for a long time but it just kind of slipped out. I'm glad it did. He confessed.

I heard his voice in my head as I read those words and I felt butterflies in my stomach. I hadn't felt like that in a very long time.

Me too.

The Snow Storm

On February twelfth of 2006, some areas of Pennsylvania saw as much as ten inches of snow. Kevin, the skater Chetna had been dating for a little over a year, and Xander had stayed the night with us at the duplex. The winter storm had hit hard the day before. They had come over for a meager but home-cooked meal provided by yours truly and my lovely assistant followed by rental movies. Their attempts to leave were thwarted by the weather so Chetna and I happily welcomed them to our beds for the night. I was so thrilled to have his warm body to cuddle up to. The seals in that old house were so poor there was a thick layer of frost inside the glass.

Devil's hour came and my eyes cracked open. I stretched and went to the window. I used a sock from the floor to clear some of the frost and peered outside. It looked as if the whole world was frozen. There were crooked tire tracks where cars had slid in the snow. The moisture in the air produced delicate halos around the street lamps. The children across the street had built a lopsided snowman with a red disposable cup for a nose. Nothing outside stirred but I felt something gently brush against my legs. I scooped up Hope and held her close to me.

As I listened to the gentle sounds of the wind outside, my cat purring, and my boyfriend softly snoring. I smiled. If my mother only knew... There I was, hundreds of miles from her and everything familiar. I had turned my back on her imposed mission for me to serve God in pursuit of a career that would make me happy. I was sinfully sharing my bed with a man out of wedlock. I was guilty of all of these selfish acts, and I could not have been happier.

I set Hope back on the floor and crawled back into bed. Xander moaned slightly. He rolled over and wrapped his arms around me. That was truly heaven.

In the morning, I woke to a commotion in the kitchen. I put socks on my feet and bundled myself in my bathrobe. I stepped into the hallway just as Chet did the same. We looked at each other, both visibly confused.

"So much for the surprise." Kevin laughed and kissed her on the cheek as we walked into the kitchen.

"Milady." Xander pulled out a chair at the table for me.

"What's all this?" I sat down.

"Breakfast!" Kevin set a glass of orange juice each in front of Chet and me. "You took care of dinner. It's our turn."

"You cook?" Chetna's skepticism was palpable.

"I can scramble an egg," Xander defended himself. "Just ignore the crunchy bits." He winked at me.

"And I made something like pancakes," Kevin chimed in.

The stack of burnt creations he set on the table in front of us only vaguely resembled pancakes and certainly didn't taste like them. I appreciated their effort. I watched Chetna and Kevin look at each other with such devotion, it made me smile. I didn't like Kevin, but he did make her happy.

After we ate, we took to the living room. Chetna and Kevin lay on the couch while Xander, Hope, and I took up the extra-wide armchair and ottoman. Everyone was nestled snuggly under a mound of blankets.

We managed to get one local channel to come in somewhat clear. We watched frozen reporters talk about traffic accidents and power outages. One reporter stood shivering with huge flakes falling around him while kids went down the hill behind him in toboggans, garbage can lids, and flattened cardboard boxes.

"I can't wait to teach my sons to snowboard." Kevin mused.

"Sons? And more than one?" Chetna looked up at him.

"Of course!"

"No. One girl is all we need."

"We'll see." He smiled and kissed her head.

"We'll see me have my way," she said under her breath as she settled deeper under the blanket.

I giggled.

"What about you, Xander?" Kevin looked over at us.

"I'm more of a skiing or ice skating man."

"Never mind him. How many kids do you want, Grace?" Chetna piped up.

I paused. "I don't know. I never really thought about it."

"Really?" Kevin's eyes widened. "I thought chicks had their whole futures figured out by the time they were like five."

I resented when Kevin referred to Chet or me as 'chicks' and became agitated.

"My life was pretty much planned out for me since the day I was born. That plan never included kids, so I never really thought about it."

Kevin clenched his mouth shut.

"I see you with two." Xander hugged me.

"Oh, yeah?" I raised an eyebrow and looked up at him.

"William and Anna," he stated frankly.

"Really now?"

"And they will have their mother's beautiful eyes and brilliant mind." He squeezed me closer.

"You seem to have an awful lot of my future planned out," I stated curtly.

The idea of yet another person guiding my life had taken root and I was starting to feel a little keyed up.

"I wouldn't call it a plan. More like a dream." He smiled as he laid his head on top of mine.

That profession did little to settle me down.

A Tie and a Dress

It was a warm but otherwise nondescript autumn day in September of 2006. I had spent my morning cleaning my room and doing laundry. I was frustrated because I couldn't find my favorite bra and pair of shorts and I had torn the house apart looking for them. Eventually, after putting everything back in its place, I was resolved that my effort was futile. I assumed I must have lost them in the dryer. Frustrated and irritated, I went to campus to study and have access to the library.

I was mulling over a picture of a Ludvig Karsten painting under a tree with Yanni coming through my headphones and drowning out the rest of the world. I didn't particularly care for the music, but I'd listened to it while studying so much when I was growing up that I'd found that it helped me focus even into adulthood. With my head in my books and music in my ears, nothing else seemed to exist until a scarlet rosebud slid onto my page. I looked up at Xander's smiling face.

"It's lovely," I said. "Thank you."

"Not nearly as lovely as you, my dear."

"Aren't we adulatory today," I observed.

"I'd hoped to request your assistance."

"So you're trying to butter me up," I suggested.

"A little," he admitted and flashed that beautiful smile.

"What do you need help with?" I sighed.

"I need a new tie."

"A tie?" I could hear the doubt in my own voice.

"Yes. It's for a presentation."

"You have lots of ties."

"Yes, but as my dad always says, 'the tie makes the man.' It has to make the right statement," he insisted.

"And what statement are you trying to make?"

He straightened his stance held his chin up before proclaiming, "I'm honest. I'm sharp. I'm making something of myself. I command presence-- without being too flashy, of course."

"I have tons of studying to do." I held up the book from my lap. "Why do you need me?"

"I need a woman's perspective and I know you'll be brutal if I pick something ugly."

I laughed a little. "True."

"Please." He dropped to his knees and said it with exaggerated supplication and puppy dog eyes.

I rolled my eyes. "Okay. Okay."

"Excellent!" He stole a kiss before standing and tugging on my arm. "Let's go!"

"What? Now?"

"Yes!" He pulled me to my feet. "I don't have much time to prepare."

"Great. Why do now what you can put off 'til the last minute?"

I gathered up my things and we left.

We ended up at a department store not too far from campus.

"I've never been here before; have you?" He shut off the car.

"Not this one but we had one in the mall a few towns over back home."

I hated when I said things like that. It made me feel like I had grown up in a cornfield. We had shopping and even a bread factory. We just weren't a bustling city or tourist destination.

"This will be an adventure for both of us then." He was grinning but his teeth seemed more gritted.

I had never heard someone describe buying a tie at a department store as an 'adventure.'

"Where do you normally get a tie?" I asked.

"The tailor, usually. Sometimes my dad's haberdasher has really good ones. Or a specialty store, of course."

"Of course…" I said. *What a silly question,* I thought.

We wandered around in the men's department for what felt like hours. He saw a few that he liked, but when he touched the fabric, he wrinkled his nose and kept browsing. I finally talked him into an emerald green with silver pinstripes. It was made of real silk but I got the feeling that he still secretly deemed it was beneath him. We paid for the tie and strolled over to the women's department.

"What are we doing here?" I asked.

"Just perusing."

He nonchalantly made his way between the racks of clothes before he spotted a navy blue, sleeveless, tea-length dress on the wall.

"Will you try it on for me?"

"Really?" I didn't think it suited me at all.

"Please."

I rolled my eyes at him again. I took the dress into the nearby fitting room. Like with most dresses, my frame was an extra small but my boobs were not. I adjusted my bra and with a little stuffing and tucking, I managed to look slightly less like a can of biscuit dough busting at the seams. When I was satisfied, I stepped out of the fitting room for him to see.

"You are so beautiful. That dress does not do you justice. And I don't think that blue is your color," he admitted.

"May I take it off now?"

"You don't like it?" Despite the statement he had just made, he seemed a little disappointed.

"It's just very… restrictive."

He laughed a little. "I see."

I eagerly ran back to the fitting room to change into my jeans and sweatshirt.

A few days later I came home from my last class of the day and found a package on the doorstep with my name on it. I took it inside and tore through the paper. In the box was a sleeveless tea-length dress that was very similar to the one I'd tried on. It was the same shade of green as the tie we had picked out and this dress was a much nicer fabric. When I held it up to myself, it looked like it was tailored just for me. I looked back in the box. There were my missing bra and shorts. Along with them was a simple note:

Dinner's at eight.

A New Puppy

I wasn't happy about the surprise dinner. I had intended to use my night off from the warehouse to get some studying done. Sometimes I got the feeling that Xander didn't see my career path as being as important as his. But then I slipped on that dress and it fit like a glove. How could I say 'no?' He had gone through so much trouble to stealthily steal my clothes to have it tailor-made for me, after all.

He picked me up at seven-thirty wearing the green tie that we had picked out and a silver shirt that beautifully brought out the pinstripes. The green made his eyes look brighter and his hair a little lighter. He was so delightfully handsome I thought of myself as truly lucky to be on his arm.

"Are you ready to go, milady?"

"Where are we going? What is this all about?" I picked up a clutch I had borrowed from Chetna.

"It's a surprise!" He beamed.

"Before we leave, are you sure you want to wear *that*?" He pointed to the quartz around my neck. "What about the silver locket I got you for Christmas?"

I sighed and set the clutch down. I went back to my room and put the locket on. I wrapped the chain with the stone around my wrist a few times and latched it as a bracelet before re-emerging.

"Absolutely stunning!" He was radiating excitement as he helped me into my coat.

He took me to a very ostentatious restaurant about thirty minutes away from campus. Everyone in attendance was dressed just as elegantly as I was. My mom had once told me that she had been to a black-tie restaurant like this before, but I had never seen one in person.

We approached the hostess's station.

"Hello!" She greeted us with a smile.

"Good evening. Eight o'clock reservation for Bonaventure for a party of four."

She looked at her paper. "Yes, the rest of your party has already arrived. This way, please."

I took his arm. "Four?"

He smiled.

We were escorted to a table with a tall, thin, blonde man in a navy blue tie and blue shirt and an elegant woman with diamonds dripping off her fingers. She was just as blonde and dressed in the same shade of blue.

"It's about time!" the man exclaimed as they both stood up.

The man shook Xander's hand vigorously.

"Eight o'clock means eight o'clock." Xander smiled.

"If you aren't fifteen minutes early, you're fifteen minutes late," the man quipped.

They both laughed.

"This is my beautiful girlfriend, Grace. Grace, this is my childhood best friend, Lucas, and his wife, Kara."

I shook both of their hands in turn.

"So nice to finally meet you in person, Grace!" Lucas exclaimed. "Xander hasn't shut up about you for at least a year now."

"What a unique bracelet!" Kara smiled.

I looked at the quartz around my wrist. I saw the look on Xander's face out of the corner of my eye. He hadn't noticed I had put it back on when I exchanged it for the locket and he seemed displeased.

"It was a gift from an old friend," I replied.

"How lovely!" The beautiful woman sat down.

Xander pulled out my chair for me and seated me properly before sitting himself.

The waitress approached. "May I have your drink orders?"

"Ladies first." Lucas insisted.

Kara smiled at the woman. "I will have a scotch and soda, please."

She looked at me.

"Just water, thank you." I felt as if Kara was judging my selection. "I don't drink pop at night," I clarified.

"Pop?" Lucas questioned.

"It's what Grace calls soda," Xander explained. "It's a Midwestern thing."

"How adorable!" Kara smiled. "Where are you from?"

"Steelville, Illinois," I said sheepishly.

Xander gracefully took the attention away from me. "I will have a glass of merlot."

"Since when do you drink wine?" Lucas laughed. "I'll have bourbon sour. I feel like living dangerously tonight."

I sat quietly glancing over the menu items. I almost immediately noticed that there weren't any prices listed next to the items. Then I looked at the top of the page. One-hundred-and-forty-two dollars for a three-course meal or three-hundred-and-twenty-seven for a seven-course meal. I almost choked on my tongue.

Somewhere amongst the artisanal cheese plate, oysters, crab bisque, Chilean sea bass, risotto, and carrot cake, I became completely lost. The men laughed loudly as they caught each other up on their lives and reminisced about things that happened growing up. I tried to be social with Kara but she and I had nothing in common. She came from old money in Connecticut and I, most certainly, did not.

In truth, I didn't really want to socialize with those people. They kept saying things like 'how quaint' my hometown sounded or how laborious my job at the warehouse must be. Xander tried to help me fit in by telling them about how good I was at golf (a gross exaggeration) and my excellent fashion sense (I don't even know where he came up with that). His attempts were sorely in vain. Try as he might to make me feel comfortable, his efforts just brought to light how different I was from his friends and family.

After the men finished arguing over who was paying the bill- going so far as to bring up money lent fifteen-plus years ago- and our coats were brought to us, we said our goodbyes.

As Kara and I stood off to the side waiting for the valet to bring the car, I overheard an exchange between Lucas and Xander. They were shaking hands about six feet away.

"Well, I have to hand it to you," Lucas said, "you weren't lying about this one. She's charming and exactly what you need. You've always had your pick of the litter and you've chosen a good one this time."

'Pick of the litter.' That was it. The presentation he had needed the tie for. It was me. That's what this whole ridiculous dinner had been about. I was Xander's new puppy and he wanted to show me off to his friends. I was angry. I was hurt. I felt degraded and indignant.

They said their final goodbyes and we drove away. I was silent in the car.

"Well," Xander said excitedly, "what do you think?"

"You tell me." My arms were crossed and I was staring out the window.

"What do you mean?" He sounded confused.

"Did your friends like your new puppy?" I heard my voice crack.

"What are you talking about?"

"I heard Lucas. 'Pick of the litter.' Am I a poodle or a Pekingese? Did I put on a good show?" I was trying not to cry.

"What? Grace, that's not what he meant."

"What then?" I almost yelled.

"He just meant that I've always had my choice of any girl I wanted. I chose you," he said as his voice elevated.

I believe that statement was mean to be reassuring or comforting. It wasn't.

"So this wasn't just to show me off to your friends?" I tried to control the anger in my voice.

"No. Well, yes." He thought quickly. "But not like that. You are important to me and so are they. They were passing through and I thought it would be a good chance for them to finally meet you. That's all."

"And what if they didn't like me?" I challenged.

"Then obviously there's something wrong with them." He let go of the gearshift and took my hand. "You are not a dog. I don't expect you to do tricks for my friends. I chose you for you."

I'm not one to let go of things very easily but I chose to accept his response. I still wasn't sure about what Lucas meant when he said I was what Xander *needed* but I wasn't going to ask. I had already picked my battle. I would find out many years later, anyway.

Different Paths

    I didn't think life could get much better. Growing up, I had never imagined I could be so happy. Despite my warehouse job, I was maintaining a four-point-zero GPA. I lived with my best friend who was essentially a sister to me and to top it all off, I had the love of a very good man. Every chance Xander could get, he would whisk me away to the Bonaventure estate where we would eat wonderful food and go to nice restaurants and hobnob with snobs at social gatherings I often didn't understand. They taught me a great deal about how to behave with higher society and pretend that I belonged. While I was never comfortable with them, they did make me feel like I was part of a family.

    It all came to a grinding halt in my fourth year of school. I came in from working the second shift at the warehouse. I was exhausted but a manila envelope on the kitchen table had my name on it. It was from the Cleveland Museum of Art. This was it. I had applied for a graduation internship there and this could either make or break my college year. I shook a little as I tore open the envelope.

Dear Miss Nightingale,

    We thank you for your interest in our internship program. After careful review of your application and conversations with your references, we would be very happy to have you on board. Internships start in June and continue for ten weeks. Please complete the enclosed paperwork prior to March 31st.

                   Kindest Regards,
                        Dr. Sonya Campbell, PhD
            Lead Curator; Cleveland Museum of Art

I looked up and saw Chetna standing in the doorway of the kitchen.

"Yes?" she asked, wide-eyed.

All of the happiness inside me exploded at once.

"Yes!" I screamed.

She ran over and hugged me. "I knew it! This is so wonderful!"

"I know! I can't wait to tell Xander."

I went to sleep smiling that night.

The following night when we met for dinner, Xander knew something important had happened right away.

"What has you so antsy?" He looked excited for me already.

I beamed. I just couldn't contain myself any longer.

"I got the internship in Cleveland!" I had to restrain myself from screaming in the middle of the restaurant.

"You what?" I thought the look on his face was astonishment, but, looking back, it may have been more shock and a little disapproval.

"The internship at the art museum in Cleveland! It's mine!"

"But I thought we were going to D.C." He looked grim.

I deflated quickly. "What? When did I agree to that?"

"I told you that all of my internship opportunities were going to be in New York and D.C. There are plenty of art museums for you to apply to up there."

"Those are extremely competitive and I don't fit in in that kind of environment. I feel comfortable at a small museum and Cleveland is perfect to get my feet wet. Not to mention they have one of the most extensive global religious artifact collections I could want to study."

"What do you mean you don't fit in? Haven't I bought you all the nice clothes and jewelry you could want? Haven't I introduced you to the right people? And what about everything my parents did to make you feel welcome and help you belong every time we go visit?"

Suddenly, it all made sense. The gifts, the lavish dinners, even his parents' clichéd behavior. He wasn't just dating me; he was grooming me. He wanted me to be a part of his world but he wanted no part of mine.

"That's not what I want." I hadn't felt so meek since childhood.

"I can't go to Cleveland." He said plainly.

I felt tears well up in my eyes. Washington D.C. and New York were massive society environments. I found the idea of dropping myself in that kind of bombastic world extremely imposing. I was a simple girl who enjoyed simple things and that was not at all what I wanted for myself.

"And I can't go to D.C.," I said with tears in my eyes.

"What are we going to do then? I can't maintain a long-term relationship over that far of a distance."

"Then I guess we can't be together." The tears were getting hard to control and I stood up. I looked at him. "I don't want this. But I don't want D.C. or New York either."

I turned and left. One of the happiest moments in my life quickly became the worst. My mind went back to Toby. All of the plans we had made for our future were for nothing. We saw different things when we looked into that crystal ball.

The next day I boxed up all of his things. I wanted to talk it out with him. I wanted to give him the chance to change his mind and join me in Cleveland, but I knew that wasn't going to happen. Chet kept insisting that we needed to watch chick flicks and drown my sorrows in ice cream but I felt more like making sure every memory of him was erased from the house.

When he came by to pick up his things and drop off a box of mine, we stood on the front porch. I wanted to hug him. I wanted him to hold me. I wanted to cry. But I held my ground and even refused to let him enter the house.

"Are you sure this is what you want?" He asked.

"I don't want this at all," I stated flatly. "But I DO want the internship in Cleveland and I do NOT want to live in Now York or Washington D.C."

"So you are choosing your career over me?"

"Aren't you doing the same thing?" I snapped back.

He looked stunned for a moment. "I do love you."

"And I love you. But we are on different paths."

He nodded and stepped off the porch and out of my life for what I thought was going to be for good.

I went back into the duplex and shut the door behind me. I crumpled to the floor and sobbed. Chetna came over and put my head in her lap and rubbed my back while I cried into her dress. It seemed so quick. It was such a little thing to end a relationship over but when I look back on it years later, we were never meant to be. He was from a nice, high society family with money and aspirations of political power. I was a smallish town girl who wanted a simple life doing something she loved. While opposites may attract, that doesn't mean they can stay together forever.

He Should Pay

"Rouse, my puppet." I woke to the low hiss of her voice.

I felt a long, scale-like fingernail trace from my hairline to the tip of my nose. I opened my eyes. They were puffy and my vision was blurred from crying, but I could clearly see the sadistic grin that was spread across Onoskelis's lips as she laid her head on the pillow beside mine. I looked past her. I could just make out the blocky red lights that spelled out three-zero-zero on the alarm clock.

"I am not your puppet." I pulled the pillow over my head.

"Tonight, yes. We are going to play."

"No. No playing. None of your games," I said from under the pillow.

"No fun? No last kiss from Xander?" she teased.

"Absolutely not! You stay away from him." I pulled the pillow off my head so I could look her in the eyes.

"Why? He hurt you."

"No less than I hurt him."

"How?"

"He didn't' want to break up any more than I did. I made that call." That was one of the hardest things I had ever admitted.

She sat up. "He could have bent to your will. Followed you. Let you have your heart's desires."

"And he would have been miserable for it."

She rolled her eyes.

"How am I supposed to live knowing I was making the man I love miserable?" I continued.

"Is that not what you just accomplished?"

I paused. She was right. No matter how you flipped the coin, one or both of us was going to be miserable. I felt the tears starting to return.

"At least this way he has a chance," I whispered.

"At what?"

"Happiness," I said a little louder.

"What of your happiness? He is the reason you are in such a state. We should make sure he suffers as you do."

"No," I said sternly through the tears that threatened to roll down my cheeks. "We are both suffering. I'm sure of that. And we'll both be happy again one day; just not with each other."

"He should not be allowed to hurt other women as he has hurt you."

"I said no." My heartache was momentarily overtaken by anger.

There was a soft knock on the door.

"Grace?" Chetna's voice drifted through the door. "Are you okay?"

"I'm okay." My voice came out as a high squeak.

"Can I come in?"

I looked at Onoskelis. "Yes."

She snarled and evaporated as the door opened.

Chet sat on the edge of the bed and took my hand. "How are you holding up?"

"I feel like there is a hole where my heart used to be."

Hope hopped up on the bed between us and purred softly.

"It will get better," she promised.

"I know. But it hurts so much right now."

She pulled me close to her for a hug and I wept into her nightgown.

Part III

Ohio

Little Fish in a Big Pond

On the first day of my internship, I was so anxious and panicky that I felt ill. Cleveland was an unfamiliar city, and I was living in a cheap hotel until I could find an apartment. I had spent my last spare dime on a meager wardrobe of office attire from a consignment shop I found in town. That morning, I dressed in the green pencil skirt and a white blouse I had found and a very special bracelet. Before we had gone our separate ways, Chetna had gifted me with what she called a chirmi bead. She said normally the beads choose their people but she felt it was okay in this case. She said the beads won't stay with an unlucky person so if I lose it, I should consider it an omen. She had strung it on a green ribbon because she said green was a color of good luck. In return, I gifted her with a silver pair of earrings with the Celtic tree of life. We cried and hugged and promised to keep in touch.

Cleveland was a much bigger city than I had imagined. I knew it wasn't going to be the tiny town I had grown up in, but I was still impressed when I had arrived. I was exhausted. I had taken a Greyhound bus home from college to collect the remainder of my clothes and my car and then turned tail and drove the clunky Crown Vic all the way back and settled in Ohio. My mother protested, of course. She had wanted me to stay home a little longer but I assured her that I couldn't. I had barely had a day to settle in and go shopping before my internship officially started.

I stared at myself in the mirror before leaving that first intimidating morning. I barely recognized myself. Only a few short years before, I had been a frizzy-haired, four-eyed outcast. Looking back at me was a woman of class and taste. The frizz was now a perfectly sleeked bun resting on top of my head. My hazel eyes were no longer hidden behind chunky glass. My blemishes and freckles were artistically hidden with careful use of the training Chetna had given me. The only thing recognizable was the silly silver chain with an old rock around my neck.

If Aaron passed me on the street, he would never recognize me. I thought to myself

My hotel was about half an hour from the museum. Hotels in the city were expensive so I had found a small, somewhat clean place to stay in the suburban area outside of the metropolis. My stomach would not settle down as I drove. I decided I wasn't really sick and it wasn't butterflies. I'm not sure how to describe the feeling but I hoped it would go away.

I pulled around the building to the booth in front of the parking garage. I showed the attendant my driver's license and he handed me my parking pass, ID badge, and pointed to where I needed to park. He was friendly and I appreciated it.

A security guard stood inside the lobby where I walked in.

He smiled at me and asked, "Can I help you, miss?"

I tried desperately to steady my nerves before I spoke. "I'm the new intern. I need to check in with Sonya."

The man's smile faded. "Oh. Up the stairs and to the right. Good luck. You'll need it."

A sudden sense of foreboding began to overcrowd my nerves. "Um. Thank you."

I turned and headed up the stairs.

I found a heavy wooden door with a gold plate that read 'Sonya Campbell, PhD. Lead Curator.' I took a deep breath and knocked.

"Enter." I woman's voice came through the wood.

I opened the door and stepped in.

A blonde woman looked up at me from behind a large ebony desk. Her curls were cropped into a bob and her bright red lips, plastic glasses, and business suit all matched.

"May I help you?" She sounded disgruntled.

I stepped forward and swallowed hard. "Yes, ma'am. My name is Grace Nightingale. I am the new intern."

She stood and walked around her desk. She approached me carefully. The air around her was thick with judgment as she looked me up and down. She held her hand out for me to shake. Her fingers were long and thin. Her nails were the same red as everything else she wore. She was a few inches taller than me but she still was clearly a formidable woman.

"Hello, Grace. I'm Dr. Campbell."

I shook her outstretched hand. "Nice to meet you."

She turned my wrist and looked at the black stone I had tied around it. She let go and motioned at the quartz around my neck. "Interesting choice of jewelry. Are you sure you wouldn't be more comfortable in a geology field?"

I wasn't sure if she was trying to make a joke or if she was being facetious. "Good luck gifts from friends."

"I suppose superstition has a place here." She opened the door. "Let me introduce you to the rest of the team."

I followed her down the hall. I already detested this woman and was questioning my decision to come here instead of going to D.C. with Xander. That thought sent a pain through my heart.

We entered a conference room with a large rectangular table in the middle. Just like Sonya's office, everything was a heavy, dark wood that was uninviting and I felt ill at ease. Around the table were four women and two men.

"Everyone this is Grace. She will be working with you as our intern for the next ten weeks. Grace, this is Joy, Tony, Elaina, Matthew, Bethany, and Candace."

They each raised their hands as their names were called.

"Nice to meet you all," I said nervously.

"Grace, please sit down. You are wasting time." Sonya gestured towards an open seat.

I sat and shoved my purse under the chair.

Sonya walked over to the corner of the conference room and picked up a small jar. She set it on the conference table carefully and almost directly in front of me.

She beamed with pride. "Our newest acquisition. This urn once held part of the shroud that Saint Sabbas was wrapped in when the Christians hid his body until it could be sent to Rome for safekeeping. We need a big display and a big story to showcase it. Who wants to be in charge?"

I looked at the urn carefully and opened my mouth to speak but when I looked up at Sonya, I snapped my jaw closed.

Her eyes shot daggers at me. "Is there something you have to say, Intern?"

I looked around the table. All eyes were on me. I was petrified but I knew I had to speak up. I looked back at Sonya.

"I don't think that's right." My voice was a timid squeak I hadn't heard since high school.

"Excuse me?" Sonya sounded incredulous.

"This can't be an urn for Sabbas the Goth."

"I have been studying this urn for months. Explain to me how you think you can debunk *my* hard work in only a few minutes."

I looked around the table again and Joy seemed to be nodding at me with careful encouragement.

My eyes met Sonya's and suddenly, I felt a surge of courage. I knew I was right and she needed to know it.

"Saint Sabbas the Goth lived in what is now Romania in the mid to late fourth century. His relics were collected in 374 CE at the request of Basil of Caesarea."

Sonya rolled her eyes. "Yes. I am well aware of this."

I turned the urn carefully so everyone could see. "If you look here," I pointed to a faint line that could have easily been mistaken for a defect in the metal, "there is a fleur de lis that has been almost completely rubbed out of the silver. The French didn't have an influence in Romania in the fourth century. The relics were collected in Rome after the body had been smuggled there. Even *if* there had been a French influence in Rome at the time, you have to understand the fleur de lis. It means 'lily flower.' The significance stems from the legend that it is the flower given to King Clovis by the Virgin Mary herself and the flower comes from Eve's tears when she cried as she was cast out of Eden. Clovis was born in the mid fifth century and died in the first part of the sixth century. That's more than one hundred years *after* Sabbas was martyred. What's more, the Roman Catholic Church didn't use the fleur de lis until Leo III crowned Charlemagne in the year 800. That's over four hundred years after Sabbas." I should have stopped there, but my mouth just kept running. "So if this urn held Sabbas's cloth, the urn was forged much later and by a French or Italian artist with no knowledge of Sabbas. Furthermore, eastern orthodox relics were preserved in wax. There's no proof that that practice was used on Sabbas's relics, but it's a very high probability and there is no residue of wax in this."

There was a stunned silence in the room. I lost my nerve as quickly as it had come and I felt uncomfortable again. I sat down and looked at all the faces staring back at me.

"How do you know all of that?" Candace finally broke the tension.

"I grew up in the church. My mother is very religious and I had to study anything and everything Christian." I conveniently left out the part about my destiny to lead the world's wayward back to the flock.

Sonya stared at me blankly before speaking with an artificially sweet voice. "Well. If you think you know more than me and all of my research, you should have no trouble proving it. I spent six months working with this urn. You have ten weeks. Fail to identify it correctly and you fail your internship." She turned and stomped as she left. I listened to her pumps angrily click down the hall.

I turned to the rest of the group.

"That was awesome!" Matthew was smiling as he stood and shook my hand.

"Oh. Um." I wasn't sure what to say.

Elaina shook my hand as well. "That was one of the bravest things I've ever seen. She's going to make your life unbearable for the next ten weeks, but I admire your moxie."

My heart sank. I had barely been an intern for fifteen minutes and I'd already started on the wrong foot.

Joy smiled kindly at me. "Don't worry. Come with me. We'll find you a workspace."

I tried to smile back at her.

"Stick close to us. We'll help you get through it." Tony smiled. "We've all been there. Interns, not Sonya's bad side, that is. But we'll try to help you there, too."

"Thank you." I didn't know what else to say.

They found a desk for me with a computer in a room that used to be used by the security guards. It was about the size of a closet but it had everything I could need. They said interns didn't usually get their own workspace but I was going to need it if I was going to identify that urn in only a few short months. More importantly, the desk was in the back of the building near the parking garage. It was about as far away from Sonya as I could get.

I went back to my hotel room that night feeling shrunken, defeated, and humiliated. I popped a TV dinner in the microwave I had purchased at the thrift shop and curled up in the bed with Hope.

"What am I doing?" I pressed my face into her soft fur as she purred. "I should have just kept my mouth shut."

I left my pot pie to rot in the microwave as I drifted off to sleep.

The next morning, I woke to Hope meowing and pawing at my face. I surely would have overslept if not for that cat. I rushed to get dressed and feed her. As I left, I was careful to remember to place the 'do not disturb' tag on the doorknob so housekeeping staff would not discover her.

When I entered the lobby at the museum, the old security guard from the day before looked at me and raised an eyebrow. "You came back?"

"Um. Was I not supposed to?" I was genuinely confused and suddenly afraid I had been fired and didn't know.

"Oh, no, Kiddo. Just that witch Sonya usually scares off the interns by the end of the first day. I like that you have staying power."

I smiled. "Thank you."

"I'm Gerald." He held out his hand."

"Grace." I shook his hand.

"Nice to meet you, Grace. You'd better get up there before that dragon starts breathing fire."

I laughed as I headed up the stairs.

Sonya was in the hall. Her red ensemble had been replaced with an impressive shade of raspberry. Her hands were on her hips and she was tapping the toes of her T-strap suede shoes against the tile floor.

"You're nearly late." She snapped.

"I'm sorry ma'am."

"See that it doesn't happen again." Her eyes narrowed.

"Yes ma'am."

She turned and started marching down the hall. "Well, come on. The morning meeting already started."

I didn't understand how the meeting could have started when it had just turned to nine a.m. but I wasn't planning on rocking the boat that day.

I took the same seat I had been in before and took out a pen and notepad in an effort to look efficient and prepared.

"Joy. What is going on in contemporary art?"

Joy looked up from her Blackberry. "We have to get rid of the Sanderson exhibit. It's old news. It's boring. I want to bring in some new pieces."

"Yes. Freshen things up a bit. Work on finding a few new pieces and have an acquisition request written by the next board meeting."

Joy's jaw dropped. "That's only a month away."

Sonya turned to me and smiled with false sweetness. "Have Grace help you."

My eyes widened. I didn't think I could be much help. I hated everything about contemporary art. Most of it required no skill to create and only had value because some yuppie with a gallery said it did or some rich idiot was willing to pay an obscene amount to show off to his friends. It wasn't art. It was a joke. I dealt with it just enough to get through my classes and even that made me sick. And I certainly didn't know how to write an acquisition request.

I smiled. "I'm here to help and learn."

"Of course you are." Sonya flashed a very impious smile at me.

"Tony. How is the restoration of the new swords coming?"

Tony interlaced his fingers. "Going to have to take a drive up to New York to check on it. May have to be out of the office for a few days."

I caught a glint of a smirk in the corner of his mouth. I got the feeling he just wanted an excuse to get out of the building.

"Take Grace. She needs to know how to deal with restoration artists."

I dropped my pen. "Me? To New York?"

"Of course! It's only a seven-hour drive and I'm sure Tony wouldn't mind the company."

I looked over at Tony. His smug smile faded. "The more, the merrier." He said flatly.

"Elaina?" Sonya turned sharply.

She sat up straight. "Working with the event planners for the benefactor's dinner. Matt is working with the runners on the plan to rearrange the layout to showcase a few things better for the event."

"Have Grace help. She needs to understand all the little details that go into an event."

So, that was her game. She was intending to keep me too busy to prove her wrong about the urn. Either that or she intended to work me to death or resignation; whichever came first. I felt my blood begin to boil. There was no way I was going to let her win.

We discussed a few more details about plans that were in the works and some financial things I didn't understand before we dismissed and I followed Joy back to her office. She filled me in on what she had in mind for new acquisitions and I feverishly took notes. My next stop was Tony's office where I acquired the provenance papers for the swords he was having restored so I could study. I spent the rest of the day systematically visiting each curator to take notes on their current projects and what their expectations of me were.

After I thought everyone had left for the day, I sat at my little desk in my closet and looked over my notes. How was I ever going to get to work on all of this? I looked up at the urn. *And that?*

There was a soft knock on my door and I looked up. Candace was standing in the doorway.

"Hi," I said.

"I was wondering if you could help me with something." She stepped forward.

Oh, boy. More help. I cringed a little.

"I can do my best." That was all I had in me.

She reached out and set a rosary in my hand. "I was told it's sixteen-hundreds and German. What do you think?"

I turned it over in my hand several times and examined the beadwork as I explained, "Austrian would be closer but the style of the cross is Bavarian. And I'd say more likely eighteenth century because that's when silver filigree like this became more popular."

She took the rosary back and looked at it. She nodded and left without saying any more. I was thoroughly perplexed.

That night on the way home, I stopped by a dollar store and purchased a day planner. I also stopped by the library and picked up a few books on modern art and medieval swords. Hope and I feasted on nuked Salisbury steak and microwave popcorn while I combed through my notes and made a plan. I worked out how I could allot time for each of the curators' projects as well as the urn. I stayed up late into the night studying the books I had picked up from the library and taking notes. I also needed to find an apartment soon. It was only a matter of time before Hope was discovered and we would be living out of the Crown Vic.

The next morning, I roused early and showered. I kissed Hope goodbye told her to wish me luck as I headed out the door. I walked into the museum with my head held high. Gerald smiled and waved as I passed by and headed up the stairs. I was the first one in the boardroom. I laid out my planner and my notes and waited. One by one the curators smiled and they filed in and saw me waiting. Matthew winked at me.

At five after nine Sonya made an appearance in a brilliant shade of peacock blue. She had a smug look on her face as she walked in until she saw me sitting and waiting.

"Good morning." I smiled sweetly.

"How long have you been here?" She raised her eyebrows at me.

"Quite a while. You were nearly late."

She snorted at my remark. It felt good. She spent the rest of the morning trying to throw me but she failed. I made arrangements to meet with Joy about the ideas I had for new pieces based on my studies from the night before. Elaina and Matthew were able to fit me in to discuss expectations for the dinner. Tony and I worked out what days we should leave to go to New York which also gave me a goal date for finding an apartment. Everything came together smoothly, much to Sonya's dismay.

This was a beautiful prelude to the next nine weeks. I had found my niche and I excelled. As long as I kept my trusty planner with me and took plenty of notes, there was nothing I couldn't accomplish. There were quite a few late nights in the office with the urn or at the library. I even worked while at the laundromat, but I knew it would all pay off.

I even managed to find an apartment before having to leave for New York. It was small, dirty, and barely larger than the hotel room. It was in a questionable area of town so I invested in some pepper spray and kept a claw hammer under my pillow.

On my last day at the hotel, I turned over the key and the portly Russian man who owned it smiled. "You take good care of you kitty."

I was a little stunned. He knew all along. I smiled and thanked him.

It all came to a head at the Benefactor's Ball. Uncle James had wired me money for some new clothes and I felt absolutely incredible. I was only a few days shy of completing my internship. I had wowed Tony and the restorers in New York with my understanding of medieval weaponry and the restoration process. I had collaborated on my first ever acquisition request and helped choose major art pieces, hideous though I felt they may be. I had helped plan this beautiful party and I had almost completed my presentation about the urn. I was on top of the world.

I was trying to be a wallflower with my glass of wine but Sonya had zeroed in on me like a bird of prey. She was in an elegant black cocktail dress like most of us, but she hardly blended in. It was strange to see her dressed in something that wasn't a power color.

"Grace! I have a few people I want you to meet!" She called to me.

I took a deep breath, painted on a smile, and met her near a small group of obviously wealthy people.

"Grace! I want you to meet a few of our board members and benefactors. These are Doctors Anderson, Zimmerman, Caine, Jacoby, Marks, and Finnian. This is Grace. She's been our intern for the summer."

I shook each of their hands in turn. They even smelled like money.

Sonya continued. "Grace has even been working on a little project of her own. Why don't you fill us all in on your progress with the urn?"

I wasn't ready. She knew I wasn't ready. All eyes were on me. I couldn't let them down.

"Of course. Let me go get it so you can fully appreciate it." I excused myself.

I cursed her in English, Latin, and Greek as I fetched the urn and notes from my closet office and returned. They cleared a space on a cocktail table for me to set it. Everyone circled it and a large crowd gathered. I took a deep breath. *Here we go.*

"There we are, Grace. You are front and center. Tell us all about it." Sonya smiled viciously.

I cleared my throat. I thought about the opening to my presentation that I had written only a few nights before. "At first glance, this urn appears to be a pretty open and shut case, but I believe it has a far more unique history than previously thought.

Even the most discerning eye could be easily fooled by its simplicity."

I shot a side-eyed glance at Sonya. I felt as if I was going to either vomit or faint. I remembered the outline that I had made and drew from that. I began with a brief history of the French Revolution and Napoleon's rise to power. With Napoleon's rise and the creation of Italy, trade restrictions decreased. I explained how the weathered decorations that I had made rubbings of and enhanced with the help of a metalwork restorer along with the general shape were more reminiscent of a silver beaker from the mid seventeenth century. I presented pictures of similar pieces from France and Norfolk that were dated from the sixteen-thirties through the sixteen-sixties. I explained that I believed the lid was, in fact, eighteenth-century Italian and it had been added later. I pointed to an oil painting on the wall nearby that I had helped Matthew move which depicted a dinner bowl with a similar lid. The more I talked and the more nods and smiles I received, the more comfortable I became. Even more, as I watched Sonya's smile fade, the more I felt my heart lift.

In the end, there was a thunderous round of applause followed by a lot of handshaking. I didn't know if I was right, but I had presented enough of a case to impress an entire room of art professionals and critics. After the crowd had dispersed and some came for a closer look at the urn, I stepped back and took my first real breath since before I had started my speech.

"Grace!" I had never heard Candace say my name before.

She was leading a slightly overweight bearded man with enough grease in his hair to lube a car engine. I smiled at them. I didn't know I had any more smiling left in me.

"Grace. This is my father, Galen Jacoby."

"Nice to meet you." I shook his hand again.

"My daughter says great things about you!" His exclamation seemed genuine.

I was a little surprised by that statement. Candace and I had had almost no contact in ten weeks.

He continued. "She says you have extensive knowledge in religious art particularly and that you were even able to correctly identify my grandmother's rosary."

I thought back to that second day. "Yes, sir."

I had been very confused by our interaction that evening, but it was clear now. Candace had been testing me. I wasn't sure if it was because she liked me or if she wanted to see what I had been capable of, but it was a test nonetheless.

"I was very impressed by your presentation. I know Sonya and I know her intent is to, shall we say, skillfully derogate people. I like what I saw. I like that you are confident in your knowledge. With your permission, I would like to recommend to the board that we make you a permanent asset to the museum."

I couldn't believe what I was hearing. A real job. A real position in a real museum.

"I- I don't know what to say. 'Thank you' just doesn't seem like enough," I stuttered.

"Just prove my daughter right. And keep Sonya in check. That's all the thanks I need." He nodded and walked away.

Graduation

Graduating with my Bachelor's degree was bittersweet. I was so proud of myself. I had accomplished four years of studying, work, and heartache and it had finally paid off in 2007. Chetna invited me out to her graduation party in California. She wanted me to meet her family and show me around her home city. I would have loved to have gone. It sounded like an amazing new experience. Unfortunately, I had no way to earn the money for such a trip. My internship had bled me dry.

Uncle James insisted on having our own little family party for me. Instead of walking in the ceremony to receive my diploma, I had it mailed to me and drove home to Illinois. I had an intense sensation of apprehension in that nine-hour drive. I couldn't shake the feeling that I was making a mistake by going back there. I couldn't understand why. Yes, that was an old life that I had left behind, but I didn't really have a reason to *fear* it. It was home, after all; wasn't it?

I pulled into Uncle James's driveway and was instantly hit with a flood of memories and a wave of sadness. The crabapple tree near the house he liked to pick fruit from was barren and dead. Garbage was piled up on the side of the house as if he had just done a frantic bout of cleaning. I stepped out of my car and peered into the backyard. The tire swing on the old sugar maple tree was dry rotted and barely hanging. Even our old classroom, the potting shed, was in disrepair and the roof was caving in. The sight was almost too much to bear.

"Holy shit. You really did come back," a voice from long ago came up from behind me.

"Jacob, don't swear. Momma could hear you," I scolded. "And why wouldn't I come back?"

"I don't know. You haven't come home in a while, let alone stayed long enough to say 'boo' to the family. I didn't see why this time would be any different." He shrugged his shoulders.

"Uncle James is happy for me and wanted to see me. We can't *both* let him down," I snapped.

"What is that supposed to mean?"

I shrugged back at him. "Probably *exactly* what you think it means."

"I knew I heard you pull up!" Uncle James came around from the back of the house and met me at the gate. He opened it wide and embraced me in a huge hug. "I'm so proud of you!"

"Thank you, Uncle James." I hugged him back.

"Let me get a look at you!" He pulled back and held me at arm's length. "My girl, you have changed! Look at this! Makeup and your hair all done! Even more beautiful than when you left! I think happiness looks good on you." He smiled.

I took him in as well. His skin was more wrinkled and his yellow button-down shirt didn't fit as well as it once had. He had attempted to comb a tangle of hair that was long overdue to be cut but he had trimmed and shaved his beard and mustache. I had never seen him with facial hair and wasn't sure if I liked it.

"Grace! You're home!" Momma came out the front door and came up behind me.

She hugged me hard. I felt guilty about staying away for so long, but I didn't want to admit it.

"Hi, Momma." I hugged her back.

"When do the rest of your things arrive?" She asked excitedly.

"Rest of my things?"

"Of course! Now that you're done with school, you're moving back home, right? I have your room all ready for you." She was beaming brightly.

My heart dropped into my stomach. I had never told her I was coming home for good and I was pretty sure I had never given her a reason to believe I was. She had just made the assumption and now I felt guilty anyway.

"No, Momma. I'm not moving back. I'm staying in school to finish my Master's degree and the museum offered me a permanent job. I'm staying in Cleveland."

I watched her smile disappear. "But, Grace-"

"No, Momma." I crossed my arms.

She stared at me in stunned silence. I saw tears begin to come up in her eyes.

"I have to go tend to the potatoes. Excuse me." She turned and went back to the house.

My heart sank further. I knew it was going to be a long time before she forgave me if she ever did at all.

Uncle James cleared his throat. "Come around back and help me get the grill started. I got us the best chicken parts in the county!"

I looked back at the front door my mother had walked through before turning back and following my uncle and cousin. I was a little nervous about sitting on the remains of the old picnic table. I grabbed a glass and poured myself some ice water from the pitcher. I could see my mother fussing around in the kitchen through the window in the back door. I turned away from her.

"Nice going. Only been back ten minutes and already made your momma cry," Jacob snickered under his breath.

"Momma and I want different things for me. She's going to have to accept that. You didn't turn out the way your dad wanted, either."

He opened his mouth to say something back but shut it back again before going and standing next to Uncle James at the grill. Somehow, my homecoming was managing to be far worse than I had imagined.

"So, Grace! You got a boyfriend yet? I want to meet him," Uncle James called over his shoulder.

I looked at my glass and thought of Xander.

"No," I said softly. "Too busy, I guess."

"That's okay." He turned and smiled at me. "Boys aren't anything but trouble anyway."

He lovingly shoved his only son. We all laughed and it felt good. Momma emerged from the kitchen with a tray of potatoes wrapped in aluminum foil. She set them on the picnic table without a word and returned to the kitchen. I looked back at my glass.

"Don't worry, Grace. She just needs time," Uncle James tried to reassure me. "Now, tell me about this job at the museum."

Happy to change the subject, I told him about my test with the rosary and all the nice people there. I told him about the urn and how good it felt to put Sonya in her place in front of such an audience. I was excited that they wanted me to stay. I caught Momma listening at the kitchen window, pretending to scrub carrots. I hoped I wasn't rubbing salt into her open wound.

"Grace, this sounds like a wonderful opportunity. I'm really happy for you." Uncle James sat next to me on the picnic table and took a big drink of water from his glass.

I suddenly wondered how long it had been since he had had anything to drink other than beer or coffee, but I was proud of him for making the effort on my behalf.

Momma emerged from the kitchen and set down a tray of freshly cut raw vegetables and ranch dressing.

"Yes!" Jacob exclaimed as he grabbed three carrot sticks and swooped up some dressing.

"Leave some for the rest of us!" Uncle James laughed as he smacked his hand when he reached for more.

It was good to see the two of them getting along. When I had left, I didn't know if interaction like this would even be possible. They never stopped loving each other but Jacob was more than Uncle James could manage. He was always getting in trouble and, instead of being there to support his father, he found more trouble. I didn't think I could ever forgive him for that part. I wasn't sure how much Jacob had matured in the time that I had been away, but I was glad to see it may have been enough to mend old broken hearts.

"James, what did you do with the corn on the cob?" Momma asked.

"I thought I put them in the pantry. Let me go have a look."

They both walked into the house.

"You really like living in Cleveland?" Jacob asked as he shoveled more dressing into his mouth on a head of broccoli.

"I do," I replied.

"Well, I guess it's good that one of us got out of here," he chuckled.

"It's not too late for you, you know. You could go to school. Get an honest job. Make something of yourself." I tried to sound encouraging though I doubted what I was saying was true.

He stood in contemplative silence for a moment.

"Nah," he finally said before turning away and pretending to scrape the grill.

"You were supposed to soak them," I heard my mother complain as she followed James out of the house.

"It'll be fine, Jan. We'll just spritz them with some water to keep the husks from burning." Uncle James rolled his eyes.

"Honestly. Can't even have proper corn on the cob." Momma threw her hands in the air and went back into the kitchen.

Despite the slightly-singed corn, we had a wonderful meal. It had been a long time since I had had a real, home-cooked supper and it was wonderful. After we had all eaten our fill, I followed momma a few miles down the road to the little yellow house I had grown up in. A few chickens scattered as I got out of my car and walked up to the familiar porch. I turned and looked across the street. Aaron's old house had been painted grey and there was now a privacy fence extending from around the back. The flowerbed was immaculate and the lawn was neatly cut in a crisscross pattern. I touched the stone on my neck. All of the memories of us together seemed like such a lifetime ago.

Inside my old home, the living room and the furniture were still the same. She had told the truth about getting my old room ready. Everything was completely unchanged from when I had left it from the hideous green carpet to the floral curtains but there was not a speck of dust to be seen. I flopped on the bed and covered my face with a pillow. I wished I had brought Hope to comfort me instead of leaving her in a cage at the vet. Eventually, I fell asleep still in my clothes.

The next morning, I showered and changed. I had to stop myself from going out the mudroom door to feed the chickens. Old habits do die hard. I, instead, turned to the kitchen where I was met with fried eggs, oatmeal, and toast.

"Good morning," my mother greeted me.

"Good morning," I said as I sat down and helped myself to orange juice.

Momma sat across from me. We said our prayer and ate in silence for a few uncomfortable minutes.

"You're really going back to stay?" she finally asked.

"Yes." My eyes didn't leave my plate.

"How long will you be here?"

"I have to go back to work on Monday so I have to leave tomorrow."

She was silent for a moment. "After church?"

"Yes, after church."

She nodded and continued to eat in silence. She was unhappy with my decision. I knew that. But I decided to cling to the small comfort that she'd at least accepted it.

What More than Blood

    I did my best to settle into my new life. My mother may have minutely accepted my decision but she still cried for hours before I left Illinois once again. She was so sure that when I'd gotten this wanderlust out of my system, I would return home and continue along the path of God. To this day, I'm not sure what she thought I could accomplish from the confines of that little town. This was in stark contrast to Uncle James who couldn't have been more thrilled for me. He asked me if I needed anything for my apartment since I would be staying there permanently. I told him no, though it was a lie. I had next to nothing. I had burned through my savings from the warehouse job and my internship had been unpaid but I couldn't take more from him; he had done so much for me already.

    My apartment was a mess. It was a studio style so all of my worldly possessions were in one room. Clothes were haphazardly thrown on top of the dresser instead of in it, in baskets on the floor, and draped over the desk chair. In the center of the room sat a loveseat I had salvaged from a thrift store dumpster. I didn't own a television, so it faced an empty wall. My old bedroom nightstand served as an end table and held the stuffed koala bear lamp I'd had since childhood. I didn't have money for curtains but a green sheet I had tacked over the window to block the view of the city (and its view of me) was falling down. A portfolio of copies of works I had made at the library spilled the papers out and all over the floor. My bookshelf was packed with volumes I had collected from used book sales, yard sales, and everything in between. Atop the bookcase rested the half-dead potted plant Chetna had gifted me as a housewarming present. It was dark. It was cluttered. It was depressing. But, it was mine.

    I surprisingly didn't feel alone in my new home city. The laundromat was a completely different world. Maybe 'community' is a better word for it. There were the regulars- those of us who would come on specific nights of the week at specific times. We barely knew each other's names, but we knew where we worked, each other's kids' names, and who was studying what. I imagined things hadn't changed much since the days of our ancestors in Greece and Egypt who would gather at rivers and fountains to wash their clothes and socialize. I would sit at the table in the corner with my headphones on and my books spread out, feverishly studying my humanities credits.

Mr. Blevins would bring leftover bagels and donuts that didn't sell at his bakery and I would take a few extra home. Ms. Cooper, the proprietor of the laundromat, knew I was struggling and would let me raid the unclaimed clothes bin once a month before she took them to the charity shop.

In return for their kindness, I would help Mr. Blevins by watching and switching out his clothes while I did mine and I would help Ms. Cooper fold the drop-off clothes. Despite their kindness and their help staving off loneliness, I needed a friend.

I missed Chet. She had flown in for a few days to celebrate my new job, but that had been months before. She had gone home to pursue her own life. We talked on the phone every day, but it just wasn't the same. I had Hope and I had made work friends, but I needed my BEST friend. She was a great motivator when I needed to study and a cheerleader when I was feeling down. Though I will admit, I was glad she didn't see what I had done to her plant.

One chilly October evening, I sat curled up on the loveseat with my textbook shoveling the remainder of a pint of mint chocolate chip in my mouth. My attempt to drown my despair in reading about kitsch art with sugary frozen dairy products was futile. I did my best to muscle through the subject matter. It was late at night and I was tired but I had to get through it.

A hard knock at the door jolted me out of my brooding state. I fell off the couch and stared at the door. The knock was harder and louder this time. I went to the kitchen area and retrieved a dirty steak knife out of the sink.

Knock...Knock...Knock...

I approached the door cautiously, cracked it open, and peered into the hall.

"You gonna let me in?" It was Jacob.

I almost would have preferred a burglar. I shut the door in his face and contemplated leaving him out there.

"Come on, Grace. Let me in," he called through the door.

I sighed and slid the chain to let him in.

"What are you doing in Ohio?" I asked and narrowed my eyes at him.

"I can't just want to come visit my family?" he asked as he flopped on the loveseat. "Been a while. Maybe I'm just checking in."

"What more is there than blood that makes us family?" I quipped as I shut the door and put the chain back on.

He ignored my question. "Were you going to stab me with that?" He gestured to the knife still in my hand.

"I might still consider it if you don't tell me what you want."

"Hey, you still got that cat?" he asked and started looking around for Hope.

"Jacob!" I crossed my arms and set my jaw.

"Okay. I need a place to stay for a few days."

"What the Hell did you do this time?" I rolled my eyes at him.

"You better not let Aunt Janice hear you say something like that. Anyways, I didn't actually do it this time," he insisted

"You have sixty seconds to explain or I'm calling Uncle James," I threatened.

"A car got stolen and they're blaming me. I just need a place to hang out while they find who actually did it."

I rolled my eyes again and threw my hands up. "Jacob…"

"No! I mean it! I got witnesses and everything. I was at Booker's and I couldn't drive home so they let me sleep it off in the back room."

"Bookers? That filthy bar out by the Carol Family's farm?" I vaguely recalled the little biker bar that had been built out of a converted house.

"Yeah. I swear I was there but there's no cameras."

"Of course not. They aren't going to record all the drug deals and bar fights."

"So I just need a place to stay until they find who actually did it," he repeated.

"What makes you think they're still looking if they think you did it?"

"Because I have witnesses and they don't have any proof that I actually did it 'cause I didn't do it," he said again. "I broke up with Crystal Martin and she told the cops it was me out of spite."

I sucked in a deep breath.

"I swear, Grace!" He was insistent but pleading.

I let my breath out. Jacob was a lowlife, but he had never actually lied to *me*.

"On Aunt Catherine's grave?" I said, finally.

He looked stunned for a second. "On Mom's grave. I swear. I did not steal that car."

"Fine." I uncrossed my arms and went back to the kitchen to throw the knife back in the sink.

"Thank you! Best cousin ever!"

I suddenly realized… "Why didn't you go to Aunt Catherine's family for help?"

His smile faded quickly and he looked at the floor. "They wrote me off a long time ago. Lost cause and all that."

I hadn't felt bad for Jacob since Catherine died but that statement hit me hard.

I firmed back up. "Well don't burn this bridge."

He looked back up at me. "Really. Thanks, Grace."

"Yeah, yeah."

I went to the bed and pulled off one of the blankets and a pillow. I threw it at him and went back to the bed. He stretched out on the little couch and turned out the koala lamp. I took my wallet out of my pocket and slid it into the case of the remaining pillow. I loved him and I felt sorry for him but that didn't mean I trusted him.

The next day I had work immediately followed by night classes so I didn't return until late. When I'd left in the morning, Jacob was still asleep on the couch and snoring loud enough to almost shake the walls. I'd half expected him to be gone by the time I returned that night. I was wrong. Before I'd even opened my door, I could smell food. *Real* food coming through the other side.

When I opened the door, I hardly recognized my apartment. My papers were all neatly tucked away in my folio. The green sheet had been replaced with a pretty blue curtain. My clothes were all put away; except for my intimate things, which remained in the laundry basket next to the dresser. The blanket I had given Jacob the night before was neatly folded on top of the pillow on the end of the couch. My bed was made, the floor had been swept, and even the plant looked perkier. Then I noticed the furniture. My nightstand and koala lamp had been moved next to the bed. In place next to the couch, there was a proper (albeit cheap) wooden end table next to one arm and a floor lamp next to the other. In the kitchenette sat a small wooden table with four chairs. He'd even replaced the two burnt-out light bulbs in the ceiling fixture (I was too short to reach them). It was clean and bright and felt like a real apartment. I stood in the doorway, stunned, with Hope happily dancing around my feet wearing a pink ribbon tied to her collar.

"You're back!" Jacob called from the stove.

"Wha- what did you do here?" I shut the door and set my book bag on the floor next to it.

"You've obviously been too busy to clean up around here so I thought I'd pitch in. Honestly, Grace, in good conscience I could not let you keep living like that."

"Where did the furniture come from?"

"Thrift store." His eyes suddenly widened. "I didn't steal it if that's what you're implying."

I looked at him. "Can you blame me for asking?"

"No. I guess not. I'm not like I was when we were kids. I don't do a lot of bad things anymore. I got a real job doing construction and making honest money. I do stupid things when I've been drinking but that's it. I promise."

I felt a little twinge of guilt for having made the accusation. "Then answer me this…"

He looked at the floor. "What?"

"What smells so good?"

He brightened up and smiled wide. "Well, I'm not much of a cook. You know Dad. He didn't teach me much but I can make one awesome bowl of chili!"

"Then let's break in this new table." I smiled back at him.

He pulled out a chair for me and I sat. He put a glass of water and a steaming bowl in front of me and sat down on the opposite side of the table with his own bowl and a bottle of beer. He picked up his spoon and was about to help himself when he stopped and looked at me.

"Should we say the prayer?" he asked.

I realized I hadn't prayed before eating since the last time he and I had seen each other.

"I'm fine if you are," I said.

He nodded and started shoveling chili into his mouth. It was like watching an ape that someone had attempted to teach table manners. Meanwhile, I skillfully spooned the rich, meaty soup.

"What do you think?" he asked in between bites.

"You've done yourself proud. You know, in some parts around here, they put chili on spaghetti and drown it in shredded cheese."

"Really?" He wrinkled his nose.

"Yeah. It's pretty popular south of here."

"That sounds disgusting."

As we ate, we tried to make small talk but it was painfully awkward. He downed one bottle of beer after another and eventually became drunk and rambling.

"What was the name of that guy you dated in high school? The one you told Aunt Janice you were tutoring?"

I felt myself get a little tense. "Toby."

"Yeah. Him. Well, remember how he disappeared?"

"Of course I remember." I could feel my heart beat faster.

"They found his remains not too long ago. Just got the identification back last week," he said nonchalantly.

I tried to look intrigued but played dumb. "Remains?"

"Yeah. Some hikers found him in the woods. Just bones and not too many of those were left. Identified him through dental records."

I swallowed hard. "What happened?"

"They don't know yet. Thinking he was murdered on account some of him was found inside an old suitcase. He was into so much stuff back then that it was probably just a drug deal gone bad. At least that what the cops are saying."

I exhaled as calmly as I could. I remembered his glassy eyes and the controller cord around his neck. Toby was a good man and, though his betrayal at choosing himself over our relationship was still a raw wound, he probably didn't deserve to die the way he had. I had made peace with what Onoskelis and I had done long ago and it bothered me his memory was being reduced to nothing more than another drug addict teenager.

I finally said, "he really didn't do a lot of drugs."

"That's not what people think of him now. You know the cops back home. They'll get any idea in their heads and run with it. That's how I ended up here."

"Yeah..."

"You know, I used to think you knew where he went and just weren't telling," he said with a casual tone.

I remembered the way Jacob had looked at me after I had been interrogated by the police.

"Oh, yeah?"

"Yeah." He finished off another bottle. "I knew he broke your heart. I was thinking about talking to him myself."

"You were?" I was surprised that Jacob would want to come to my aid let alone admit it more than a decade later.

"Yeah. I wasn't going to let you know though. I love you like a sister but that doesn't mean I like you. Anyways, I didn't have to talk to him since he went missing and now I know you had nothing to do with it." He shrugged.

"What makes you so sure of that?"

"Oh, come on, Grace!" He laughed an obnoxious, drunken laugh. "You were half his size! No way you could have hauled him in a suitcase out to the woods."

I could with a little help. I thought.

I feigned a laugh. "Yeah. Guess you're right."

He drank almost an entire case of beer by himself that night and passed out on the couch. I sat up in bed with headphones on to drown out his snoring while I studied.

The next day, I left him still snoring on the couch early in the morning again but I didn't return to a home-cooked meal. The apartment was clean but empty. On the table sat a vase of dyed flowers from the grocery store and a note that said simply 'thank you.'

I smiled. In just two days I'd seen a side of Jacob I hadn't even known existed in over twenty years.

Home

Life was coming together in a chaotic sort of way. I had rescued a small desk from the curbside and set up a proper study area in the corner of my tiny apartment. This allowed me to keep the rest of the apartment somewhat tidy after Jacob had worked so hard to show me what it could be. I'd been working rigorously on my capstone for my master's degree. Hope wasn't happy about how busy I'd been but I assured her it would be worth the late nights and microwave dinners.

I was feverishly typing away on my laptop. I had a mountain of notes for my project and it was due in only four days. Other women got to enjoy their Sundays. Mine were typically spent on the phone with my mother. She liked to call after a particularly meaningful sermon to pass along God's glorious message. I would put her on speakerphone and pretend to listen while doing chores. Thankfully, she would get too wrapped up in preaching to me to ask how church was for me. I wasn't attending. After I'd make my excuses to get off the phone with her, I'd decompress with a cup of tea and a sandwich before setting to work on my studies. There was a light at the end of the tunnel. I had thought that day would be the same as every other Sunday and, though it had started out that way, it ended tremendously.

A soft knock at the door drew my attention from the screen. I looked at Hope. She was hardly disturbed. I grabbed the pepper spray from my nightstand. The addict on the ground floor had recently taken a shine to me and I wasn't sure if he would get brave enough to do more than gawk at me from around corners and follow me to my car. I cracked my door and peered out. Nothing. As I was closing the door, a splash of color on the doormat grabbed my attention. I slid the chain and opened the door to pick up the orchid.

"I figured you would have killed that fern by now." A sweet, condescending, yet oh-so-familiar voice teased.

"Chet!" I almost dropped the flower in my rush to embrace my friend.

"Sweetie, I can't breathe."

"Sorry!" I released her. "Come in!"

She stood just inside the door as I closed it behind her. She looked around.

"This looks much more cozy than the last time I was here," she observed.

"It's a work in progress."

I wasn't going to dare give credit to Jacob.

"I'm not going to lie. I've always been a little concerned for your safety. The fact that you just met me with that proves me right." She pointed to the pepper spray in my hand.

"Oh. Right." I set the pepper spray and the orchid on the end table and we sat on the loveseat.

"I thought the money at the museum was pretty good."

"It is."

"Then why stay here?"

"It's cheap so I can save up for something better. And small. Between school and work, I don't have time for something bigger. And after so long, it's really felt like home."

"That makes sense. But you're almost done with school," she pointed out.

"That's true." I felt the need to take the focus of the conversation off of myself. "What are you doing here? And where's Kevin?"

"He stayed back home. He's started another new job. He doesn't like it so I doubt he'll stay at this one either but it pays well." There was a hint of irritation in her voice.

"That's only part of my question." I raised my eyebrows at her.

"Well, I want to complete my doctorate, as you know." She turned more to face me and sat up straighter.

"Yes. You've been talking about how you need to find a research position."

"I found one!" she blurted out.

"Here?"

"The Botanical Gardens are looking for research associates. My interview is tomorrow!" She was almost screaming.

"The Gardens? That's right next to the museum!" My volume matched hers.

Words cannot express how high my heart leaped. My best friend- my sister- could be right next door.

"Do you need a place to stay for the night and get ready in the morning?" I tried to steady my voice.

"I got a hotel near University Circle. I don't know what traffic is like and a cab will be cheaper."

I sensed she was trying to spare my feelings, but it still stung a little. In truth, I didn't have much besides a loveseat and hot water to offer her so I didn't allow myself to become too upset.

"And there's more," she announced.

"Oh, God. You aren't pregnant are you?" I didn't mean for that to slip out let alone sound as nasty as it did.

"What? No!" She held up her left hand.

Her ring finger was encircled with a silver band. It was poorly etched with elephants walking trunk-to-tail and exaggerated with a rough patina. Overall, I was surprised the ring hadn't turned her finger a lovely shade of sage.

"That is a huge leap!" I exclaimed a little too loud.

"I know! He completely caught me by surprise!"

"Are you sure about this?" I honestly didn't mean to sound so unsupportive.

"I know we have our arguments. I do wish he would spend less time skating and more time helping me plan our future. And, I really wish he would stick with a job for more than a year. But I love him and I can't imagine my life without him."

I was hesitant. I honestly didn't think Kevin was good for her for all of the reasons she listed and then some. He had never actually finished college and had no real direction in life. But, he had moved across the country just to be with her and he did make her happy.

"Okay," I said, finally. "Let's get you the job and then we'll plan your wedding."

She squealed. "I'm getting everything I ever wanted! And you are going to look so beautiful in seafoam as my maid of honor!"

I tried to force a smile but I honestly couldn't imagine myself in such a fetid color. We spent the next few hours giggling and gossiping like teenagers. We talked about work, school, and Kevin. It's funny how even though we talked on the phone several nights a week, we could still find more to chatter about. Eventually, we called a taxi to take her to the hotel. After she left, I suddenly realized that I felt more like myself than I had in a very long time. I knew I missed her, but I hadn't realized just how much of me was missing without her. When she was there, I was more than just a study robot.

Needless to say, she got the position. No one in their right mind would deny Chetna.

The next month went by in a blurry instant. By some miracle, I did well on my capstone and achieved my master's degree. I helped coordinate Chetna and Kevin's big move and in the process of finding their condo, we came across a sad, dilapidated little ranch house. It was about nine hundred square feet. It had three bedrooms and an eat-in kitchen. The hardwood floors were in near disrepair. Only a few of the windows still had glass in them and the living room walls were a rainbow of graffiti. There were no appliances and the kitchen walls and ceiling were coated in an oily residue. The bathroom walls had exposed studs and I will spare you the details of the toilet. It was being sold for land value only but there was something about that house that kept nagging at me. A week after we finished moving Chetna and Kevin into their new condo, I found myself signing my life away on a deed to that shell of a domicile.

My former study time was spent painting walls, learning how to refinish floors, and scrubbing every surface. Kevin proved himself to be more useful than I had ever known he could be. In between half-hearted job hunting, he built the walls in the bathroom and even tiled around the bathtub. He had picked up quite a few skills in his constant job-hopping. He took me appliance shopping and helped me get them installed. Chetna insisted on being allowed to landscape my flowerbed out front. Getting the house ready to live in felt like such a mountain to climb, but I loved seeing my best friend almost every day and even her fiancé made me feel less alone.

My first night in the house, however, felt completely empty. With my bed and nightstand in the bedroom, the only furniture in the living room was an end table, a lamp, and a loveseat. I had two whole bedrooms in the house that were completely empty. I hadn't realized how much going from having all of my worldly possessions in one room to spreading them throughout a house would feel like opening a great void. I had all of this space and time to make my own and no idea what to do with it.

Steadily, I accumulated a nice living room set, dishes that actually matched, and even a television. I set up one of the extra bedrooms as a home office complete with a file cabinet and book shelves. The third bedroom was turned into a guest bedroom using the old air mattress I had started my new life on and purchased a brand-new bedroom set for myself. I had saved up a lot of money by staying in that rat-hole in the city while finishing my master's and, while I admittedly burned through it more quickly than I wanted to, I felt like the end result was something to be proud of.

With a new house full of all my own things and my best friend only twenty minutes away, I finally felt like I was home.

My Father

Church changed as I grew older. I sat in Lenten mass year after year when Momma would come to visit. Purple adornments were draped along the walls, pews, and pulpit. But each year as I looked around, the pews became more and more vacant. Devout blind faith was for the old and fewer young people carried on the traditions of their elders. Even on Easter, when people closer to my age came purely out of obligation, there were fewer voices in the hymns and prayers. I didn't blame them. It was easy to lose faith or doubt his existence. God is a mad scientist and we are an experiment in a Petri dish.

Much to my mother's dismay, I followed them and steadily stopped making an effort to attend church. I knew God was real. Onoskelis was every bit of proof that I needed. But the church itself drove me away. Cult-like ceremony and skewed interpretations of carefully selected gospels became more than I could bear. Some churches tried to become more relevant with music and then corporate churches and megachurches became a thing. Free coffee, Wi-Fi, jumbotrons, and televangelists spewing corrupted nonsense. I was done with it all.

When I was an adult, the only thing that could move heaven enough to get me into a church was my mother. Every few years throughout school and a little after, I had gone home to visit her. I had to attend church, of course, and I was all but locked into confession in an attempt to save my soul and remind me of how important I was. One year, during the Sign of Peace, she told a very attractive man in the pew in front of me that he should feel honored to shake my hand. I was mortified. So I had stopped going home for anything other than Christmas. That didn't work. She would come to me nearly every spring under the pretense of visiting for my birthday. I decided if she was going to come to me, there was no reason for me to go home at all and made my excuses even at Christmas.

2010 was no different. I had found the most gaudy cathedral in the city and she loved it. It had been built in the eighteen-fifties and looked completely out of place amongst the modern buildings in the city. We sat in Lenten mass and listened to the same three stories about the Samaritan and the well, the blind man, and Lazarus's rising. These were the same three stories that had been told for lent for two thousand years. I could recite them from memory. I stopped paying attention and let my eyes wander over the huge white columns and blue and gold vaulted ceilings. Statues of the Blessed were tucked into alcoves and stained glass windows depicted angels in vivid color. But the skull was what really piqued my interest. In a glass case were the skull, skeleton, and broken vial of blood from a thirteen-year-old girl who died sometime around the year 300 CE. She was St. Christine. She was a gift from the pope himself to the people of Cleveland. Most people would find it macabre to display the remains of a dead child, but I found it fascinating. She was a shrine to innocence. In truth, she was ultimately what had led me to choose this church. After all, relics like her were my specialty.

At the end of mass, my mother and I exited the church onto the street arm-in-arm.

"Oh, Grace!" She was grinning wide. "That is such a lovely church! And a wonderful no-nonsense sermon! I can't wait to go back."

"Uh-huh. I thought you might like it." I guided her towards the car.

"Your father would be so impressed by this!"

I stopped in my tracks. "My father?"

"Oh, yes. Shame he didn't live to see this." Her expression changed to a faraway look over a stone face. "So much blood."

That was it. I had spent nearly twenty-six years on Earth and the only thing I learned about my father was that he seemed to have died a horrible death.

"I'm still not sure about this career of yours." She had snapped out of her haze and dove into one of her particularly critical moods.

"We talked about this. I am more likely to find my path outside of the convent."

"But you've changed so much since you went to school." She whined. "You talk different and so much makeup and your clothes!"

She was right. College and a career away from home had changed me a lot and I felt like it had definitely been for the better.

"Momma, I have to dress for work," I stated.

"I don't believe cleavage is part of the dress code," she retorted.

"Momma, I have to dress in modern attire. There are a lot of expectations of me in my field. God will understand that." I could hear the exasperation in my voice.

"Well, I sincerely hope you dress more modestly when you meet with bishops and the pope."

"Of course. And the fact that I do meet with them at all is proof I'm on the right path. When have you ever met a pope?"

"I hope for the sake of your soul that you are right."

Shawn Bullocks

I had finished my master's degree in the summer of 2009. For more than a year afterward, I remained an underling that Sonya still seemed to hold in contempt after the incident with the urn. Despite her, I was rapidly gaining a reputation in my field and the contribution to the museum as a result of my notoriety could not go ignored. Dr. Jacoby had even sent me to Italy for the acquisition of a particular painting. That was when I had met the Pope. I had my picture taken with him and set it back to Momma and Sonya. She resented me even more and took every opportunity to remind me that she was still my superior. It wasn't until Bethany moved on to warmer climates and left a vacant office that I was finally permitted to leave my closet in the basement and have a real office with my peers. I'm sure Candace had pulled a few strings to make it mine. She and I weren't what you should call 'friends,' but we had a wonderful respect for each other.

On sunny days, Chetna and I would often stroll over to Little Italy for lunch. Sitting out on a roadside patio in the fresh air with warm, homemade bread, risotto, sometimes a glass of wine, and topped with handcrafted cannoli was pure heaven. Each time I would return, I would take the scenic route through the museum back to my desk (often to walk off that Italian wine). Every day I would see the same man admiring different paintings in different areas.

He was a black man of average height but had a build like a wrestler and looked to be maybe a few years younger than me. His hair and beard were neatly trimmed and he almost always wore a clean, white shirt. The satchel he regularly carried suggested he was probably a student who came wandering over in his downtime. He never seemed to have someone with him or talked to anyone. Some days, I'd stop myself and realize I was studying him almost as intently as he was studying the paintings. There was something captivating in the way he meditated on the art so intently.

One warm, July day I finally decided I had to talk to him.

"Hi. I see you in here quite a lot."

He turned and smiled politely. "I love it here."

"Are you an art student?"

"No ma'am. I wish though. I'm studying pharmacy." There was something sad in his voice when he said it.

"You don't want to be a pharmacist, do you?" I observed.

He looked at the floor. "Not really. But, it's interesting and it pays well."

I looked up into his eyes. "So does art."

"Pops says a real man works a real job and art is just a hobby."

I laughed a little. "I work with a couple of men who would have something to say to your pops about that."

Tony was the first to come to mind.

"He perked up a little. "You work here?"

"I'm a curator. My specialty is Christian art and artifacts." I held out my hand. "Grace Nightingale."

He, at once, became energized and stood up straighter. I almost felt like a celebrity as he shook my hand vigorously and grinned wide.

"Shawn Bullocks."

He finally released my hand.

"Hello, Shawn. It's nice to meet you."

His satchel slipped off his shoulder and spilled a few items on the floor. We stooped down to pick them up. Among the textbooks and notepads, I caught a glimpse of a pencil sketch. I picked up the drawing. It was a beautiful African American woman with curls piled on top of her head and big hoop earrings. It was clearly unfinished, but amazingly well done.

"Is this your work?" I handed him back the drawing as he stood.

"Yes, ma'am. That's my sister, Ashley. She went and joined the air force this year. I miss her. First time we've been apart since we were born."

"Twins?"

"Triplets, actually. But my brother Michael has kind of always been the odd one out. Ashley and me were always close. She bought me my first real charcoal set."

"It's good to have family like that. You are very talented."

"Thank you." He beamed. "What kind of art do you do?"

I laughed a little. "Oh, no. My talent rests solely in recognizing it in others."

"Well, thank you for seeing it in me. I've got to get to class now. It was nice to meet you, Miss Nightingale."

"You too, Shawn. And call me Grace."

He nodded and headed towards the exit.

"Who was that?" Candace walked up behind me.

"His name is Shawn. He's an art enthusiast who has a lot of talent."

"Sounds like you need an assistant."

"Yeah, right!" I laughed at the notion "As if Sonya or the board would let me hire an assistant."

"Maybe not hire but Dad always says 'you can't say no to free labor.'" She walked off towards the East wing.

I thought hard as I headed up the stairs. I *could* use some help. All this new popularity was keeping me busy. But he might not want that kind of work; especially not to do it for free. He also had his studies to consider. By the time I reached the third floor, I decided it couldn't hurt to ask him. Sonya's door was open and she was scribbling at her desk so I marched straight into her office.

"I want to bring on a volunteer assistant. He seems to really have an eye for art and-"

She didn't even look up. "Email Legal and tell them to draw up a volunteer contract."

She dismissed me with a flick of her hand.

"Oh. Thanks." I turned and left. That was far easier than I thought it was going to be.

The following Monday I found Shawn staring at *The Devil and Tom Walker*. It was one of my favorites.

"Good afternoon, Shawn."

He turned towards me and smiled that big, happy smile. "Hello, Miss… Grace."

"Do you like this one?"

He turned back to look at the painting. "I can't decide."

"Have you read the story it's based on?"

"No, ma'am." He cocked his head slightly. "I know the picture is telling a story, but I didn't know it was based on any writing."

"What story do you see?"

"Well, this man with the walking stick seems to be happy but something about him says he's not too bright."

I laughed. "What else do you see?"

"This guy with the axe looks evil. Kind of predatory, in a way. And I feel like this skull in the path is foreshadowing. Like if he stays on the path, he's going to die or at least something bad is going to happen."

I clapped. "Bravo."

He smiled.

"I was hoping to find you today. How would you feel about coming to work under me? It's only a volunteer position but you would have access to more of the art and behind the scenes."

His eyes widened it his whole body lit up. "Really?"

"There's something about you. I can't put my finger on it, but I think you need to be a part of this museum. I'm not suggesting a career change and we can work around your class schedule. But, there is a fire that lights in you when you are here and I think I may be able to offer some new tinder to keep it going."

He was silent for a moment and I almost thought he might start to cry.

"When do I start?" His voice cracked a little.

"Well, come with me and we'll get you set up with the paperwork for your background check and work out a schedule around your classes." I turned to escort him upstairs.

"Grace?"

I turned back to him. "Yes?"

"Can I give you a hug?"

I laughed. I don't think anyone had ever asked me that before.

"Yes," I said.

He wrapped me in a big bear hug and lifted me off the ground.

"Thank you," he whispered.

When you least expect it

It was a beautiful summer day in University Circle. Chetna and I liked to meet at our favorite coffee stand and walk to work. It was nice to work a three-minute walk from your best friend's office.

"I can't believe Rob just totally flaked on you like that." Chetna took a long draw from her morning mango spinach smoothie. "I mean, just a breakup text? What a coward."

Rob was my most recent failure at love. We had met through an online dating service. I know it's a bit cliché but I was coming up on thirty in a hurry and I was lonely. Unfortunately, he, like so many others, was looking more for one thing and it wasn't long-term.

I smiled. "Come on, Chet. We were only barely dating and only for a few months. It is what it is. Honestly, I'm beginning to feel like I have a six-month expiration date. This keeps happening."

"You going to try that dating site again?"

I choked a little on my coffee. "I don't think so. I think I should just accept my fate and be a spinster forever."

We were standing in front of the employee entrance to the botanical gardens. Students and locals were out on their morning jogs and headed to class on their bikes.

"Don't be ridiculous. You just haven't bumped into the right guy yet."

I laughed. "Easy for you to say. You and Kevin have been together for, what? Eight years?"

She smiled as wide as her face could stretch. "I did get lucky." She got a far-off, dreamy look in her eyes.

"If it weren't for bad luck, I'd have no luck at all," I said mockingly.

"Don't be ridiculous. The right guy will find you when you least expect it."

I Promised

The following two years are a blurry memory. Shawn had settled in as my assistant and was excelling. I had wanted to nudge him away from his path towards a career as a pharmacist and more towards a position in museum studies, but I didn't feel it was my place to interfere so much in his life. Chetna and Kevin, thankfully, had yet to set a date for the wedding. She had only just told her family about the engagement. She had been biding time for them to accept Kevin and after having stood by four years after he'd asked her to marry him, she grew tired of waiting and made the announcement. I had dated here and there but nothing ever stuck. I wasn't exaggerating when I had told Chet that I had a six-month expiration date. I was burying myself in my work and even traveling in the name of art. Staying so busy meant a relationship was difficult to maintain.

It was a beautiful March day in 2013. I sat in the atrium of the museum for lunch. There was, of course, an employee lunchroom, but I liked the atrium so much better. The thirty-foot glass ceilings and tall windows made the space feel open and welcome. There were always people to watch as I sat on the benches hidden in the bamboo plants.

I was contentedly munching on my sushi. The chef at the cafe always made me something special. I twirled my quartz stone in my fingertips as I flipped through my notes. Over the years, the stone had gotten smaller from my constant rubbing but it had become a habit that I could not control. I particularly did it when I was focused on something important and this was a big one. A new relic was due in and I was having trouble authenticating it. Most of these things came with some assemblage of provenance and only required a little research. Not this one. Because it contained human remains, this was potentially going to require me to deal with the Vatican directly. I hated trying to work with the Vatican more than I could possibly explain. They had more red tape to dodge while playing phone tag than any bureaucracy in Washington D.C.

I had just popped a spicy tuna roll in my mouth and turned a page when I heard him.

"Gracie?"

Only one person in the whole of my life *ever* called me that. I turned and my eyes met a tall tanned man of lean but muscular build. His square jaw met with a messy mop of brown hair. I took in this not-unattractive man for a moment before I looked at his eyes. Behind thin wire-rimmed glasses were the same maple brown eyes I had known all those years ago.

"A-Aaron?"

He smiled the biggest, most beautiful smile I had ever seen. "I promised."

I think I must have quite literally flown into his arms. He seemed taller now and my head pressed against his chest. Strong, warm arms wrapped around me. I couldn't believe it. I felt pure joy welling inside me and spilling into my eyes but I kept the tears at bay.

When we finally released our embrace, he smiled down at me. He reached out and picked up the quartz. My skin felt electrified when his fingertips brushed against my chest.

"I was afraid you hated me." He held the stone in the palm of his hand.

"How could you think that?" A rush of sadness washed over me.

"Every time I called, you would never come to the phone. I finally stopped calling when your mom said you didn't want to talk to me anymore."

"You called?" I suddenly realized that *she* had struck yet again and my sadness turned to chagrin.

"Every day after we set up in Boston."

"She never told me," I said angrily.

"I'm kind of glad for that. I rather she lied to you than you hate me," he admitted. "I honestly thought that even if I found you, you wouldn't even look at me."

"I can't believe you are really here," I murmured as I reached up and touched his face.

I felt a tap on the shoulder. I turned and saw Shawn looking not at me, but at Aaron straight in the eye. He almost seemed like he was protecting me.

"I'm sorry to interrupt but Miss Grace has a conference call with the Executor of the Jerome estate and Dr. Jacoby in seven minutes." He stepped forward.

I put a reassuring hand on his shoulder. "Thank you, Shawn. I'll meet you up in my office in a moment."

He broke eye contact with Aaron and looked down at me. I nodded. He nodded in return and walked towards the escalator. He stopped before stepping on to wait for me.

"He's a cheerful fellow," Aaron remarked as he watched him go.

"He's the best assistant and bodyguard I could ever ask for," I mused.

"Can we have dinner tonight? Catch up?"

"That sounds lovely!" I could barely contain myself.

I reached into my padfolio and pulled out a business card. I haphazardly scribbled my cell phone number on the back. He held my hand for a few seconds as he took the card from me.

"I'll call you later, Gracie." He turned and left.

I packed up the rest of my sushi to finish in my office during the conference call. I met Shawn at the escalator and he motioned for me to step on first.

"You know him?" he asked as we rode upwards.

"He's a very old friend. I haven't seen him since we were children."

"I don't like the way he was looking at you," he asserted.

I paused. "How was he looking at me?"

"Like a dog that just found his favorite ball."

I felt like I should have been insulted at having been compared to a chew toy. But, I knew Shawn and I knew he was only looking after me.

"Like I said," I iterated, "we haven't seen each other in a very long time."

"I'm just saying if he hurts you, I'll fry him up like Saint Lawrence," he snorted as we stepped off the escalator.

"Lawrence was roasted, not fried. I think we need to spend some time on some Buddhist artwork. You need to calm down." I laughed.

He didn't seem to find the humor.

After a very unproductive conference call in which Dr. Jacoby volunteered me to meet with the executor to select which artworks we wanted from the estate, I lost my ability to focus on any other tasks. My mind kept wandering back to Aaron. It was as if a dam in my mind had broken and hundreds of memories came pouring in.

Aaron called a little after four-thirty and we made arrangements for him to pick me up from work for dinner. As we headed out of the garage in that familiar old white 4Runner, I saw Chetna walking towards the museum. I had completely forgotten we had made plans to go dress shopping that night.

I text messaged her. *So sorry! Something came up! I'll explain later.*

Old Friends

We ended up at one of my favorite seafood restaurants, The Blue Point Grill. The high ceilings and white pillars stood in contrast to the red of the bare-brick archways. I loved it there because even at its most crowded, each booth felt like a little room of its own. It was privacy while surrounded by a hundred other people, though I'm not sure I would have noticed them even if we had been standing bare in the middle of the room. My old friend had me completely captivated.

Aaron and I had an amazing dinner. I couldn't believe that underneath that handsome façade was the same chubby little boy from across the street who taught me the joys of playing in the dirt. He was still playing in the dirt. As a somewhat accomplished archeologist, he had found his way to Cleveland- and me- to teach at the university.

"Your mom still believe you are the chosen one?" he asked as he cut a slice off of the loaf of bread on the table.

"Oh, yes. I am a Holy Child. Now she is convinced that God has led me down my current path so that I can discover the one artifact that will lead his flock of wayward sheep home."

"I wish I didn't know you were serious," he confessed.

"Believe me, I know." I shook my head. "Why do you think I settled down so far away?"

"That makes sense. You like it here?"

"It's definitely not the flattened farmland of Bufu Illinois. I like going out to the lake and everything I could want is here. My job, my house, my cat, Chetna…"

"Husband?"

I smiled. "No. No husband. Or boyfriend, currently."

"Why on Earth not? You're successful and beautiful, and I'll bet you're just as funny as you were when we were kids."

I laughed. "I don't know where you think all of this flattery is going to get you but, please, continue."

He laughed too. "I mean every word."

I swirled my wine in the glass. "So. Is there a missus Akakios?"

"Only my Aunt Sophia. Mom and Dad had a messy divorce so she's no longer a missus. Not a lot of time for meeting women when I'm traveling so much. Came close but that was a long time ago."

"Oh, I bet you meet plenty of women." I smiled coyly and took a drink of wine.

"I'm not really the one-night-stand and flee the country kind of archeologist."

I raised one eyebrow at him. "So will you be fleeing Cleveland any time soon?"

"I don't intend to." He stuffed some buttered bread into his mouth. "When the university asked me to come teach, I looked up the city on the internet to see if it was something I'd even want to consider. There you were in some article about the museum. That was when I knew I had to take the offer. Now I've got a job in a real building. I found an apartment yesterday. And I finally found you after more than fifteen years. I'd say I really don't have a reason to go anywhere at all."

I felt electricity go through my body when he said that he finally found me and my hair stood on end. Then a dark thought crossed my mind. How hard had he honestly been looking? I forced the judgment aside.

We closed down the restaurant. We simply couldn't stop talking and managed to catch each other up on over fifteen years of happenings. We may have changed on the outside, but our hearts were still old friends. We'd had a little too much wine and he called a cab for each of us. While we were waiting, he gave me a strong hug that felt like it embraced my soul.

"I've been waiting for too long to do this," he said as he pressed his face into the top of my head. "I kind of don't want to stop."

I wrapped my arms around his waist and buried my face in his chest.

"Me too." I breathed deep.

My taxi arrived and he helped me into the vehicle. He tipped the driver straight away and looked at me in the back seat.

"Can I see you tomorrow?" he asked as if he had done or said something offensive.

"Of course." I smiled.

He smiled back at me and tapped the roof of the car.

When I got home, I couldn't stop smiling. Aaron Akakios was back in my life. The little nagging voice in my head wanted answers as to why it took him so long but I told it to be silent. I shuffled out of my shoes, stripped down, and crawled into bed.

It was dark when I woke. Hope was on the pillow next to mine. She hissed and ran towards the living room. I rolled over and looked out the window. The moon was round and bright. I looked at the alarm clock on the nightstand. Three o'clock.

"Where are you?" I shot upright in bed.

"I'm here." Onoskelis was standing in the darkened corner of my room across from the bed. "Tell me the name of the handsome suitor you dined with this evening."

"Aaron Akakios."

Her eyes widened and she rushed to the edge of the bed. She knelt on the mattress and looked me closely in the eye.

"*The* Aaron?"

"Yes. Back up, will you?"

She jumped off the bed and stood staring at me. "The Aaron who gifted you that hideous stone you wear?"

"It's not ugly." I reached up and touched it. "He made it when we were kids. And yes, that's him."

She clapped her hands together in excitement. "Out of bed! I wish to meet him!"

I shook my head. "Absolutely not."

Her eyes narrowed. "And why not?"

"It's been a decade and a half. I'm not going to scare him away by introducing him to the murderous she-demon that pops up every now and then."

"I have no intention of scaring him," she hissed.

No. Of course, she had no intention of scaring him. I suddenly felt rage boiling up inside me.

"You can't have this one," I stated defiantly through clenched teeth.

"I want him."

"I don't care. I've waited two-thirds of my life for this man to come back into it. Like Hell am I going to let you take that away from me!"

"'Like Hell.' Well put. I will have him."

"No. I won't allow you to," I argued as I stood and crossed my arms.

"Why? Why is this one so special?"

I stepped directly towards her and screamed, "he was my best friend!"

"Fifteen years ago!"

"We still have so much in common." I steadied my voice. "I haven't felt this good in a long time."

"You seem to forget that he abandoned you," she growled.

"He didn't abandon me." I heard my tone raise an octave. "We were kids. He had to go where his family took him."

"He left you all alone with your mother and Jacob," she persisted.

"He didn't have a choice!" I was screaming again and I felt like my blood was boiling.

"What of the last fifteen years?" she rebutted. "Have you fooled yourself into believing that with all modern contrivances he could not come to you sooner?"

"He had a life that he had to move on with. I did the same. I didn't exactly go looking for him either." I had never admitted that out loud and it kind of shocked me to feel those words pass over my tongue.

"You made no promises. He made a promise that took nearly two decades to keep."

I stepped towards her again. "But he still fulfilled his promise."

She sneered. "I will have him, Grace."

"No!" I hurled a pillow at her and her form disappeared before it could hit her.

I lay back down on the bed. She had a point. He could have found me sooner. But I could have gone looking for him, too, and I hadn't. I rolled these thoughts in my head for hours until the sun came up and told me I needed to prepare for work.

Very like a cave

Aaron had come back to me and she was not going to ruin that. I had let her have her fun in the past but not this time. I had come to terms with what she and I had done before and no, I was not proud of it, but I had accepted it. This time was different. She would be gone for another month at the very least. Her visits could only correspond with the full moon so I at least had that much time to mount a defense against her. She didn't possess me, so seeking out a priest for an exorcism would be useless and I couldn't just *stop* being a Holy Child. Maybe when she returned I would be able to placate her with a random guy from a bar. I hated the thought of sacrificing a stranger, but if I chose carefully, he wouldn't be missed.

Hope pawed anxiously at my leg for breakfast. I rolled out of bed and followed her down the hall and towards the kitchen. She stopped suddenly, hissed, and ran back towards the bedroom.

No.

I turned the corner into the kitchen and Onoskelis was sitting at the table.

"How?! You have to return to your cave at the end of every full moon!" I shouted in disbelief.

"A well is very like a cave," she smiled wittingly.

I froze. The cistern. My house had an old cistern from before it was connected to the city water system but the old pipes still ran through the walls.

I shook my head. "It's not even three in the morning. How can you be here?"

"I never crossed back over so I do not need your slumbering mind as a doorway."

"This can't be real." I buried my face in my hands.

"And I will not be sated by a drunken stranger. I want Aaron."

"Well, you can't have him and since you are trapped here until the next full moon, I'll keep him away from the house."

"You called me here and then you deny me!" She stood and stared down at me.

"I didn't call you." I met her gaze with the same aggression.

"I can only come when you need me," she reminded me.

"I don't need you! Not this time!" I yelled and refused to break eye contact.

She growled. "He needs to pay."

"No, he doesn't, so stay in the fucking well!"

She seethed as she disappeared.

The Garden Party

Chetna was practically buzzing at breakfast that morning. I had taken a cab to meet her since I'd left my car at work. My fight with Onoskelis had energized me but I could still feel the sleep deprivation. We were sitting outside at a bistro table with our customary coffee and smoothie respectively.

"What's gotten into you?" I stared at her.

I swore if she smiled any harder, her face would crack. She kept fidgeting, poking at her smoothie with her straw, and tapping on the table.

"Tell me EVERYTHING!" she finally blurted out.

"What are you going on about?" I looked at her wide-eyed.

"The guy! The guy I saw you with yesterday! Who is he? Where did you go? Are you seeing him again?"

I choked a little on my coffee. I hadn't known Chetna had seen Aaron and me together but I shouldn't have been surprised. There were days when I swore that woman had cameras hidden on me.

"Remember me telling you about my best friend when I was a kid? The one who gave me this?" I held up the quartz.

"Yeah. Alan."

"Aaron."

"Yeah, that's it." She paused and her eyes widened. "That was him? You said he was a little fat kid."

I laughed. "He grew up." *Did he ever,* I thought.

"Oh, my God! This is so cool! Wouldn't it be so awesome if we have a double wedding?"

I choked on my coffee again.

"Are you coming down with something? You should get that cough looked at." The woman was brilliant but sometimes utterly oblivious.

"Chet." I set my coffee on the metal table. "I just had dinner with the man for the first time after not speaking to each other in over fifteen years. Planning a wedding may be jumping the gun just a little."

"Hear me out." She interlaced her fingers, decided against it, and started talking animatedly with her hands. "They write romance novels with this exact storyline for a reason. It's kismet. Destiny. You two found each other after more than fifteen years. What brought him to Cleveland, of all places?"

"A job offer."

"See! Call it fate or will of God or whatever you want, but you two were meant to be together again."

I rolled my eyes. She really needed to lay off the cheesy romance novels.

"If you say so," I finally sighed.

"I do say so." She stated matter-of-factly. "And you know I'm right. Why else would you have held on to that rock all these years?"

I instinctively touched the quartz. She may have had a point.

"See," she continued.

I thought about Onoskelis. "I don't think everyone is going to see it that way."

"Everyone who?"

"There's an… old acquaintance I talked to last night who says Aaron abandoned me and blames him for some of my misery growing up."

"Well, tell this 'old acquaintance' he can choke on an egg!"

I laughed a hard, earnest laugh. That didn't usually happen when Onoskelis was a presence.

"Now," she continued, "I insist you bring him to my engagement party next Saturday. No excuses. I want Ishwar to feel him out. He's an excellent judge of character and he'll tell me everything I know you won't."

I felt a little embarrassed about asking Aaron to join me at Chetna's engagement party. He had only just returned to my life and I was already asking him to be that friend who accompanies you to social gatherings because you don't have a significant other; my private 'plus-one.' I told him I wouldn't be mad or upset if he said 'no' but he didn't seem to mind at all and I was grateful. He even softened it a bit further by bringing up that he had no friends in Cleveland yet and this would be a good way for him to meet new people.

Aaron pulled into my driveway in his dad's old Toyota and knocked on my door. I obviously couldn't let him in knowing Onoskelis was lurking beneath the house. He looked amazing in a pair of khaki pants and a nice navy blue button-down shirt. We hadn't planned to dress to match, but I just so happened to be wearing a dark blue dress and tan shoes. I knew Chetna was going to have something to say about that.

I opened the door quickly after he knocked and squeezed out onto the porch. I looked at the 4Runner.

"I'll drive," I said.

Of course, Chet's party for her and Kevin was a most elegant affair. She had set up her backyard as a lovely informal event center. Her yard was always perfectly landscaped with violet, cobalt, and lemon-colored blooms the names of which I couldn't pronounce, tall wisps of ornamental grass, and hand-blown glass hummingbird feeders. She had lighted paper lanterns strung around the lawn, ornate wrought-iron tiki torches lit amongst the tufts of ornamental grasses, and twinkling Christmas lights flowing along the red wooden privacy fence. It gave a very fairytale feel to her tiny patch of earth. She had silver trays of specially requested finger foods she'd had catered lined up on a table interspersed with carved fruit and flowers. Smells of spiced chicken, crafted cheeses, a vegetable soup, and fresh bread intermingled with the sweetness of the flowers and fruit. She seemed to be glowing in a beautiful purple sleeveless dress, gold earrings, and her hair sleeked and tied up in a ponytail. Kevin being Kevin had worn jeans but, to his credit, he had at least worn a clean shirt.

    Immediately after we arrived at the party I took Aaron directly to meet Chet. She would never forgive me if I hadn't introduced them straight away. We found the happy couple, each with a glass of wine in their hand, hobnobbing with guests near an **hors d'oeuvres** table. I pushed my long bangs back over my head as I escorted Aaron through the house and into the yard. Chet caught sight of him almost immediately.

    "Oh my god! Oh my god! You're here!" She skipped up to me with her long black hair bouncing behind her. She hugged me as she squealed in my ear, "you were supposed to be here early. I've been waiting for you."

    "I know," I said. "I'm so sorry. I got caught up doing some things for work."

    "Oh, whatever." She smiled and her eyes turned immediately to Aaron. "Introductions!" she exclaimed.

    "Aaron. This is my best friend in the world, Chet. Chetna Mehta-"

    "Soon to be Alexander," Kevin interrupted.

    I glared at him as I continued, "this is Aaron Akakios."

    "Oh, you are not just Aaron!" she exclaimed. "You are *the* Aaron!"

    "Chet," I scolded.

    "What? I've heard about this man since the day I met you. He was the one thing that kept you from completely losing your mind when you were kids."

    Aaron looked over at me and straightened up a little. He seemed to be beaming and I'm pretty sure I could watch his ego inflate like a balloon.

"Well, Chetna. It's very nice to meet you. I'm sorry to say, I haven't heard quite as much about you, but I just got into town and I'm sure you and I will be getting to know each other better." He shook her hand.

Chetna smiled. "Of course we will!"

Kevin stiffened at the sight of another man touching his fiancé. He put his arm around her. "Hello, Grace." He smiled, pretending to ignore the other man.

"Hello, Kevin. I'd like you to meet my friend, Aaron. Aaron, this is the groom to be, Kevin."

Aaron shook his hand. "It's very nice to meet you, Kevin."

"Chetna! Come here!" a voice from across the yard called.

"Please, excuse me. Aaron, I look forward to getting to know you better." Chetna smiled.

"Likewise." Aaron nodded his head to her.

When Chet and Kevin had wandered off, Aaron turned to me.

"So, Kevin, huh?" his brow wrinkled above his glasses, just as it had done when we were children.

"Yeah. That's the groom." I think my voice was more half-hearted than it should have been.

"You don't seem to be very happy about this."

I sighed. "It's her happiness that matters, not mine."

"Grace!" A familiar voice called.

I turned and saw Ishwar walking towards us. I smiled as he bent down to hug me.

"Ishwar, this is my friend, Aaron. Aaron, this is the brother-of-the-bride, Ishwar."

"Nice to meet you," they said together as they shook hands.

"When did you get into town?" I asked.

"Last night. I had to be here early to help set up. It wasn't a bad flight from New Jersey."

"Chetna told me you left California! Do you like it on the other coast?" I wasn't very good a small talk.

"Not really." He laughed. "But it's still new and it's on the other side of the country from the rest of our family."

"Grace! Come here for a moment!" Chetna called to me.

I excused myself and went to stand with her and a group of her friends from the Botanical Gardens. I knew why she had done it. She was intentionally leaving Aaron and Ishwar alone. From the corner of my eye, I watched them laugh and seem to genuinely enjoy each other's company. I must say, I was very relieved. I didn't know why Chetna- and Ishwar's- approval meant so much to me.

At the end of the evening, we said our goodbyes and began the drive back to my house.

"Did Ishwar put you through the wringer?" I asked.

Aaron laughed hard. "As soon as you walked away, he said 'My sister wants me to judge you and make sure you aren't going to hurt her friend.'"

I rolled my eyes. "Well, at least he was honest about it."

He smiled. "I think it's sweet. She wants to protect you."

"I don't need protecting," I stated flatly.

"It turns out we both like fishing, comic books, and had a few other things in common so I think I made a good impression."

I tried not to let my relief show.

"I don't think Kevin likes me very much, though." He looked at me to gauge my reaction.

"I really don't care what Kevin thinks. He's always been kind of possessive of Chet. Even had their lives planned out when we were in college." I had a split-second flashback to being snowed in at the old duplex.

"Still," he said, "his peacocking was a bit much."

I smiled. "I'm glad I'm not the only one who noticed it."

We pulled into my driveway. He turned and gave me a hug. He felt warm and solid.

"Thank you for introducing me to your friends," he said.

"You know if you stay, Chetna will insist on inviting you to more things," I warned him.

"I don't mind. And you don't need to say 'if I stay.' I'm not going anywhere." He hugged me again before turning to the 4Runner.

I breathed deep. He was back for good.

I Will Not

Aaron and I spoke on the phone at length or went to dinner almost every night for the following month. I was absolutely captivated by his animated retellings of all of the places he'd traveled, both for work and fun. Not to be outdone, of course, I talked about the Pope I'd met and some of the celebrities I'd authenticated things for. My travels were nowhere near as exotic and, by comparison, were pretty boring if not for the people I'd met along the way. The way he looked at me made me feel like I was truly important. Those dark honey-colored eyes looked right into my ego and I loved it.

Onoskelis primarily kept to the cistern. Periodically she would surface when I was home to remind me that she was still waiting. She still wanted me to give in and serve Aaron up to her like a hog to slaughter. I would refuse or sometimes ignore her completely. These responses seemed to only enrage her and she would pout and plot for several days before returning to try again.

One night, he and I had planned to meet for dinner but he had canceled. He said he was still working on getting settled into the new job and needed the time to work on his lesson plans and make a strategy for grading papers. I was very disappointed, but I told him I understood. On my way home from the museum, I came to a roadblock resulting from a ruptured water main. It felt a bit like adding insult to injury, but I followed the detour. On the highway, there was an accident that blocked the right two lanes. Rerouted traffic during rush hour is always a disaster, but this was fairly exceptional. My normally thirty-five-minute commute took nearly three hours. Every time cars started moving, I was hopeful that the worst was behind me, but that was quickly dashed when I became trapped at another full stop.

When I finally reached home, a very hungry and very indignant black cat was meowing at me before I'd even had the chance to set my things down.

"It's not my fault!" I defended myself to her.

After appeasing her with a spoonful of chicken baby food on top of her kibble, I called for pizza delivery and started a hot shower. I simply wasn't in the mood to cook anything so late at night and I just wanted to relax. The little bathroom filled with steam and I stood and let the hot water wash away my tension. The sweet herbaceous aroma of the lavender oil I kept in a reed diffuser on the back of the toilet intermingled with the water vapor. My muscles relaxed and my mind cleared. Not wanting to completely lose myself before the pizza arrived, I eventually shut off the water and stepped out of the tub. Through the steam, I could see her and my heart missed a beat from the surprise.

"Why are you here?" I felt the tension returning.

Onoskelis hissed. "You had a tryst arranged for this evening. He made something else more important."

"It's hardly a tryst and I am not the only thing he has going on in his life.'

"You are hurt."

"No, I am disappointed." I slipped on a t-shirt and flannel pajama bottoms. "There is a big difference."

"Let me at least taste his flesh," she pleaded as we walked out into the living room.

I pointed at the big picture window in the living room. "Tomorrow is a full moon. By Thursday morning you had better be on one of those beams and out of my life for good."

She smiled a toothy, sinister smile. "I *can* only travel by light of the full moon. I do not *have* to do so. I quite think of this well as home."

"What about Persephone? Won't she be mad?"

"I told you; she granted permission for my visits only when you need me. She will not be angry."

"What about Xander?" I felt a pang as I said his name. "You left without killing him."

"You did not truly need me then. As you said, you broke his heart too."

"I don't need you now, either," I asserted.

"You do. Whether you realize it or not is a different matter entirely."

"Leave," I repeated.

"I will not. Not until I've had what I am here for."

Thaumaturgy

"It's here! It's here!"

Shawn burst in through my office door like a child on Christmas morning. He was carrying a large box that was covered in tape and shipping labels. He carefully set it on top of the papers I was looking at and stepped back. I looked at the box and back at him. I don't believe he could have smiled any wider. I opened my desk drawer and pulled out a penknife. I held it out to him.

"Why don't you do the honors?" I invited.

He took the knife from me.

"Are you sure?" he asked.

I nodded. "I think this could be one of the most important pieces in this museum's collection and I'd like you to be a part of that."

Tears welled in his eyes. "Thank you."

He very carefully cut along the seams of the tape. Once through, he gently lifted out the foam that had been molded specifically to fit the treasure inside. After he had meticulously cut along the foam, he lifted off the section and almost gasped.

I gingerly lifted the object from the remaining foam. I should have worn gloves. It was mildly damaged already, but I couldn't help myself as I carefully examined it. It stood almost a foot-and-a-half tall. The base was a polished, flat stone. The reliquary itself was ornately carved wood with flourishes that resembled wings at the base of the pedestal. The pedestal itself was almost heart-shaped and supported a rococo-style shield. At the top of the shield stood a very plain crucifix. The entire thing was silver-gilt with great expertise except for the center. The center of the shield was what made the entire piece so important. In the heart of the shield was a small, rectangular glass window. The glass was slightly yellowed, but inside we could clearly see the tooth.

"Well?" Shawn was practically bouncing.

"Eighteenth-century baroque Italian. It fits the timeline."

"Yes! I knew it!"

"Hold on, now. That could be porcelain or a pig's tooth for all we know. The only provenance we have is word of mouth. We have a lot of work to do before we can claim this is the missing piece of St. Agnes."

"Where do we start?"

I laughed. "Same place we always do. We need pictures, weight, measurements... all of the normal cataloging."

"I'm on it!" He reached for the foam but stopped short. "Unless you would rather? I know this one is kind of a big deal."

"Have at it. I'm supposed to be heading to dinner anyway."

I tenderly set the artifact back in the foam and he excitedly carried it away.

I met Aaron at Taki's for a light Greek dinner. I could hardly contain myself as I sipped my water. Aaron was droning on about something archeology-related but, I'm ashamed to say, I wasn't listening. My mind was reeling. I had done vast amounts of research into Agnes of Montepulciano in preparation for the arrival of the reliquary. Transfer of ownership and getting it through customs had taken far longer than usual. Now that it had finally arrived, I felt as if I hadn't done any work at all. I would need to reach out to the family that donated it for a written testimony about where it came from. I needed comparative photos from other pieces made in the same area and time frame. Of course, I would have to contact the Catholic church for a statement, which was likely going to be a fruitless endeavor.

"Okay. I get that stratigraphy maybe isn't the most fascinating of topics, but I get the feeling you aren't even in the room right now. You kind of have the same look on your face that my students get when I'm lecturing."

I snapped back to the present and looked at him.

"I'm sorry. It finally arrived today and I guess my mind is still at work."

He pushed his glasses higher on his nose. "What arrived?"

"St. Agnes's reliquary."

"Oh, yeah." He recalled. "I remember you saying something about that."

"She's a lesser saint, but this relic could be really important."

"Why's that?"

I sat upright. "Okay. Quick history lesson. Agnes of Montepulciano was a Dominican who had mastered thaumaturgy at the end of the thirteenth century in Italy."

"Mastered what?"

"Thaumaturgy. She was a miracle worker," I clarified.

"Snake handler." He attempted to correct me.

"Not quite. She died at the beginning of the fourteenth century. Despite a botched embalming, when they moved her body some years later, it had been completely unchanged. No decay or anything. Half a century later, a Dominican friar wrote Agnes's biography and hinted that one of her teeth had been stolen by one of the men from the church who moved her body."

"Why steal a tooth?" His eyebrows pulled together in confusion.

"A souvenir of the miracle, I suppose. Like the theft of Eva Peron's fingertip." I shrugged. "The tooth was kept hidden and passed down the family of the perpetrator in secret until she was canonized in 1726. Supposedly, the tooth had come into the possession of a wealthy family who had a proper reliquary made to display it. It gets lost for a while after that but turns up in New York in the nineteen fifties. It was purchased by a Maybelle Sansom and taken back to her home in England where it's been until now. Her granddaughter is American and inherited a lot of her things, including the tooth. She said she had grown up with the story of its origin and felt like it belonged in a museum. She admitted she tried to donate it to several others that didn't show any interest. Then she found me."

"Okay. I still don't understand. Doesn't the museum already have things related to St. Agnes?"

"Wrong Agnes. That's St. Agnes of Rome; the saint of chastity. Agnes of Montepulciano is a lesser saint. If I can authenticate this, it proves all the myths and rumors about *this* Agnes's missing tooth are probably true."

"Can't the church do that?"

I scoffed. "They aren't going to admit that one of their own henchmen stole a body part. For over a century they've refused all requests to exhume and examine her body to see if the tooth is even missing."

"How are you going to prove it?"

"First, I've got to prove the reliquary itself is over two hundred and fifty years old." I sighed. "That's the easy part. The rest is going to be difficult."

"It sounds exciting." His voice was encouraging.

"It's a gift and a curse. I prefer to study art from Hindu and Muslim countries. It's so intricate and beautiful. But, thanks to Momma, Christian art and history are what I know best. It allows me to keep my work separate from my passion."

"It sounds like you have your work cut out for you."

"If I play this right, it could really put me on the center stage but it's going to take years of work."

"If you play it wrong?"

I shrugged and feigned nonchalance. "The church can cry fraud and destroy me."

"Yikes. Sounds like you need a little thaumaturgy."

- 220 -

You Can Leave

Aaron had declined dinner with me for the third time. I was beginning to feel like he either didn't enjoy my company anymore or there was something he wasn't telling me. I had buried myself in work to dull the sting of the rejection. It was getting late and I was exhausted. I was hidden behind a mound of paperwork at my desk. I had several requests to guest lecture that I was procrastinating replies to, two budgetary proposals that I had no control over but needed to familiarize myself with, and a menagerie of other documents that were vying for my attention.

I suddenly felt a chill down my spine and my hair stood on end. I turned to see Onoskelis standing by the wall behind me. I shoved some of the papers on my desk aside and looked at the calendar. There, highlighted in neon pink, were the words 'full moon.' I had forgotten. I turned back towards her.

"Why are you here?" I asked, exasperatedly.

"You were not home for dinner. I worried," she lied.

"Since you've left my house, you don't have to go back."

"But I will."

"It's been months. You can leave on any full moon you want. Why won't you just leave my cistern and not come back?"

"I will leave when I have taken what I want." She sneered at me. "I have told you this before."

"The last remnants of my sanity?" I asked sarcastically.

"Aaron's last breath."

Just as I opened my mouth to clap back at her, there was a knock at my office door and Shawn stepped in.

"Everything okay, Miss Grace?" he asked.

I looked over my shoulder and saw that Onoskelis had disappeared.

"Yes; just talking to myself." I smiled at him.

"You've been stressed. You should go home soon. It's getting late." He sounded concerned.

"You too."

"See you on Wednesday." He nodded as he shut the door.

Onoskelis stepped out of a shadowed corner. "Shawn is quite handsome-"

"Absolutely not," I interrupted. "You cannot have him either."

"No matter. He is not deserving of my talents."

"If I have my house blessed, will you go away?"

She cackled hard and loud. "You think the chants of some mortal man who thinks himself the voice of God could stop me?"

"Holy water?"

"I shall have a bath!" She laughed.

"I won't give you what you want," I said defiantly.

"You will. You may not like it, Grace, but we are connected."

A Really Rough Day

I was already sleep-deprived and feeling disheartened. Nothing I had been working on was moving in the right direction, Hope's kidneys were failing at her last checkup, and she didn't like her new food. I was exhausted and frustrated and Sonya was in rare form that day. She'd spent all morning and immediately after lunch critiquing our various projects. I had gone through less than half of the Jerome estate collection and moving so slowly was simply unacceptable for her. How dare Elaina wear *that* to the tour and luncheon with our guests from Charleston? Apparently, Tony's write-up on that horrid new-age folk-art piece of garbage he had acquired sounded like it had been written by a kindergartner. No one was safe from her fury that day.

At around three in the afternoon, those of us who could do so collectively decided we'd had enough and abandoned her to continue her judgments by screaming at the walls. I headed down the hill and across the street towards the botanical gardens. I was painfully aware of the rapid clicking of my heels against the cold, wet pavement. Fifty-three degrees in a frigid May drizzle was miserable in a skirt and heels. I was irritated and I just wanted my best friend to listen to my woes and help calm me down. The cold bit at my bare legs and I heard my step quicken even more.

Just as I reached the entrance to the Botanical Garden's lobby, I heard a voice behind me.

"Miss Nightingale!" Amy ran towards me from across the grounds.

Amy was one of Chet's favorite assistants. She often left her in charge when traveling for her lectures and conferences. She opened the door and ushered me in.

"Too cold." She shivered. "I'm sorry, Miss Nightingale. Dr. Mehta isn't here. She is at the zoo today to help them plan their autumn floral exhibit. I don't think she is coming back here today."

I sighed. I'd known that. We hadn't met that morning before work because she wasn't going into the office that day.

I smiled. "Thank you, Amy. I'd completely forgotten. I'll call her later."

I wiggled my toes inside my stilettos to check for feeling before heading back out into the cold. There was no way I was going back into work to put up with more of Sonya's lunatic ramblings. I went straight to the parking garage and got in my car. I turned the heat on full-blast before backing out. I'd fully intended to go home. I was annoyed and angry and I just wanted to walk in the front door, hold my cat, have a hot shower and a cup of tea, and call my best friend when she got off of work.

That isn't at all what happened. I came out of my angry haze just in time to realize I was pulling into the university parking lot. I'd driven seven minutes in one antagonized blink of an eye. If one friend wasn't available, maybe the other one was. I fished around in my glove box to find a parking pass (benefit of the museum working so closely with the school) and parked as close to an entrance as I could.

I maneuvered through chatty students down well-lit halls. That atmosphere was very different from when I had been a student but the institutional feel of the drab tile floors and grey walls was still the same. I pushed through a heavy steel door at the back of a dead-end hallway. I tried to keep my steps from echoing too loudly as I headed down the stairs to a corridor of more steel doors. I followed along until I came to the one labeled *"Anthropology Dept."*

I giggled a little. I remembered at dinner one night when Aaron had gone on a random rant about being lumped in with the anthropology department. Apparently, the department chair didn't like the idea of sharing the work area and even though the two disciplines overlapped, archeology wasn't entirely welcome in their office space.

I didn't need to read the names on the cubicles to figure out which one was his. In the very back corner sat a cube full of books haphazardly stacked on almost every surface. Papers were scattered over the keyboard and a monitor peeked out from a curtain of sticky notes.

"Gracie?"

I turned to face him and sighed. "Hi."

"You look like Hell."

"Thanks," I said wearily.

"Sorry. You look like you need a hug."

That did it. I nodded. He pulled me to him and wrapped his arms around me. I took a deep breath. He smelled like wood and honey and I breathed him in deeper. I stood there and let his warmth melt away all of my tension and frustration. He buried his face in the top of my head and I closed my eyes. I'm not sure how long we stood like that before he released me. He lifted my chin until our gaze met.

"Are you okay?"

I nodded again. "Just a really rough day."

"Want to come to my place for dinner tonight and tell me all about it? I make a pretty mean manicotti."

I felt myself smile. "Okay."

"Great. Seven p.m. Be at this address."

He made a pad of sticky notes and a pen materialize from the mess on the desk. He handed me an address scribbled in a script that hadn't changed since he was eight years old.

I felt oddly relaxed on the drive home and even more so when I'd changed out of heels and a suit and into jeans, sneakers, and a fluffy sweater. I put food in Hope's bowl and patted her head.

"Dinner for one, tonight. Mommy's got plans."

She looked up from her bowl, hissed, and ran. As I watched her go, I saw a shadow move in the corner of my eye.

Onoskelis was seated at the kitchen table. Her arms were crossed over her chest and her jaw was set.

"No." I held up my index finger at her. "I've had a crappy day. I'm finally in a better mood. Don't you dare ruin it."

I grabbed my coat and left without giving her a chance to explain her appearance.

His apartment was on the eleventh floor of the high-rise complex on St. Clair. The main entry was white and clean-looking. Residents headed from the gym to home strolled through the halls and the whole place smelled like rose air freshener. All of the people smiled as if they knew me. It was completely different from the rat-hole I'd called home when I'd moved to Cleveland but I had been a struggling student and he was a successful archeologist. We'd walked such different paths and yet they'd still crossed.

I knocked on the door of number eleven-zero-two. He greeted me in red flannel, blue jeans, and a smile. He took my coat and rushed down the hall. I looked around. Immediately to my left was a small kitchen area. There was water boiling on the stove and something smelled like garlic and cheese. The kitchen was separated from the main living area by a counter with a built-in sink. There were two empty glasses and a bottle of pinot grigio waiting. In the main living room, a cream-colored, plaid couch faced a dusty television. A stereo in the corner gently played melodic jazz notes. Along the walls were boxes stacked on top of boxes. A floor lamp and an end table seemed to be the only evidence that the room was intended to be used for habitation.

He re-emerged from the hallway.

"You know, you've been here a while now. You could unpack."

"What do you mean?" He pushed his glasses up higher on his nose. "I've got clothes in a dresser and dishes in the cabinet. What more needs doing?"

I wandered over to the T.V. The grey layer of dust suggested it hadn't been turned on since it had been placed there. On top of a box next to the T.V. was a framed picture. Two familiar but long ago faces looked back at me. A pudgy little boy with messy hair and thick glasses and a frizzy-haired redhead sat with their arms around each other and corndogs in their hands.

He handed me a glass of wine.

"Seems like a lifetime ago." He pointed to the picture.

"That trip really was the highlight of my childhood though. And if your mom hadn't taken us to the museum, I may not have ended up here."

"It was a great weekend. I'd never seen you happy like that. Where do you think you would have ended up if you hadn't found art?"

"If Momma had her way, probably in a convent. But in all likelihood, a cashier at K-Mart watching my life go by."

"Well, that's depressing."

"But the truth. That trip showed me more than just art. It showed me a whole world. That's how I realized I wanted to go to college and explore it all."

He nodded and looked thoughtful. "Hey, remember that time we snuck out and took my dad's spirit board into the woods?"

I thought back to the first time Onoskelis had contacted me.

"Oh, yes," I said.

"I gotta say, you freaked me out for years after that."

"*I* freaked you out?"

"Yeah. Moving that glass eye around. Making it say we were talking to a demon." He chuckled. "I was a little old to believe that but it still got to me."

He thought *I* had moved it. I opened my mouth to protest but stopped myself. It sounded too absurd to explain that we were communicating with a four-thousand-year-old demon that was currently living in an old water reservoir under my house. I pretended to laugh.

"Yeah. Sorry about that." I took a big sip of wine.

"Enough about the past. Our dinner needs my attention and you need to tell me about your horrible day."

He escorted me to a barstool at the counter by the sink. As he cooked, I poured out all of my frustrations with Sonya, the new exhibit that wasn't coming together at all, even my unhappiness over Chetna's engagement. It was as if those stuffed noodles and Italian wine were some sort of truth serum, though it may have been the company and how long I'd been stewing over those things. As he cooked and throughout dinner (which was eaten on bar stools at the counter next to the sink), he listened intently. He didn't interrupt me. He didn't offer his two cents. He just listened and occasionally asked 'how does that make you feel' or 'what would you like to be able to do about that?' The ability to just openly vent made for one of the strangest but most liberating conversations I'd ever had.

Even after the food had been eaten and the dishwasher had been loaded, we sat on opposite ends of the couch and kept talking. We changed topics a little and he talked about teaching and his students. He said he felt a little unnerved about having such a routine. It didn't feel natural to him but he still had every intention of traveling when he could and he wasn't going to die without seeing Turkey first.

Around two in the morning, my eyes got too heavy and I couldn't stop yawning. He offered to call a taxi for me, but I insisted that I was fine to drive home. He helped me into my coat and gave me another wonderful hug goodbye.

When I returned home, Hope didn't meet me at the door like usual. I assumed it was because she was mad at me for staying out late. I was wrong. I hung my coat in the hall closet and went to the kitchen for a glass of water. *She* was there; still sitting in the same chair with her arms still folded.

"I'm happy. Don't ruin this." I rolled my eyes at her and selected a glass from the cabinet.

"He believes you forged the spirit board."

"Of course he does."

"He thinks you are a liar."

"We were kids." I filled the glass. "It was a game. I wouldn't believe it if I were him either."

"What are you going to do about it?" She sounded indignant.

"What am I going to do about what?"

"Telling him the truth."

"If I tell him we were actually communicating with a man-hating, homicidal she-demon, he'll have me committed." I stared at her.

"If he truly values you, he will believe you. If he does not, he obviously does not deserve your… friendship."

I didn't like the way she ended that sentence.

"You're crazy and I'm tired," I snapped.

I took my glass of water and turned out the kitchen light.

Her voice came from the darkness. "You will see. He does not care for you at all."

The Invitation

From the far end of the East wing, I could look out over the street. Gothic turrets jutted into the sky from the university on the left and the cathedral in the distance on the right. It was warm sitting in the sun, surrounded by glass. Below, I watched hospital employees in black scrubs strolling on their lunch break. Joggers darted across the crosswalk. Directly in front of me, on museum grounds, was a small square cement and marble courtyard surrounded by square hedges. I saw two lovers steal a kiss In front of the Bacchanale statue. I sighed and smiled at them before returning to my desk.

Just as I took my seat, my cell phone buzzed. It was Aaron.

Dinner tonight? He asked.

I looked at my desk calendar. Highlighted in bright green for the day's date were the words 'full moon.'

Sorry. Have to work late tonight. I lied.

I hated lying to him. I wondered if he would ever catch on that I declined his company only on the full moon. I may have to lie to him more if that were to happen. I wondered if I could convince him that I was a werewolf. That seemed more plausible than telling him that I had a succubus Hell-bent on revenge living in the cistern under my house.

Tomorrow? He asked.

I smiled. I appreciated that he wanted to make up for lost time with me.

I should be free then, I answered.

Excellent! Came his reply.

The next evening, we had dinner at a burger joint that wasn't far from University Circle. I had a pepperoni pizza burger while he had some kind of barbeque, mushroom, and cheese-laden atrocity.

"So," he said in between licking sauce from his fingers, "I had an ulterior motive for wanting to see you."

"Oh, yeah?" I gently dabbed some marinara from the corner of my mouth. "What motive did you have?"

"I need a favor." He clasped his hands together in front of him as if to begin a prayer.

"I'm not going to like this, am I?"

"Melanie is getting married again. I have never been to a family wedding with a date…" His eyes turned pleading.

"So you need an escort?" I laughed.

"I need to not be trapped alone with my family for five hours." He laughed.

"Hmm." I pretended to ponder. "What's in it for me?"

"An all-expenses-paid trip to Michigan." He grinned.

"Oh! How exotic! How could I say 'no?'" I laughed at him.

"Really? Oh, Gracie! You are a life saver!"

The Wedding

I was strangely looking forward to seeing Aaron's family again. We hadn't been particularly close when we were kids; his sisters did bully him relentlessly, after all. But, I was excited for that sense of familiarity. They were one of the only consistent points of sanity in my childhood before they left.

It was a short flight from Cleveland to the upper peninsula of Michigan. All the while I anxiously fidgeted in my seat. Would they recognize me? Would they remember me at all? I had a million thoughts, feelings, and emotions coursing through my head but excitement was at the forefront of it all. He had rented a truck to take us to our hotel. We picked up our key cards at the concierge and headed to our rooms which were right next to each other. He put his hand on the handle of his door and turned to me.

"Pick you up at five-thirty?"

I giggled. "It's a date."

"Can I have a peek at the dress beforehand?"

"I'm pretty sure that's bad luck."

"Only if you're the bride."

I felt a mischievous grin spread over my face. "You never know where things might lead."

I brought my bags inside the door and stared around the room. It was small and a little dingy. The walls were adorned with cheap minimalist art prints but the bed was made and the windows that overlooked the city were clean. I set to work. As Chetna had taught me, a properly made-up woman is a work of art and requires time.

For the next several hours I waxed everything from the waist down, my lips, and my eyebrows. I smeared a protein mask on my face while I took a scented bath. I carefully manicured all twenty of my nails. When everything was washed and dried, I set to work on the last part of the art. I sculpted my hair into a very classy ponytail and I put on my favorite little black dress. Every woman has that dress. I carefully painted my face and finished off with a pair of silver heeled sandals just in time for a knock at the door.

I opened it. Aaron was wearing a simple black suit with a grey shirt and black tie. He had tried to gel his messy hair into something stylish and had failed but still looked amazing. His eyes widened and his jaw dropped.

"Damn!"

I smiled. "You don't look half bad yourself."

He reached out and touched the quartz stone. "This really doesn't match though."

"It doesn't have to. All that matters is how I feel when I wear it."

He stood a little straighter and looked pleased. He held out his arm and I accepted. He escorted me down to the truck and we headed to the venue. It was not a long drive, but I felt so nervous. I kept my hands folded in my lap and hoped that Aaron wouldn't notice. He parked the truck and turned his head to me.

"I know I probably should have said something sooner, but my mom is a little different from when we were kids." The worry lines over his glasses were deep.

I realized that in all the dinners that we had had, all of the walks we had taken, and all of the card games we had played, he had rarely mentioned Elizabeth.

"Oh. Okay. Anything specific I should be prepared for?"

"After my dad left, she kind of blamed me. My sisters are still her favorite. She just doesn't try to hide it anymore. She drinks a bit more, too."

I squeezed his hand. "Then let's get this over with."

He smiled.

No sooner had we entered the hall than I heard a voice like a ghost from my past say, "you would show up in something that looks like that."

Elizabeth still looked very much the same as she had fifteen years ago. Her skin was a little more saggy and more wrinkly and her hair was a little thinner but still dyed blonde and styled like it was still the nineties. But, those eyes and nose were still the same.

"Hello to you too, Mom." He hugged the woman and kissed her cheek.

"Well, don't be rude. I raised you better than that. Who's your date? Your sisters were all buzzing when you added a plus-one to your RSVP."

Aaron stepped back and held his hand out between us. "Don't you remember Grace Nightingale?"

Her eyes widened much the same way his had when he saw me. "Grace Nightingale? The little girl from the old neighborhood with the crazy mom?"

I blushed a little.

"Mom. Don't be so rude," he chided.

"It's okay," I reassured him. "I know my mother is crazy."

Elizabeth laughed. "I'm sorry. Please come in and enjoy the evening."

She held out her arm and motioned for us to go inside while she stayed behind to greet guests.

The hall was lovely and undoubtedly expensive. The chapel was laid out in beautiful ivory. I recognized Stephanie and Tiffany as a bridesmaid and the maid of honor. They may have been wearing some fairly heavy makeup and Stephanie had dyed her hair blonde, but they were still just as cavalier as ever.

"Oh. My. God. No way!" A short woman with long, curly brown hair wearing brown slacks and a white blouse was running towards us from across the venue. "Grace!"

I was stunned for just a moment before I blurted out, "Nicole!"

I held out my hand to shake hers but she grabbed it and pulled me in for a hug. I hadn't expected such a welcome from any of Aaron's family; least of all his sisters.

"When Mom told me you were here I almost called her a liar."

I laughed. "I wouldn't have believed her, either."

Aaron stepped closer to me. His arm brushed mine and I felt my hair stand on end.

"Aren't you even going to say 'hello' to your baby brother?" He narrowed his eyes at her.

"Yeah. Yeah. Hi. Hi." She smiled and embraced him.

"You two certainly get along better than we were kids," I observed.

"When Mom started drinking and blaming me for dad leaving, Nicole stood up for me." He gave a very appreciative glance towards his older sister.

"Yeah, well, as big sister it's my job to make you feel like garbage, not hers. She just couldn't handle that she's not perfect and needed a scapegoat," she huffed.

I wanted to know what happened with Elizabeth and more about why she blamed Aaron for her divorce, but I decided that was not the right time to pursue it and changed the subject.

"You aren't a bridesmaid?" I asked.

"This is her third wedding. She's lucky I came at all. Told her I'd get her on the next one." She laughed.

"I'll bet that went over well." Aaron chuckled.

"She told me to go to Hell and Mom called specifically to tell me I'd be out of the will if I kept it up. As if I'd want any of her junk."

We all laughed.

Two photographers rushed around carefully timing photos to perfectly capture the day. I think their haste and fastidiousness had more to do with fear of incurring the bride's wrath than pride in their craft. One focused on the bridal party. He keyed on the obligatory staged photos of the dress and the shoes. One of the mother of the bride pretending to surprise her with 'something blue' (which happened to be one of the clunkiest pair of sapphire earrings I'd ever seen). The best photo was of the bridesmaids sliding on their shoes. They were all seated in folding chairs awkwardly trying to lace their silver ballet slippers. They had all been drinking fuzzy navels and mimosas since eleven in the morning and had switched to harder liquor at the venue. As if on cue, they all drunkenly slid out of their chairs and onto the floor, just as the shutter clicked.

The other photographer focused on the guests. He insisted on taking my and Aaron's photo together. He told us we were the best-looking couple there. Rather than correct him, Aaron turned me to face him. He put my hands on his chest and his on my waist. Even in three-inch heels I barely came up to the top of his tie and had to look up to look him in the eye. When I looked into those pools of maple brown, I felt my hair stand up again.

"Absolutely stunning!" I heard the photographer say as he snapped a few pictures.

Aaron suddenly looked as if he had just woken up. He cleared his throat and released me.

The ceremony was very short and nondenominational but quite classy. A pianist played the music to introduce the couple and played them out. The groom looked every bit as anxious as you would expect but he never stopped smiling. I hoped my future husband would look at me in that way.

The reception was held in the ballroom. Centerpieces of peach-colored roses and ivory feathers with ivory bows sat on every table. Elizabeth escorted us to a table off to the side of the wedding party.

"I had a feeling you would seat us at your table," Aaron remarked.

In a crass tone, she replied, "Of course I want to sit with my only son who never visits me."

"I visit plenty." He rolled his eyes.

"No you don't," she said flatly. "You are always off in some faraway land and now that you're rooted back in the United States, you never come to see me."

"I'm busy." The pitch in his voice rose a few octaves.

"That's always been your excuse."

"Mom-" Aaron started.

"Not enough that you had to drive your father away. Then you had to go abandon me too." She took a large gulp of wine.

"I had nothing to do with Dad leaving. You know that."

"Of course you did. All he ever wanted was a son. Instead, he got four daughters and *you*."

Aaron was getting visibly agitated and I had no idea how to diffuse the situation.

He smiled slightly and said, "Excuse me for a moment. Grace, would you like a glass of wine?"

"Yes please," was all I could manage to say.

He took his leave from the table.

"I just don't know what to do with that boy," Elizabeth said bitterly as she shook her head.

"What do you mean?" I asked from the other side of the round table.

"He never really made anything of himself. He's just a college professor. He is over thirty years old and never married and or given me grandchildren. He has no direction with his life."

I felt resentment towards her welling inside me. "Your son is one of the top in his field and that's why he is an educator. He has positively influenced the world with his findings and most people can only dream of traveling as much as he has. Not everyone is meant to settle down. Maybe instead of being disappointed in the man he has become, you should be proud of the son you raised. Excuse me."

I stood up and walked out onto the balcony. I was still seething and shaking a little as I looked out over the water. A glass of wine appeared in front of me.

I took it from him. "Thank you. I'm sorry." I held the stemware in one hand and stabilized it with the other.

"What are you apologizing for?" He put his hand on my shoulder.

"I said something inappropriate to your mother." I looked at the ground.

"No. You said something no one has ever said to her before." He used his finger to lift my chin till my eyes met his. "No one besides Nicole has ever stood up for me like that; especially not to her."

"You heard what I said?"

"Every word." He kissed my forehead.

We stood on the balcony a moment longer in silence and sipped our wine. From inside the ballroom, I could hear Sinatra starting to play. Aaron smiled wide at me.

"Come on!" He said with brightened eyes.

He took my glass and set it with his on a table and pulled me into the ballroom. We danced close together very inelegantly. While I had learned to be graceful and poised in my time with the Bonaventure family, Aaron was still as refined as the teenage boy I used to know. Before the next song, I kicked off my heels, threw them towards a wall, and stood on his feet.

He laughed. "Am I that bad?"

I smiled up at him. "Let's just say I think this might make things a little easier. And safer."

His cheeks pinked slightly but we danced to two more songs that way. When the music picked up, I collected my shoes and we went back out to the balcony with two new glasses of wine. Nicole was leaning against the railing and smoking.

"If Mom catches you doing that, I won't be the least favorite anymore," Aaron said as he nodded towards her cigarette.

She huffed. "You make that sound like a threat."

He laughed. We all stood outside together. The two of them bantered as they caught each other up on their lives. I was repeatedly invited into the conversation but preferred to just listen. After a few more cigarettes, we said our goodbyes. We didn't stop to see the bride or tell anyone we were leaving before we headed down the stairs and to the parking lot. Nicole and Aaron hugged for a long time and promised to keep in touch.

Nicole turned to me and pulled me in for another hug.

"Take good care of him," she whispered in my ear.

"Of course," I whispered back.

When we returned to the hotel, he hugged me tightly and rocked me a little.

"I cannot tell you how much it means to me that you were here tonight," he said softly.

"I'm glad I was," I said back. "I'm sorry it didn't go a little better."

He pulled back and looked down at me. "Are you kidding? I got to dance poorly with my best friend and hang out with the only sister I like. And the frosting on the cake, my mom got told off. This was one of the best nights of my life!"

Trick or Treat

    Growing up, Halloween always held a forbidden magic for me. All of the other kids got to dress as their favorite characters and parade around the neighborhood for candy. I, of course, could not be allowed out when evil was lurking around every corner on the night that demons could visit the Earth. Momma conveniently ignored the fact that Halloween is not mentioned in the bible and had no reason to believe it was significant, but Uncle James always saved a little candy to sneak to me.

    As a teenager, it was a little different. I didn't have any friends to invite me out to parties so I stayed hidden in my room with my books. Aaron and his dad had an annual tradition of staying up too late eating pizza and watching horror movies. It was the one thing his dad made sure he made himself available for every year and Aaron was more excited about it than Christmas. Every year Jacob would wait until he thought Momma was asleep and sneak out to toilet paper and egg houses. One year, the wind blew the mudroom door shut just enough that the latched clicked and he was locked out. At a little after three in the morning, he knocked on my bedroom window. Fortunately for him, I was already awake. I helped pull him through the window and he stood looking down at me for a moment.

    "You going to tell Dad and Aunt Janice?"

    "Why would I? I don't care what you do."

    He nodded and went back to his room.

    In college, I enjoyed going to Halloween parties with Chetna. I could be anyone I wanted to be in costume and it was liberating. She could make friends with anybody and she would drink too much, flirt too much, and we would go home together.

    As an adult and employee of the museum, Halloween was usurped by the Haunted Gala. On October thirtieth of 2013, Sonya called me into her office. She was standing wither arms crossed and her jaw set. She took a deep breath and looked me in the eye.

"Do I need to remind you how important this gala is?"

"No, ma'am but you do every year anyway."

She continued without hearing me. "Our biggest donors will be there. Be sure to mention your work with the new reliquary and the Jerome estate and everything else you can think of to schmooze them. We are counting on this to be big to round off the fiscal year with a bang."

"Schmooze the donors. Big bang. Yes ma'am."

She looked at me. Obviously, I hadn't hidden my note of facetiousness well enough.

"Go." That was all she had to say.

I hated that Sonya had to do things like that to make herself feel important. We both knew I had become too valuable for her to fire and so she wouldn't even threaten it.

The following night, I was admiring myself in the mirror. My white, flowing gown was perfect as the little flecks of silver shimmered in the light. My tiny wings were straight, the feathers were lying flat, and I had neatly hidden the straps that held them on. My halo was suspended by a wire on a headband that dug in behind my ears but I was willing to tolerate the discomfort for just this night. I had managed to paint my face respectfully and even broke out a little glitter for my cheeks. If it had been for a church function, even my mother would have been proud. I turned from the mirror and saw Onoskelis on the bed.

She shook her head. "Angel's do not look like that, you know. They are corporeal light."

"You don't really look like a beautiful woman, either."

"This is true." She stood up and followed me into the kitchen. "I do not understand why you have combined so many feasts and traditions into something that makes no sense and parade around in costume on a day with no meaning. Do you realize how many cats are going to die tonight as sacrifices we demons do not want?"

Hope hissed at her from under the couch.

"Well, I'm not sure what you want me to do about it, but I am sure I'm going to be late if I don't leave now."

The mezzanine had been reinvented into an opulent ballroom. Dinner tables had been set up on the end nearest the café. Little placards with gold lettering ensured no enemies sat near each other. The world of philanthropy was savagely cutthroat but most were willing to pretend to set their differences aside and shake hands when the photographer came by. A string quartet played in the center of the bamboo groves while projectors cast moving images of ghosts on the walls. Catering staff circulated with trays of alcohol and hors d'oeuvres. Each of them was dressed as a famous artist or artwork.

I helped myself to a glass of white wine from Vincent Van Gogh. I carefully pointed out that his bandage was on the wrong ear as I accepted the glass. I looked around at all of the donors and miscellaneous other guests. Like it or not, the board's event committee knew how to throw a party.

A tall, dark, and handsome nineteen-twenties bootlegger in a very dapper grey suit found me.

"Look at you, Shawn. I'd swear you just stepped right out of a speakeasy."

"Thank you. I do clean up a bit, don't I?" He pretended to buff his fingernails on his coat.

Marilyn Monroe waved at him from across the hall and he excused himself to join her.

"I don't believe alcohol is looked at as very angelic." A voice came from behind me.

I smiled and turned to see a handsome bespeckled face under a brown fedora.

"Really? Indiana Jones? You couldn't be more original?" I raised my eyebrows at him and shook my head.

"Don't be ridiculous. Indiana Jones didn't wear a bandana around his neck or a blue shirt." He stepped back and held his arms open so I could get the full effect of his costume.

"Then who are you supposed to be?"

"The paleontologist from Jurassic Park. Sam Neill's character."

"I'm pretty sure that was a Stetson hat."

"Okay, fine. I was Indiana Jones last year. Actually, every year. I didn't have time to come up with something else so I threw something together and recycled the hat."

I laughed. "You didn't tell me you were coming tonight."

"I didn't know until today. Mark, the campus president, told me this afternoon that he had a few tickets for select faculty members and I was to be sure to represent the school wisely and carefully. I guess a lot of our benefactors overlap."

"Why did he wait until today to tell you?"

"Who knows?" He shrugged his shoulders.

"Well, I applaud your creativity."

"Your mother would be horrified at you in costume but I think she would be proud of your choice. You are quite angelic, if I may say so."

I giggled. My mother would be more than horrified at this spectacle regardless of how I was dressed. All things Halloween were evil in her eyes.

"Ah! Grace! Could you come here for a moment?" Marie Antoinette in heavy-rimmed red glasses motioned to me from a group across the room.

I sighed. "Duty calls."

I chugged my wine and handed Aaron the empty glass.

Sonya was shamelessly flirting with D'Artanion the musketeer in a very elaborate masquerade mask. Her dress, though long-sleeved, was tight-fitting and low cut. She looked as if she would pop out of the top at a moment's notice and I prayed she wouldn't dare bend over. She was lavishly decked out in gold and jewels with an elaborate wig and crown. She did Madam Antoinette proud in appearance and personality.

"Grace, I'd like you to meet-"

"Milady." He cut her off.

There was something familiar about his voice. I held out my hand and he kissed the back of it.

"A true angel. I'd hoped I would meet you here. May I have this dance?" he asked.

He led me away before Sonya could complete her introduction. I let him lead me around the dance floor for a few moments.

"I'm sorry. Are you a donor?"

"If I need to be. That's not really why I came tonight."

I was getting a little weary of the mystery. "Can I at least know your name?"

He spun me out and pulled me back to him again.

"Still graceful in every sense of the word."

I froze. I dropped his hand and stepped back.

"Xander?"

He removed the mask and hat. The face beneath was a little older and the hair had a few flecks of grey, but it was still him.

"Hello, Grace."

He moved forward as if to hug me, but I stepped back.

"Why are you here?" I choked.

He held his hat by the brim in front of him and looked at the floor. "Is there somewhere we can talk?"

I didn't want to do it. A flood of emotions from pain, to love, to sorrow, to excitement hit me like a force of nature. It had been six years since we broke each others' hearts. Six years had passed and I had finally forgotten about all of the pain he had caused. I had a new life; a happy life without him. Why was he there? I finally admitted defeat. I needed to know.

"My office," I said flatly as I turned to lead him away.

I passed Shawn.

"Are you okay, Miss Grace?" He stepped forward as if to follow us.

"Yes. Thank you, Shawn. We're just going to discuss some things in my office."

Shawn looked apprehensive but nodded and stepped back.

I caught a glimpse of Aaron watching us ascend the stairs near the Far East exhibit. When we reached my office, I realized I didn't have my keys with me. I backtracked and took him to the board room. I knew Sonya would leave it unlocked during an event so we could milk money out of the donors in relative privacy.

I locked the door behind us and turned to face him. The Xander I remembered oozed confidence and charm from every orifice. The man who stood before me seemed nervous and insecure. I looked into his magnificent green eyes and, for a moment, lost myself in them. I wanted him to hold me like he used to. I wanted to breathe him in. I started to feel weak. I suddenly felt a jolt from within and I pulled myself together.

"Why are you here?" I asked again.

"I miss you, Grace."

He set his hat and mask on the table and returned his gaze to my eyes. He stepped towards me but I stepped back. There were about seven feet between us and I wasn't ready for that gap to be any smaller, no matter how much a part of me wanted to be in his arms.

"Missed me? It's been six years. I haven't heard from you at all."

"I've been focusing on my career. Trying to move past you. Trying to move on."

"And?"

"I can't. I've tried other women. They aren't you. Everything I've ever wanted has always been you."

My heart melted. I found it to be a struggle to keep my composure.

"We talked about this." I swallowed hard. "We want different things."

"Hear me out." He stepped forward again but I held my ground. "We can find a little house in a suburb. We don't have to live in the city. There are plenty of small art museums that I'm sure would love to have you and once I get my seat in the Senate, we'll have plenty of time to travel and you can do research."

I felt myself waver and I looked down to the floor. I think he sensed it too and he pushed on.

"Come on, Grace. We're perfect. You're the beautiful small-town girl from the rural Midwest who made it to be an authority in, not just art, religious art. The public expects men in my family and status to marry women from money. That isn't you."

I suddenly understood what he was saying. "So you marrying beneath you would really resonate with the voters."

He fumbled a bit. "Not beneath me but... Uh. Yes, they would love you."

"And you?"

"Of course I love you, Grace."

I closed the gap between us and looked up into his eyes. "I don't think you ever loved me as much as you love your career." I stepped back to the door, unlocked it, and held it open. "But I do think you need to leave."

He opened his mouth to say something but changed his mind. He picked up his hat and mask and headed for the door.

When he reached the doorway, I spoke up. "Xander?"

He turned to face me.

"Was I always a career move?"

He broke eye contact, clenched his jaw, and walked out of my life for good.

I tried to stand strong. I tried to hold myself together but I felt my whole body tremble as tears streamed down my face. I took a deep breath and stepped into the hallway. Aaron was waiting for me.

"Want to talk about it?" He asked.

I shook my head, still fighting tears.

"Want a ride home?"

I nodded.

He took the handkerchief from his neck. He gently dabbed my face. He handed me the damp cloth, put his arm around me, and escorted me down the back hallway away from the prying eyes of the donors and Sonya. We stopped at the coat check to get my keys before disappearing into the parking garage.

We didn't speak a word in the 4Runner as he drove me home. When we pulled into my driveway, he squeezed my hand.

"Thank you," I said softly.

"I'll always be here for you, Gracie."

Something about that sentence stung a little even though I knew he didn't mean it to. I got out of the vehicle and let myself in the living room door. Onoskelis was standing in the corner of the kitchen.

"Maybe you should have let me kill him when we had the chance," she sang.

"I'm not in the fucking mood!"

I ripped off my halo and hurled it at her like a Frisbee. I stormed down the hall and slammed the bedroom door shut behind me. I cried myself to sleep. At three a.m. I pulled my pillow tight over my head so Onoskelis couldn't try to convince me to let her have Xander. In the morning, I woke to Hope purring softly on the pillow next to my head. I rolled over and dug the phone out of the white robes of my angel costume. I went straight to the text message from Sonya.

I don't know where you went last night but I'll forgive you in light of the twenty-five-thousand dollar Bonaventure donation.

Twenty-five-thousand dollars. A parting gift instead of a wedding present, I supposed.

The Dress Fitting

"I shouldn't be laughing," Shawn cackled.

He had helped me up to stand on the shipping crate he had brought into my office. The seamstress for my bridesmaid's gown for Chetna's wedding needed to do more pinning and cutting but I wasn't going to have time to go to the other side of town, so we paid extra to have her come to me. I stood on the crate in the gaudiest, seafoam green, ruffled taffeta monstrosity you could imagine.

"No, you shouldn't. This isn't funny." I put my hands on my hips. "This is a travesty."

He only laughed harder.

The seamstress pulled at the bottom hem of the skirt. The dress was originally designed with someone at least half a foot taller than me in mind. She seemed annoyed at how much fabric she was going to need to scythe off the bottom.

"How tall will your shoes be?" she asked.

I hadn't even thought of shoes. What color even goes with such a putrid shade of green? I'd honestly hoped Chet would have backed out before we got this far.

"Oh. Um. Probably three inches."

She huffed. "Probably."

Shawn stifled a giggle.

"Chet is lucky I love her," I sighed.

"You don't like Kevin, do you?" Shawn took a seat at my desk chair to watch.

"It's not that I don't like him. He's a nice enough guy. But he's never grown up and she may not see that as a problem but I do."

"Have you told Chetna?" He asked as he started doing half-spins in my chair.

"Nope."

"Why not?" He stopped swinging. "Shouldn't your best friend know how you feel about the man she wants to spend her life with?"

"In theory, but there are a few problems." I held up my index finger. "First, it's her relationship, not mine. I don't see what he's like when they are alone together. He may be a better man than I give him credit for."

"Please refrain from moving so much. I have to start over and I do have other things to do today," the seamstress grumbled.

"Sorry." I stood up straight.

Shawn rolled his eyes. "Second?"

"Second, 'love is blind' isn't just an idiom." I thought briefly of Xander. "She knows his inability to hold a job for any length of time is a problem. She knows the amount of time he spends playing games with his friends instead of helping with the house isn't normal. But, she justifies it all. Rationalizes it. Makes excuses for his behavior. They've been together for so long that pulling herself out of it is going to be impossible or, at best, improbable. Hearing it from me won't change her mind because her rationales are made."

Shawn looked like he was contemplating my explanation.

"I don't want to see Chetna hurt," I continued, "but it's what will happen if I'm right regardless of whether I open my mouth or not."

"I get it, but that sucks. I like her." He shook his head.

Someone knocked on my office door.

"Come in," I called.

Matthew opened the door while looking at a paper in his hand.

"About that grant from the Weaver Foundation-" He looked up and stopped in his tracks. "Oh, my." He smiled.

I held up my index finger and aimed it at him. "Don't. Just, don't."

He tried to suppress his laughter. "I'll come back later."

He shut the door behind him but we could hear his roaring from my welcome room.

"There. Finally," the seamstress said. "Do be careful not to lose any of the pins when taking it off."

I looked at Shawn. "Get me down and out of this thing."

He snorted from stifling his laugh as he interlaced his fingers to give me something to step down onto.

The rest of the afternoon was a mess of meetings. How to spend the grant from the Weaver Foundation had everyone at odds, but we needed to come to some compromise that we could all agree on to take to the board. Instead of helping us decide, Sonya had told us to work it out for ourselves and watched from the sidelines for her own sick amusement. By the end of the day, the only thing we could all agree on was that it should not be spent on a fundraiser. At around a quarter to seven, I was in my office getting caught up on emails since the debate had recessed until the following day.

My cell phone buzzed.

Dinner? That was all the text message said.

I looked at the clock on my computer and my stomach rumbled. I suddenly realized I hadn't eaten anything since the granola bar I'd had with my coffee at nine a.m.

Seven-thirty at The Cantina, I replied.

The Cantina was packed. There was some sports event or another playing on the televisions and rowdy patrons were yelling and pounding on the bar. I was grateful we had been given a comparatively quiet booth in the corner. The alternative seating was barstools at four-foot-high tables in the middle of the commotion. I wasn't in the mood to feel like a child dangling my legs off a tall chair nor did I want to be surrounded by all the noise.

I watched our server skillfully navigate through the crowd with a tray of chips and salsa and two glasses of water.

"Can I start y'all with a drink?" he asked as he laid out our table for us.

'I'll have whatever the special on tap is," Aaron answered.

"Okay. And for you, ma'am?" He turned to me.

"Raspberry daiquiri with the strongest stuff you've got."

The server smiled. "You got it!"

Aaron looked at me. "Liquor? Must have been one Hell of a day."

"You have no idea. We just can't agree on how to spend this grant money. Joy and Matthew want to expand on our already-too-big modern art area. We got new pieces for it several years back that didn't draw nearly as large a crowd as they had wanted so I think they are trying to redeem themselves."

"You oppose that idea?"

"Absolutely. The garish, kitsch abominations they like to call 'art' are an insult to the word."

He laughed. "What do you want?"

"I'm backing Candace and Tony. We need more cultural art; particularly Native American or South American pieces. The grant isn't enough to purchase too many artifacts but we could get some on loan from another museum to fill in the gaps for a really nice unveiling."

"Well, if it's artifacts you're looking for, you might be able to sweet-talk some help from a well-connected archeologist."

"Oh, really?"

He leaned back in his seat and crossed his arms over his chest. "If you make it worth my while."

"You know a well-connected archeologist who could help me?" I snickered.

"Now, that's just cold."

I laughed as our server set our drinks in front of us. "Do y'all know what you're having?"

"Ladies first." Aaron gestured to me.

"Chicken taquitos. No beans. Extra rice."

"And for you?" The server turned to Aaron as he scribbled in his notepad.

"Beef enchiladas.'

"Very good. I'll have those right out for you." The server turned and left.

"So, what else is under your skin?" Aaron asked as he shoveled a mound of salsa on a chip into his mouth.

"What do you mean?" I sipped my fruity drink.

"Come on, Gracie. I can read you like a book."

I sighed. "I had another fitting for my dress today."

"Oh. Is she still insisting on that hideous green thing?"

"Yup."

"I'm sorry. I know the prospect of being seen in that thing is awful but what's really got you down?"

I began swirling my drink with the straw. "It's the whole idea of her marrying Kevin."

"Still can't bring yourself to like the guy, huh?"

"No. I really can't. He's a nice enough guy and they've been happy together for ages but I honestly don't think he's good for her. Maybe there's something wrong with me."

He cocked his head at me. "What do you mean?"

"Maybe I don't want her to be happy. Maybe I secretly want her to be alone and miserable like me." I stopped swirling and started poking my drink with the straw.

"I'm no psychologist, but you are one of the best people I know and I have no doubt your concern is genuine and comes from a good place. Besides that, you most certainly are not alone." He reached across the table and took my hand. "And I hope you aren't miserable."

I looked at my hand inside his. "I guess not."

"Good." He let go. "Have you talked to her?"

"Shawn asked the same thing. I've said little things here and there but we haven't *talked* about it. She sees the same problems I do but she's convinced herself it's not that bad so I feel like I'd be wasting my breath."

Aaron nodded. "Or you're afraid she'll hate you for it and choose him over you."

That comment hit like an arrow to my heart. He was absolutely right.

"What do you think I should do?" I looked up at him.

"Well," he shoveled more chips and salsa and chewed for a moment. "I think you're right. She's not going to listen. She's headstrong and in love and living one of those romance novels she reads all the time. But I don't think it's good for you to keep all this bottled up. She's your friend. You two love each other and I think that's stronger than you realize."

I thought for a moment. It was decidedly not a conversation I wanted to have.

"When did you get so wise?" I finally asked.

"Always have been. You just don't listen." He smiled and down half his beer.

My stomach reminded me how empty it was so I started munching on chips and we changed the subject.

The next morning, Chetna and I met for coffee as usual.

"How did the fitting go?" she asked excitedly.

"I don't think your seamstress realized how short I am."

She giggled. "She'll get over it."

I looked at my coffee cup for a moment.

"Chet," I finally said.

"Yeah?"

"You're sure this is what you want?" I asked timidly.

"I always get a smoothie."

"That's not-"

"I know that's not what you meant," she interrupted. "I know Kevin has his flaws, but I really am happy."

I sighed. I should have put up more of a fight but I didn't have it in me. I lost all of my nerve when she confirmed that she was, in fact, happy.

"Okay." I nodded.

"I'm glad I have you looking out for me." She hugged me.

I hugged her back. "I only want the world for you."

"I know." She smiled as she released me.

"Then I have one more question," I said.

"What's that?" She cocked her head slightly.

"What color shoes am I supposed to wear with that dress?"

Happy Birthday

I stood out on the dock in the freezing spray. I watched the waves crash against the little peninsula where the lighthouse stood. The sky was grey and heavy. The rain had not begun yet, but the threat was there. I pulled my coat close against me and lowered my umbrella to try to stay dry. I shouldn't have been out there, but I needed to escape the confines of my office.

I would be thirty years old soon. I had a constant, crushing weight of emotions about that. Thirty years old. Alone. Childless. And *that* night. On April fifteenth of 2014, there was a full lunar eclipse starting shortly after midnight. and reaching its peak at three forty-five a.m. Onoskelis could leave my house on full moons by traveling by the light. I had been careful to be home or, at the very least, not with Aaron ever since she had taken residence beneath my house. I had no idea how an eclipse would affect her powers, but I knew I did not want her to make an appearance at my birthday party.

I had not wanted a big affair made of my thirtieth. It was the marking of another year gone and, for all of the reasons listed above, I had no desire to commemorate that. Of course, Chetna was hearing none of it. She insisted it would be something small and tasteful just before she offered to fly Momma, James, and even Jacob into town for the occasion. I assured her that was quite all right. Momma had already canceled her nearly annual trip on account of Uncle James. He had been sick and in and out of the hospital. Since she was the only person who could care for him, she would be staying in Illinois that year.

It was a week before my birthday. I had been on and off the phone all day and Shawn was neck-deep in paperwork. I had finally managed to schedule a meeting with the Catholic Bishop about the reliquary. Since it did not arrive with any provenance more concrete than hearsay, we were desperately searching for some shred of evidence to present for authentication. With our noses buried in papers, we both jumped when Chetna burst through the door without knocking.

"Hey!" I greeted her. "Did I forget a lunch date?"

"Nope! I'm actually here to see Shawn."

"Me?" My assistant perked up from a pile of papers he had been sorting through on the floor.

"Yes!" She smiled. "April fifteenth is next Tuesday. What are you doing?"

"I've got classes 'til four."

"At six p.m. be at this address for dinner." She handed him a small greeting card with a floral design. "It's Grace's birthday and you *must* be there. Do you have a girlfriend?"

"Oh. Um." He looked a little sheepish. "I've kind of been seeing this girl from my pharmacokinetics class named Kiara."

"Great! Bring her too!"

"Uh, okay," he reluctantly agreed.

She turned to me. "See you for coffee in the morning. We can talk color schemes for dinner!"

I stood up in protest. "Chet!"

She smiled and ignored me. "Toodles!"

With that, she dashed out of my office just as quickly as she'd entered. That woman really was a force of nature.

Shawn looked at me. "You don't want a party, do you?"

"Of course not but I'd like to see you try to rope her under control. You'd have better luck hogtying a rodeo bull."

He laughed.

"Never mind that," I continued. "Why am I just now hearing about this Kiara?"

That night, I sat in my favorite chair with a cup of tea and some light reading. I was trying to relax at the end of my day. I had the big window in the front of my living room cracked open. The April night air was cool and quiet but my tea and flannel pajamas kept me warm. Hope purred contentedly next to my legs in the chair. The peace was not to last.

Buzz. Buzz. Buzz.

I looked at my phone on the end table in annoyance. It was Aaron. I sighed. We hadn't spoken at all that day.

"Hey! What are you doing?" His voice was light but not happy.

"Reading." I closed my book. "What are you doing?"

"Heading home from the school."

I looked at the wall clock in the kitchen. It was almost nine.

"A little late, aren't you?" I asked.

"Departmental faculty meeting. We had to brainstorm ideas to help keep students engaged and make them feel like they are part of the program while they are still in their core classes."

I swore I could hear his eyes rolling through the phone.

"What did you come up with?" I baited.

"This was *not* my brainchild but guess who got nominated to oversee the new archeology club?"

"Archeology club?"

"Oh, yes." His voice was high-pitched and emanated agitation. "It's the new small student body in which we are going to pair students close to graduation with newbies for mentoring."

"How do you fit into all of this?"

"I'm the 'faculty advisor.' I get to oversee all club activities, help them hold elections, and coordinate whatever else they come up with." The agitation was giving way to complete discomposure.

I giggled, though I knew I shouldn't have. "Congratulations?"

"Can you hear the excitement in my voice?" That was said with pure sarcasm.

I laughed harder. "I'm sure it could be worse."

"We'll see. I'm dragging you along for the ride."

"How do I fit into this? I don't even teach."

"They're talking about guest lecturers and day trips outside of class time to keep the students engaged." He paused for my response. When he didn't get one, he continued. "Where do our archeological finds eventually end up?"

I sighed. "Museums."

"Exactly!"

"I guess we can talk about it at dinner on Tuesday when Shawn's there."

"Tuesday?" All of the irritation in his voice was gone and replaced with confusion.

"My birthday dinner at Chetna's house."

He was silent for a moment. "I'm sorry, Gracie," he finally said. "I'm supposed to be heading over to Boston to help my dad. When he and mom split, he kept Grandma's old house but with all his traveling, it's been neglected. I told him I'd come out this weekend and help him fix some things. Don't know when I'll be back."

"Oh. Okay, then we'll talk about it when you get back."

To tell the truth, hearing him say that hurt far worse than I thought it could. I didn't want a big fuss for my birthday, but I knew I wanted him there. Knowing he would be six hundred miles away instead made a hole open in my chest.

"I'm really sorry, Gracie."

"It's okay. Honestly," I lied.

"We can do something just the two of us when I get back." He offered. "I'll take you to a nice dinner."

"That sounds lovely." There was an awkward silence. "I think I'm about ready for bed," I lied again.

He sounded completely crestfallen. "Okay. Goodnight."

"Goodnight." I hung up the phone.

I settled deeper into my chair and reached to pet Hope, but she was gone.

"He cares so little for you," Onoskelis said. "I do not understand why you refuse to see it. You are like your friend. Refusing to see these men for what filth they are."

She was sitting on the far end of the couch. Her long, black hair was draped over her shoulder and coiled in her lap. She stroked it like an animal as she stared at me.

"Not now." I threw my head back and stared at the ceiling.

"Why do you refuse to see it?"

"Aaron has his own life to live. I respect that. You're just mad because he won't be at dinner. And it's a full moon so don't you dare even think about coming."

She emitted a low growl. "I cannot leave that night. A shadow will cast on the moon and break its light. I would not be able to control my travel."

"Then maybe that would be the perfect night for you to leave. Find yourself a nice cave instead of my cistern. Or another holy child to torment. Play a little Russian roulette with moonbeams and end up somewhere far away."

"I am needed here."

I turned my head to her. "You are neither needed nor wanted."

"Deny me all you will. I see your secret thoughts. I know your heart's truest desires," she insisted.

"I don't want Aaron dead," I retorted.

"But you long for retribution."

"Why can't you just leave me alone?"

I rubbed my face and when I looked back at the end of the couch, she was gone.

I have to hand it to Chetna; she had an incredible talent for making an intimate gathering of friends into a beautiful affair. She had adorned her dining table with yellow fabric napkins that she had painstakingly folded into tulips. A bountiful basket of yellow tulips, roses, little white flowers, and fern fronds sat in the center of the table with a candlestick on either side. I was seated at the place of honor at the head of the table with Chetna and Kevin to my left and Shawn and Kiara to my right. Chetna had insisted on cooking the meal herself.

There was chicken in a spinach cream sauce, homemade bread, rice, and little orange potato cakes that were nothing short of divine. She truly outdid herself with a death by chocolate cake as an homage to my age.

The evening was as quiet as I had hoped. We sipped zinfandel as we ate. We joked about work and hopes for travel that summer. Kiara was a very sweet girl and melded into our group beautifully. Despite it all, the empty chair at the other end of the table stared back at me. Chetna had Kevin (regardless of how I felt about him). Shawn had Kiara. And there I sat surrounded by my friends but utterly alone.

At half-past ten, I made my excuses to go home so I could get up for work in the morning. Everyone agreed and thanked Chetna for a wonderful evening. After a few more 'Happy birthdays', I finally was able to leave.

Just before midnight, I lay in bed on the cusp of sleep. I was still a little woozy from the wine and the room was still spinning. Hope suddenly sprang from the bed and ran towards the living room. I stared down the hallway after her in bewilderment for a few seconds before there was a pounding on the door.

I pulled the hammer out from under the pillow on the bed next to me. My neighborhood was safe, but it was still an old habit that I hadn't lost. I wandered into the living room. Hope was happily dancing in front of the door.

I opened the door and Aaron stood on the other side holding a cupcake with a single lit candle. "Do you have any idea how many speed limits I had to break to get here before midnight?" he asked.

I couldn't believe he was there. I stood in the doorway with my mouth wide open.

"You going to blow out the candle or wait for the frosting to catch fire?" He laughed.

I could feel Onoskelis behind me. The lunar eclipse was almost beginning. Hopeful she was still confined to the house, I stepped out on the porch. I closed my eyes and wished for her to go away before blowing out the tiny flame.

"Hopefully, your wish will come true." He smiled.

"Hopefully." I glanced over my shoulder. "You know, we could have just had dinner or something tomorrow."

I sat on the porch step and motioned for him to join me.

"I've missed too many birthdays." The tone in his voice was solemn.

He sat beside me and tore the cupcake in half. We leaned against each other under the eclipse in silence as we ate the cupcake. The heat from Onoskelis's stare burned holes in the back of my head as she stood in the picture window behind us. I chose to ignore her as I savored the hours that Aaron and I sat in silence watching the eclipse. I didn't want a big fuss for my thirtieth birthday and I couldn't help but feel that that was the perfect way to spend it.

The People vs. the Church

    I wasn't looking forward to meeting the bishop. Contacting any member of the Catholic diocese was always a chore. Locally, he was the highest rung in the ladder that I could reach. In most cases, the former bishop would authenticate Catholic relics for me. We had a mutual respect for how we viewed each other's work. However, there were a few pieces he was unwilling to associate his name with, no matter how much I pleaded. Inevitably, I would have to work my way up the ladder of command and navigate a sticky web of red tape until I found a cardinal who was willing to at least speak to me. With only a little over two hundred cardinals in the world, this was difficult and painstaking. Twice, I'd had to leave the country to meet with them. I didn't HAVE to have the church's blessing for an artifact, but it made all the difference in the world to enthusiasts, collectors, and benefactors. The church's blessing sometimes exponentially increased the value of a piece and the more valuable our collection was, the deeper patrons' pockets became. It was a cycle.

    I didn't have much faith in this new bishop. He had already rescheduled multiple times purely to inconvenience me. Rumor had it, he was a pompous misogynist. That was further cemented in my mind when he insisted that, instead of meeting at the diocese building on East Ninth Street, we would meet in a private office he kept at St. Peter's.

    I didn't like the way he was looking at me. I couldn't quite put my finger on his facial expression-- boredom perhaps, but his body language spoke volumes. He was turned slightly to the side, so as not to address me head-on. His hand wasn't resting on his hip, but the outside of his wrist. Not only was he displeased with the idea of having to speak to me, but he had no intention of shaking my hand. Instead of wearing an informal cassock, he was dressed in full liturgical garb, complete with stole, to remind me of his rank. I couldn't help but notice the touch of gold peeking out from his vestments. Call me jaded, but I never did understand how so many clergymen of so many faiths around the world could call to the lower classes to give what little they have to charity while displaying their own wealth. So many of the artifacts I worked with were decadent displays of porcelain, gold, and jewels. If the wealthy who commissioned them were so devout, why not follow the biblical teachings? The church was not exempt from this duplicity.

Our mutual disgust for each other hung in the air like a heavy cloud. I despised the hypocrisy of the church while he despised the fact that I was a woman with such public authority on it.

"Hello, Miss Nightingale. Your reputation precedes you. May I offer you a drink?" He gestured to a pitcher of water on a sideboard behind his desk.

We were going to feign civility. I understood that.

"Thank you for such hospitality, Bishop, but I do not wish to take up too much of your time." I twisted my face into a sickeningly sweet smile as I said it.

He snickered slightly as he took a seat behind a mahogany desk. I recognized it as nineteenth-century with brass work. I doubted a ten-thousand-dollar desk had just been donated. I carefully set down the box and gently removed the relic. His eyes widened when he saw the tooth contained within.

"I cannot confirm that relic is real," he said dismissively.

"No, but you can acknowledge it for what it is and request a historian from the Vatican to work with me."

"I can. But I won't." He narrowed his eyes.

"Please. I do not wish to desecrate or destroy this relic to carbon date the tooth."

"I'm sorry. Please see yourself out." He sat back in his chair and waved his hand at me.

I leaned over his desk and looked him in the eye. "You and I both know it's real."

"Yes, but we both know the Vatican will never send someone to authenticate it without provenance- which you don't have- and I will not put my reputation on the line, nor will I risk losing my position to acknowledge such a myth."

I felt myself get angrier. "Then why did you agree to meet me? Why waste both of our time?"

"To at least have a look at what you will undoubtedly raise a fuss over and to offer you-"
he paused, "some advice."

I glowered at him. "Enlighten me."

"The church has a great deal of power over people in your position. It would be wise to not make enemies."

I stepped back and threw my hands in the air. "I came here in good faith." The irony of that statement struck me. "I grew up in the church and I'm very familiar with both the public and private side. I am not here to make enemies. You have chosen to make me one."

He lifted an eyebrow at me and gestured towards the reliquary. "What do you hope to accomplish by authenticating this?"

"I only want the world to see what it could be and for the world to know Agnes's story. I may not be able to prove without a shadow of a doubt that it is hers, but even if I put that seed in people's minds, it will grow."

"You sound as if you are taking the church to trial." He narrowed his eyes at me again.

"Only in a court of public opinion." I stepped closer to him and looked directly into his villainous eyes. "You can threaten me all you want but destruction of my career only gives credence to the myth. The church will successfully implicate itself in a cover-up and I will still win." I stepped back and returned the reliquary to the safety of its foam in the box. "Now, as you suggested, I will see myself out. See you in court."

I held my head high as I walked out with all dignity and pride intact. But, when I got to my car, I crumbled. I sobbed uncontrollably the entire ride home. I was proud of myself for handling the situation so well but, in truth, I knew what the church could do to me. I was terrified. In the back of my mind, I knew they wouldn't be bothered with someone as insignificant as me ruffling a few feathers. At most, I was mild annoyance. This time, however, I controlled something significant. I had to believe they would disavow the possibility that I was right and leave it at that. I would tread lightly and word things carefully from that point on and hopefully, they would leave me alone.

By the time I reached home, I had stopped crying but I was still shaking. I set the reliquary on the floor and I picked up Hope as she met me at the door. I held my face in her fur and listened to her purr. I felt myself relax slightly. I carried her into the kitchen and fixed her dinner. I had a long shower after that and felt a lot more of my angst wash down the drain.

I sat in my favorite chair with Hope on my lap and a much-needed cup of chamomile tea.

Buzz.

I sighed and looked at my phone. It was Aaron.

How did it go? He asked.

About as well as I expected, I answered.

Wow. That bad?

I felt myself tear up a little again but I swallowed them.

Worse, I replied.

Want to have some dinner and talk about it?

I didn't want to tell him 'no.' Being close to one of my best friends sounded like a good idea, but I just couldn't bring myself to do it. I wasn't hungry and I truthfully just wanted to wallow in self-pity for a little while.

Maybe next time.

Fishing

I was feeling extremely disheartened after my talk with the bishop. I had only just managed to roll out of bed around ten in the morning that Sunday. Hope was displeased by my lack of motivation. She had been pawing at my head and meowing in my ear for several hours before I dragged myself into the kitchen to make her breakfast and my coffee.

I was leaning against my kitchen counter feeling the warmth from my mug move into my fingertips. My hair was completely disheveled from a night of restless sleep. My makeup wasn't done and I was wearing a rumpled old baggy t-shirt that hadn't been washed in a while. I was in no fit state at all to see company so when I heard a familiar engine pull into my driveway and watched Hope excitedly run to the front door and start pawing at it, my heart fell into my stomach.

Knock. Knock. Knock. Ding-Ding. Knock. Knock.

I stood frozen for a moment.

"Gracie, open up," Aaron yelled through the door.

I was in a foul mood and I looked like a reanimated corpse. Aaron was probably the second-to-last person I wanted to see; just behind my mother. Only just. I thought about Onoskelis seething in the well below us.

"Gracie either you let me in or I'm going to get the key I'm betting you've got hidden in a flower pot and I'm going to let myself in."

I looked out the kitchen window at the Boston fern that was hanging from my patio roof. It wasn't exactly a flower pot but he wasn't wrong.

I looked at the floor. *Stay down there.* I thought.

I huffed and pushed myself up from the counter. Hope was excitedly prancing in circles in front of the door when I opened it.

"Whoa." He stepped back. "You okay?"

"Why are you here?" I turned and headed back for the kitchen.

He let himself in the storm door and followed.

"Good morning to you too, Sunshine." He looked around as he followed me. "You know, I've been in Cleveland for a year and never been inside of your house before. Not as many knick-knacks as I imagined."

He systematically opened all of my kitchen cabinets until he found what he was looking for. He took a mug out of the cabinet to the left of the refrigerator and helped himself to some coffee. I raised an eyebrow at him. He was far too cheerful and I was too under-caffeinated for his nonsense.

"I'm here because you are stressed," he continued.

I cringed a little as I watched him heap spoonfuls of sugar into his coffee and dilute it with milk. What was the point in coffee if you're just going to ruin it?

"I'm always stressed." I resumed my place against the counter and tried to hide my disgust with his beverage.

"And it's not good for you."

I sighed. "Still not answering my question."

"I'm going to help you un-stress." He mimicked my lean against the counter.

"The word is *de*-stress. And how do you plan to accomplish this?"

His eyes lit up. "Put some jeans on, Gracie, 'cause we're going fishing!"

It took me a moment to process the words that had just come out of his mouth. "Fishing?"

"Absolutely!"

I looked at him with mild disgust at such enthusiasm. "I've never been fishing in my life."

"So? Never too old to try."

I shook my head. "I have work to do."

"Not today. It's Sunday. Day of rest and all that. Now go put on some pants."

I looked him square in the eye. The set in his jaw matched my own and I knew I wasn't going to win this one without a fight that I was too tired to have.

"Fine." I threw my free hand in the air in defeat, set my coffee on the table with the other, and stormed back down the hall towards my bedroom; ignoring his victorious grin.

I grabbed a pair of jeans that had been wadded up in the corner for God knows how long and bundled my hair on top of my head. I stared in the mirror for a minute before I decided to change my shirt. I wasn't going to put on makeup though. I drew the line there. When I came back out, Aaron was sitting on the couch with his mug of milky coffee while Hope lying in his lap purring with her belly exposed.

Traitor. I thought.

When he looked up and saw me, he smiled. "I made your coffee to-go. No milk or sugar. Black. Just like your mood today."

He handed me a travel mug. I resisted the urge to take off the lid and dump the scalding liquid on him. I was worried the cat might end up as collateral damage and I didn't want to have the couch cleaned.

I sat in silence on the passenger side of the old eighty-six 4Runner. I remember it being so much fun when I was a kid and Mr. Akakios would take us for ice cream. Now the antique was a miserable prison. It was awkward and loud compared to my A5. Being trapped in that vehicle for no less than an hour in complete silence while Aaron grinned at whatever was inside his head did absolutely nothing to improve my mood. Eventually, we passed a sign that said 'Mosquito Lake Creek.' How much fun could we possibly have at a lake named after a vampiric insect?

He found a parking space and we got out of that awful vehicle. It was cloudy and the air smelled like exhaust. A loud group of kids ran past us as he handed me a cooler and unloaded a small tackle box, another cooler, and two rods.

"Blue cooler is lunch. Red cooler is bait. Don't mix them up." He laughed.

A man in a uniform who looked like he took his job far too seriously walked up to us. "Y'uns going fishing today?"

No. I thought. *We've got all this gear just to look the part for a movie.*

Aaron smiled politely at him. "Yes, sir! Going to be a beautiful day."

I looked up at the dreary rain clouds. I had my doubts.

The ranger looked at me and back to Aaron. "Got licenses?"

"Yes, sir." Aaron set the rods against the car and pulled two folded pieces of paper out of his back pocket. He handed them over. "Mine and hers."

The ranger looked over the papers and handed them back. "Y'uns have a good day, now."

"Thank you. We will." Aaron put the papers back in his pocket.

The ranger nodded and walked away. Aaron turned to face me. I must have been staring at him.

"What?" He asked.

"You got me a fishing license?"

He shrugged. "Of course. Did a pretty fine job of forging your signature on it, too."

"What if I had said 'no' today?"

He laughed. "You weren't going to say 'no.'" He picked up the rods and tackle box. "Grab those coolers."

I grudgingly picked up the coolers and followed him to the boat docks where a graying man in a blue polo shirt was waving at us.

"I was beginning to think y'all weren't coming," He called to us.

"Sorry about that." Aaron set the poles down and shook the man's hand. "Had a little trouble moving this morning." He winked at me.

The man smiled at me. "Saw old Barney Fife giving you trouble too."

"Just doing his duty." Aaron grinned.

They both laughed.

"Well then." The man clapped his hands together. "Let's get y'all on the water."

It was then that I realized he was standing in front of a small fishing boat on a trailer at the back of a pick-up truck. I watched Aaron guide the man as he backed the truck and trailer to the shore and they slid the boat off and into the water. They motioned to me and I brought all of the gear. We loaded the boat and Aaron helped me get in. It was one of the least graceful things I'd ever done.

"Back here at five?" the man asked.

"Yup. Thanks, Ben."

The man, who I now knew was named Ben, nodded, got back in his truck, and pulled away.

Aaron turned to me. "You ready?" He was grinning ear to ear.

I sat down on the bench seat. "Do you even know how to drive this thing?"

"Of course! Have you ever actually seen Indiana Jones? There's nothing an archeologist can't do."

He had a few false starts as he tried to figure out the motor.

"Good job, Indy," I teased.

"Hush."

It was several more minutes before he was finally able to get the motor started. I must admit I smiled a little. Eventually, the little boat carried us away from the crowded shoreline and out past the wave brake. I closed my eyes and felt the water spray on my face. The clip holding my hair fell out and it whipped and waved in the wind. I was actually starting to feel a little better but there was no way I was going to tell him that.

He steered us into a quiet, tree-lined alcove.

"We're here!" he exclaimed as he shut the motor off.

He opened the tackle box. I watched his fingers skillfully weave intricate knots to secure the hooks to the end of the fishing line. He next opened the little red cooler and released a putrid smell of rotting meat.

"Oh, my God! What is that?" I gagged.

"Spoiled chicken. Best bait there is for channel cat fishing."

He hooked the meat, closed the cooler, and rinsed his hands in the water.

"Are there channel cats in this lake?"

"Don't know. Hope so." He pulled me to my feet. "First thing is to aim away from the trees."

He put his hand on my hip and turned me around. He pulled me against his chest and I could feel his heartbeat and the hairs on my arms and the back of my neck stood on end.

"Then?" I tried to make my voice sound level.

He placed a rod in my hand and wrapped his fingers around mine. His hand was warm and rough and I felt my heart beat faster.

"Then you're going to hold this little trigger and pull back like this." He drew our arms back. "When you get about here" he moved our arms back forward, "you're going to flick your wrist and release the trigger." He stepped back. "Give it a shot."

I took a deep breath and my heart rate slowed. I followed the motion I was instructed in once as a practice and then gave it my all. I watched the rotted meat sail through the air before landing with a splash. I turned to Aaron. He was smiling even brighter than before.

"Excellent! Congratulations on your first cast." He kissed the top of my head and cast his own line.

The kiss caught me completely off guard and I momentarily froze before I found my voice. "Now what?"

"Now we wait." He sat back in the boat.

I sat down too. "That's it?"

"Relax and let your stress roll out with the tide," he said as he leaned back in the bottom of the boat.

"We're on a lake."

"Hush. You'll scare the fish away," he chided.

I settled down in the bottom of the boat. The clouds parted and the sun warmed my body. Every twenty or so minutes, we would check the bait and recast. I ignored Momma's weekly call. I would pay for it later, but I just couldn't handle her that day. We paused a little after one to eat the sandwiches and chips he had packed in the blue cooler. We tried a little while longer before heading back to the loading dock. We didn't catch a single thing. We hardly spoke all day but, by the end of it, I had forgotten to worry about all of the things that were waiting for me in the office the next day.

Aaron helped Ben secure the boat back on the trailer while I put the gear back in the 4Runner. We rode in silence back to my house and he walked me to my door.

I turned to face him. "Thank you."

He wrapped his arms around my shoulders and I hugged him around his waist.

"Sometimes you just need to be reminded to breathe." He squeezed a little before stepping off my porch and heading down my driveway.

I let myself into my house. I put my keys in the bowl by the door and went back to the bedroom to get out of my dirty clothes. I flicked on the light. Onoskelis was sitting on my bed.

"No," I said firmly.

"You'll change your mind." She smiled slyly as she walked towards the living room and disappeared.

When she was gone, Hope came out of the closet. I picked her up and kissed her head.

"No. I won't."

My Patient

"What are you most looking forward to?" I asked

Shawn and I were sitting on opposite sides of my desk in my office. It was pouring rain outside and the gentle pounding of the drops on the glass had made the whole day feel lazy. We both knew I had phone calls to return and emails to reply to, but neither of us really cared. Shawn was in his last semester of school now. I was very proud of him. Since I had taken him under my wing, he had become the little brother I never knew I'd always needed. He was wonderfully professional when he needed to be but had been known to bounce paper wads off the back of my head when it was just us. I had also grown an appreciation for his protective nature.

"I don't know. I'm ready to be done with studying but I've been thinking about continuing on with a second degree."

"Oh, yeah? In what?"

"Art history." He smiled.

"Really?" I felt myself light up. "What about your Pops?"

"It's my life, not his. Being here with you has really shown me a lot about myself."

I grinned wide. "Well, you know I'm not going to discourage it."

He leaned towards me. "Thank you for seeing something in me."

"I'm just glad you finally see it in yourself. You just let me know where I need to send the letter of recommendation."

He beamed.

The rest of the day was just as unproductive. It's hard to find motivation on a dreary Thursday. I left work feeling a complete lack of accomplishment but oddly fulfilled. I text messaged Aaron to ask him about his day.

Not feeling too great. Went home early, was his reply.

What's wrong? I asked.

Head is pounding. Stomach won't settle.

I'm sorry. Can I get you anything? I asked knowing he would never let me take care of him.

Nah. I'm going to sleep it off, he answered.

I knew he would say no.

Okay. Feel better, I told him.

The next day was far more productive. We were making real progress on a new exhibit design after we had finally settled on spending the money from the Weaver foundation on expanding the Native American art section.

As I walked through the parking garage towards my car, I text messaged Aaron to see how he was feeling.

I'm dying, he answered.

Is it really that bad? I rolled my eyes as I keyed in the words.

Yes, he said.

That was it. Whether he liked it or not, someone needed to take care of him. I went home to feed Hope and grab a few things from the cupboard before doubling back to the city.

When he answered the door, he looked like a warm cadaver. He wasn't wearing his glasses. His eyes were heavy and dark-rimmed but his face was pale.

"Gracie?"

"You look terrible." I pushed past him. "Get back to bed. Let me handle things."

He did as he was told while I went to the kitchenette. I laid out all of the items in my canvas bag on the counter before raiding his cabinets and drawers for pots and utensils. In true bachelor form, he had the bare minimum but I really only needed a big pot and some spoons. I cut the chicken and started broth while I cut celery and carrots and rinsed the peas. The noodles were the last to go in the pot. When I was satisfied with the soup, I fixed a bowl for each of us and carried them back into the bedroom.

I had never been in his room before. It was just as sparsely furnished as the rest of the apartment. His bed and nightstand were on the far wall. Near the closet was a tall, narrow dresser with a small tube television on it.

"You do watch TV!" I exaggeratedly exclaimed.

"Sometimes when I can't sleep." He looked at the bowls in my hand. "You didn't have to do all that."

"Of course I did. God knows you aren't going to take care of yourself and there is no better medicine than my chicken soup. Now, be a good patient and take your medicine." I crawled into the bed next to him.

"Aren't you afraid you'll get sick?" He asked as he took the bowl from me.

"I'll live."

We sat in his bed and watched old fifties black and white sitcoms. I'm not sure what time we dozed off but I woke a three in the morning. I felt uneasy and light-headed as if Onoskelis had been mucking around in my brain again. I turned my head. Aaron snored softly beside me. It felt good to be sharing a bed with a man again but quickly reminded myself that it was Aaron. I considered going home but my head was too unsteady to drive. I nestled down and laid my head on the pillow before drifting back to sleep.

Around eight a.m. my internal clock sounded the alarm and I woke again. It took me a moment to realize that the weight on my abdomen was Aaron's arm. I was lying on my left side against his chest. His arm held me close as he snored into the top of my head. In that moment, lying with him, I had a complete sense of peace and contentment that I hadn't felt in a very long time. I didn't want to move and I definitely didn't want to leave, but I had an angry cat at home and I had promised Chetna I would spend the day with her.

"Aaron," I said softly.

"Hmm?" he moaned.

"I have to go home."

"Mmhmm," he moaned in acknowledgment.

"That means you have to move your arm." I heard myself giggle a little.

He grunted as he rolled over and released me. I put on my shoes, put our bowls in the dishwasher, and slipped out the apartment door.

I couldn't stop smiling as I drove home. I had no idea why. Aaron and I had spent a lot of time together. But, spending time with him always did seem to make me happy.

As I pulled into my driveway, I heard my cell phone buzz.

I read Aarons' message. *You didn't have to spend the night.*

I smiled wider.

I didn't mean to but I didn't mind, I replied.

You really shouldn't have, he responded.

Did he mean I *shouldn't* have or I *really* shouldn't have? I hoped it wasn't the latter. Falling asleep with him genuinely had been an accident but it was one I was glad had happened. Was he mad at me for staying? I decided to put it out of my mind and went inside. Hope hissed at me and ran into the bedroom. Either she was that mad at me for such a belated breakfast or… Onoskelis marched angrily out of the kitchen, directly towards me.

"You spent the night in his bed? How dare you?!" She yelled in my face.

"How dare I fall asleep?" I asked with mock innocence.

"Do not play games with me!" she growled.

I shrugged. "Okay. I won't."

I turned down the hall and closed my bedroom door behind me. She barreled through the still-closed door as if it wasn't even there.

"He is the enemy! Why do you refuse to see it?" she continued to yell.

I finished pulling my sweater off over my head and stood glaring back at her.

"Enemy?" I put my foot down. "He is my best friend!"

"Even now as you arrived home he told you he cares not for your gestures of 'friendship!'"

I didn't like the way she used that word. "Get out of my head! And that wasn't what he meant!"

"You lie to yourself more than you lie to me!"

"Grace! You ready to go?" I heard Chetna's voice ring from the living room as she let herself in the front door.

I turned to Onoskelis. "Go back to Hell!"

She growled as she disappeared.

I walked out in the living room, still in my bra.

Chetna looked me up and down. "You okay, Honey?"

"Give me a minute. I need to shower and get changed. I just got home."

"Just got home?" She cocked her head at me. "Where were you?" I looked at her and before I could say anything she squealed, "Oh, my god! Oh, my god! Oh, my god! You were with Aaron!"

I rolled my eyes. "Yes. Will you feed Hope while I'm in the shower?"

"Yes. You shower. I'll feed the cat. Then we're going to get coffee. Then you're going to tell me everything!"

She was practically dancing as she left the living room and headed into the kitchen to feed the cat. When I was dressed, she virtually shoved me into the car to get coffee. After we went through a drive-through for a plain cup of Columbian and a smoothie, we headed towards downtown.

"Well?" she finally asked.

"Well?" I repeated back to her.

"Grace Nightingale I will stop this car dead in the center of I-90 if you don't spill!"

"There's nothing to tell! He was sick. I went to his apartment to make him some soup. We fell asleep watching TV."

"And?" she prodded.

"And what?" I asked, getting annoyed.

"We've been friends for how long?" What are you not telling me?"

I sighed. "When I woke up this morning, he had his arm around me."

She squealed again.

"Really, Chet?" I set my jaw.

"Yes, really! Anyone who knows you two knows this has been a long time in the making. Almost twenty years at this point."

I touched the quartz and rolled my eyes once more. "Don't I keep telling you to lay off the romance novels? And don't get your hopes up. He told me I shouldn't have stayed."

"Seriously? What were his exact words?"

"That I shouldn't have stayed. Do you want to see the text message?" I held up my phone.

"I doubt he meant it like that," she insisted.

"Maybe." I shook my head. "Anyway, like I said, nothing happened. All clothes remained on."

"*This* time." She laughed.

"I swear to God, Chetna. I'm going to dump this hot coffee in your lap."

She cackled harder.

We spent the day looking at wedding bands. She and Kevin had decided that, in lieu of getting a matching set, they would each choose one they felt was the best fit for the other. They were also writing their own vows and Chetna kept pulling a wallet-sized spiral notepad out of her purse to scribble down ideas as I told her which were good and bad. I was certain Kevin was not putting so much effort into searching for her ring, nor looking at such expensive options. I also had no doubt his vows would be copied from the first thing that popped up in an internet search the morning of the wedding.

We stopped by the seamstress's shop. She sneered when she saw me. I remembered that, at my last fitting, she had heard my true feelings about Kevin and I was glad she hadn't told Chetna. Thankfully, we weren't there for me to try on that hideous frock again. Chet emerged from behind a curtain wearing a beautiful emerald and gold saree.

"What do you think?" she asked as she spun in a mirror.

"I've never seen you look so beautiful," I admitted. "But I thought the traditional color for weddings is red."

"Depends on where you're from. I'm American. I get to choose. Green is the color of luck, happiness, and new beginnings. I couldn't think of a better color to wear on my wedding day." She was smiling.

I thought about the chirmi bead on the green ribbon she had given me for my first day at the museum and the horrible seafoam thing she was asking me to wear. Luck, happiness, and new beginnings were all the things I wished for her and she wished for me.

We stopped by the florist next. The wedding had been pushed back again and was still seven months away, but she wanted to finalize the design well ahead of time. She said the last thing she wanted was to fuss over details at the last minute. Being a botanist, she had designed her own bouquets and centerpieces and managed to find one florist in the city that hadn't acted indignant about it.

The more time I spent helping Chet with her wedding, the more I felt I should be grateful I had never married. Her guest list was over two hundred people long. I wasn't even sure I knew two hundred people. I couldn't' imagine having so many eyes on me for an entire day. I thought about what could have been if Xander and I had married. It hurt a little to imagine, but I knew I would have ended up in a dress worth more than half my salary. My wedding party would have included people I barely knew or didn't know at all, like Kara, simply because I only had one person I would want to be a bridesmaid. There probably would have been well over five hundred people and I wouldn't have known any of them. My side of the church may have had two people if I was lucky. Momma would have insisted on a Catholic wedding which probably would have been a point of contention. The more I thought about it, the more I was comforted that I had never become a Bonaventure.

After visiting with the florist, the seamstress, and twenty-three jewelry stores, we had dinner and a glass of wine. Throughout the meal, we went over her notes for her vows. We changed and re-worded a few things. Most of her ideas were based on things she had read in her absurd romance novels and trying to change her thought process was like trying to reprogram a computer.

It was late when I finally arrived home. I fed Hope immediately and then lay on the living room floor. I was only there for a few minutes before I heard my phone buzz in my pants pocket.

I didn't mean to come across so harsh this morning. Aaron's message said.

It's okay I replied.

I wasn't going to let him know just how much thought and over-thought I had put into his earlier message or that I had confided in Chetna. He didn't need to know that he had left me very confused and a little hurt.

I think I was groggy still. Thank you for taking care of me, he said.

The Heart of the Piece

It felt blasphemous to open the reliquary but I could not see an alternative. Unfortunately, we had to know if the tooth was even human and, if it was, the age of the molar. I had made arrangements with a DNA lab in Washington D.C. to attempt to extract any genetic material that may be remaining while hopefully still leaving enough of the tooth intact. I was wholly terrified that they would destroy the artifact, the tooth, or both. I had insisted on at least accompanying the reliquary and handing it over personally and they had agreed.

"Departure is at five p.m. the day after tomorrow." I held a plane ticket towards Shawn.

"For real? I can go?" He stood up from the little desk in the old security guard's office he was sitting behind.

I laughed. "I know you have exams coming up but we are escorting the reliquary and coming right back so hopefully you won't miss too much."

"Wow! Washington D.C.? I'm in!"

That night, I sat in my pajamas with Hope in my lap on our favorite chair. I desperately tried not to fall asleep as I read the proposal Sonya had given me to review. It was only a formality. She couldn't have cared less for my opinion on it but I had learned that I needed to stay on top of her to keep her in check.

Buzz. Buzz. Buzz.

I didn't know why Aaron liked to call so late at night. I answered.

"Hello?"

"What are you doing?" he asked with a 'hello' back.

"Trying to read through this nonsense that Sonya gave me to evaluate. What are you doing?"

"Lying on the living room floor. Staring at the ceiling," he answered.

"Why?"

He sighed with heavy exaggeration. "I'm bored."

"Why don't you watch some TV?" I offered.

"Nah."

"Read a book?"

"Nah," he said again.

"Take up knitting," I retorted.

"Now you're just being absurd."

"I don't know what to tell you, then." I could hear the smile come out in my voice.

"I need to go somewhere," he replied.

"I'd invite you to D.C. but I'm leaving Wednesday night and coming back first thing Friday morning so it won't be much of a trip."

He suddenly sounded interested. "What are you going to D.C. for?"

"Shawn and I are taking the reliquary to a lab to have it analyzed."

I thought I heard his tone change. "You're *both* going?"

"Sure. It'll be a great learning experience for him. That and he's kind of my partner on this project, regardless of how much Sonya likes to remind me that he's just a volunteer assistant. He doesn't need to know that I paid for his plane ticket, though."

His voice had lost the lightheartedness from moments ago. "Why does he work so hard as just a volunteer?"

"He has a real passion for art. And a talent for it. He even told me he's thinking about getting a second degree."

"So you think he works twenty hours a week while going to school just for fun?" he asked cynically.

I didn't appreciate the way he said that. "What do you think it is?"

"I don't know. *You?*"

I felt myself become agitated at the implication. "What are you talking about?"

"Maybe he spends all of his free time hanging around you because he likes *you* not the art."

I rolled my eyes. "Now who's being absurd?"

"Am I?" He sounded accusatory.

"What is your problem?"

He was quiet for a moment. "I don't know. I'm going to bed. I'll talk to you later."

The phone went silent. He didn't even give me a chance to tell him goodbye, good night, or go to Hell. I didn't understand how he could think there were feelings between Shawn and me. We had developed a closeness. That was true. But, it certainly wasn't anything romantic.

Aaron didn't answer my phone call the following day. I decided it was best just to let him sulk and not push him any further. I didn't understand why he was so offended but I had more important things to tend to than his ego.

I was incredibly happy to get out of the office. The flight was just under an hour and a half long which didn't give me much time to relax. It had been quite some time since I had traveled for work and I missed it. Shawn had taken the window seat and sat with his nose pressed against the glass like a child. He insisted he'd flown before, but every time was a new adventure. I admired his enthusiasm. I had left Hope in the caring hands of Chetna and Onoskelis to sit in the well, giddy that Aaron and I had had a disagreement.

I periodically looked up at the overhead compartment above me. There was a treasure up there and I knew this was one of the most important things in my career. I knew I could have shipped it to D.C. but this needed my personal protection.

Our rooms were on the fourth floor on opposite sides of the hallway. I saw Shawn slide his keycard in and open the door. He immediately ran in and took a flying leap onto the bed, leaving his suitcase in the hallway. I laughed. I was genuinely glad I had brought him with me, regardless of how Aaron felt. I let myself in my room and looked around. It wasn't the nicest room I had ever stayed in, but it was far more modern than that first hotel in Chicago all those years ago. There was a small entertainment center with a flat TV and a small desk. There were lamps in every corner except in the kitchenette. A big, king-sized bed was laid out with a fluffy white comforter that was calling my name. I resisted the urge to copy Shawn's maneuver, but I did lay down and hug the pillow after stowing my suitcase and the reliquary in the closet. We ordered room service on the museum's tab and ate on the floor in my room while we worked out a plan for the next day.

The following morning, we met in the lobby for the continental breakfast before heading to the lab. The building was tall and made of white cement and heavily tinted windows. We entered the main lobby and gave our identification for inspection before the receptionist called a technician named Daniel.

Daniel closely resembled a hairless ferret. He was extremely tall and thin and seemed almost enveloped in his lab coat. He had a long, pointed nose, dark, bulbous eyes, and very round ears that sat high on his polished head. He took both of my hands in his to welcome me and introduced himself while subtly glancing at my left hand before releasing them.

"How's a pretty little thing like you single?" The technician's unnerving grin exposed slightly yellowed teeth.

Such pompous arrogance never ceased to amaze me. 'Pretty little thing.' Was that supposed to be a compliment? What kind of woman was actually flattered by words like that?

"I'm married to my work." I struggled to smile as sweetly as I could.

"You shouldn't have to work. You should have a good man to take care of you. You would want for nothing if you were my wife."

He reached out and put his hand on my forearm. I was instantly disgusted. I thought of Xander trying to make me his trophy wife. I thought of letting Onoskelis have this man but the thought of seducing him made my stomach churn. I opened my mouth to let him know if he didn't remove his hand, I would do it for him, but I saw muscular fingers wrap around his wrist and twist it back.

"Ow!" he yelped.

Shawn stepped between us. "Miss Grace is one of the best at what she does. People come from all over for her opinion and I'm sure right now she'd like to give you one so I suggest you behave more professionally."

He clamped down on the technician's wrist harder.

"Sorry!" the weasel-like man yelled.

"That's better." Shawn released his arm. "Please go and see what's keeping your boss."

The technician shot me a dirty look before he headed down the hall. I stepped next to Shawn. He looked down at me.

"Guys like that should have their nuts cut off. They give us all a bad rep," he snorted.

"I know better from you." I smiled and nudged him with my elbow.

The doctor in charge of the project was far more cordial. He escorted us back to his office and I set the reliquary on his desk. He took a pair of glasses out of his pocket and examined the artifact carefully.

"Hmm. This one will be tricky. I think the best course of action will be to remove a section of the glass and then have a restoration artist seal it back," he finally said. "In this condition,

I'm afraid if we try to drill a pinhole through, it might shatter the glass."

"So, you don't think it's impossible?"

"Oh, my dear, nothing is impossible. That tooth is the heart of that piece and, like any heart, it has to be handled delicately. We do work like this for the Smithsonian and NGA regularly. I promise your piece is in good hands."

I felt much lighter as the weight of concern was lifted. We toured the facility and I felt most of my apprehension wash away with every step. I thanked the doctor profusely for putting my mind at ease. He promised to keep in touch throughout the process and let me know when I could come and retrieve the art.

That evening we had a superb dinner at Le Diplomate. Shawn had too much French wine and admitted that, as much as he loved Kiara, he didn't see a future with her.

"What do you mean?"

"I just think we want different things. I want my career. She wants to start a family before she's thirty. I get that. And it's not that I don't ever want kids but that ain't a goal right now."

"I understand that. Have you talked to her about it?"

"Sort of." He poked at his empty plate with his fork. "We've been spending less time together so I think we both know what's coming."

I thought about what Aaron had said. "You don't have someone else in mind, do you?"

He drunkenly laughed. "Hell no! I just need to focus on getting my own life together."

I smiled inside. I knew Aaron was fretting over nothing. But, then, why was he upset? We weren't a couple, after all.

After dinner, I saw Shawn to his room safely before going across the hall to mine. I'd barely stepped out of my shoes when I heard it.

Buzz. Buzz. Buzz.

It was Aaron. We hadn't spoken in two days. I answered.

"Hello?" I flopped back on the bed and put my feet on the pillows.

"How's D.C.?"

"It's been busy. We got in late yesterday, spent the whole day at the lab today, and our flight back leaves at six-twenty tomorrow morning."

"Damn," he said. "Haven't been able to have any fun?"

"We had a nice dinner tonight. Can't say 'no' to French food. Goat cheese is amazing."

"Where's Shawn at?" His tone changed again.

I felt a twinge of annoyance. "Probably in bed."

"Where are you?" he asked.

"In bed."

He sounded surprised when he asked, "are you in separate rooms?"

"Of course."

"Oh," he said humbly.

I stared at the ceiling and tried not to burn a hole in it. "Why would we be in the same room?"

"I- I don't know. And when you said you bought his plane ticket but you didn't say anything about getting him his own room... I just thought-"

"Thought what?" I snapped. "Shawn and I are not romantically involved. Period. What is your problem anyway?"

"I don't know. I just don't like the thought of the two of you together."

"Well, get over it. Okay?"

He was silent for a minute. "Okay. I'm sorry."

"You should be. And you need to think about how you're going to react the next time I do start dating someone. I'm not staying single forever. Understood?" I was still fairly irate, despite his apology.

"I hear you."

"Good." I settled down. "Now tell me what I've missed over the last two days."

The Family I Built

Around six weeks after the trip to Washington DC. Chetna and I were having our customary luncheon together near campus. It was summer break, so there were few students out but this was the time of year the museums were busiest. Unescorted teenagers ran rampant and talked loudly without appreciating any of the art. Exhausted parents tried to keep their children entertained through the summer and tourists who came for the lake wandered freely. But, outside, it was peaceful and refreshing.

Buzz. Buzz.

I answered my phone. "Hello?

"Missus Nightingale?"

I rolled my eyes at 'missus.' "Yes."

"Hi. This is Dr. Watt's assistant with Handschuh Laboratories."

I sat up. "Yes."

"Dr. Watt asked me to call and inform you that we were able to retrieve enough sample without altering the tooth too much. We'll have some answers for you, hopefully, within the next few weeks."

"That's wonderful news!" I was almost yelling. "Thank you for the call!"

"You're welcome, Missus Nightingale. Have a good weekend."

I almost leaped out of my seat. "Yes! Yes! Yes!"

Chetna stared at me wide-eyed and smiled. "What? What? What?"

"They got the sample! They'll be able to provide me with some genetic information on that tooth!"

She looked thoughtful. "From the reliquary that jerk bishop refused to help you with?"

"Yes!" I screamed again.

She paused and looked confused. "But isn't DNA only helpful if you have something to compare it to?"

"Not exactly." I sat back down. "This will tell me if it's male or female or even if the molar is human at all! Plus I asked them to shave off a little extra to send to a lab in Miami for carbon dating."

"Explain why you are doing all of this as if you were explaining it to a botanist." She said. "I know what carbon dating is but I'm a little confused."

"If it's human, it'll tell me if the sample is from a man or a woman and how old it is. That won't tell me exactly *whose* tooth it is, but it'll at least tell me if the claims made on it fit the timeline."

"Oh! I get it! Well this is great news! We'll celebrate with dinner at your house! I'll call Kevin. You call Shawn and Aaron. See you at seven!" With that, she took off towards the gardens.

Dinner at my house? I'd never hosted dinner for more than just Chetna before. Even that was usually takeout and movies. My stomach lurched. Onoskelis. I couldn't let Aaron in my house for too long. I couldn't be sure of what she would do. I didn't think she could or would be so careless as to hurt him while other people were there, but I refused to underestimate her rage. A food truck pulled up in front of one of the office buildings as I walked past. Suddenly, the solution was obvious.

At seven o'clock, everyone piled into my backyard. Shawn brought a charcoal grill. Chetna brought fresh vegetables from her garden. Aaron brought steak and veggie burgers. I provided the wine and beer. Kevin had stayed home because he said he was too tired to come out, so it was just the four of us. Chetna and I sat in my comfortable porch chairs with our wine while Aaron tended the grill. I insisted that I knew how properly cook meat but *he* insisted that I would just turn a perfectly good steak into shoe leather and he would have none of it. I resented the remark, but I didn't argue. Shawn did card tricks and talked about his classes. He and Chet bonded over a shared love of organic chemistry. I understood about a quarter of what they said.

As we sat and enjoyed ourselves, I could feel Onoskelis seething inside the house like a rabid animal in a cage. She wanted Aaron dead but she couldn't leave the house. If he had to use the bathroom, I would make sure I stayed outside. I didn't think she could hurt him without me. I wasn't certain, but it was the only plan I had.

We ate a wonderful dinner and had far too much to drink. Shawn's card tricks turned into a friendly game of bullshit. I looked around at those wonderful people and realized that this was it. This is what I had always wanted. I finally had a normal life. I had created this family of wonderful human beings and despite the monster inside my house, my life was pretty close to perfect.

When the last drink had been drunk and the embers in the charcoal had died, everyone said their goodbyes and headed home. I shut the door behind Shawn and turned. Of course, she was standing there. Her arms were crossed. Her normally black eyes seemed to have a hint of red.

"You mock me!" Onoskelis screamed!

"I did no such thing." I protested. "I wanted to have dinner with my friends. You gave me no choice but to have it outside."

"You tease a cat by putting a mouse too close," she hissed.

"Why won't you just go away?" I clenched my fists and attempted to maintain self-control.

"Not until I have had what I want."

"Maybe I'll get a priest to bless this house and cast you out," I suggested.

She laughed maniacally. "You truly believe that works? We've discussed this before."

"Fine. I'll move. I'll buy a house without a cistern. Where will you live then?"

"You think you can avoid him every full moon for the rest of your life?"

"I can try!" I declared.

I stormed down the hall and slammed my bedroom door. I was not going to let her tear my new family apart.

Beilin's Takeout

I arrived at Aaron's apartment at six-thirty. We had made plans to play cards and split some takeout to round off the week. I'd stopped by Beilin's for the best Chinese-Korean fusion takeout in the state. When he answered the door, he looked drained, soulful, and old. The worry lines on his forehead stood out prominently over his furrowed brow. The long sleeves of his blue button-down shirt were rolled up over his elbows. He stood wringing his hands and rubbing his wrists.

"Rough day?" I began setting the food out on the counter.

"I have thirty-seven term papers to grade. I've been at it for two days now. I'm worn out. Half of these kids copied verbatim off of the internet and virtually none of them can form a properly structured sentence. How do they think they're going to write research papers after they graduate if they can't do it now?" He rubbed his face. "I'm trying to push through them but their stupidity and laziness is just exhausting."

I had never heard him speak so ill of his students before. This was bad.

"Well, sit down and eat. Momma always said 'good food is good for the soul,'" I recited as I pulled out a stool for him to sit on.

"Your mom couldn't cook, if I remember correctly," he said flatly.

"No, but Beilin can so get over here before it gets cold," I snapped back.

"I'm sorry. I'm just a bit crabby."

He took a seat and started portioning out chicken and rice on our plates. I carried the majority of the conversation. He was so frazzled and spent, he was even eating slowly. I don't think he could have formed a clear thought to add to the conversation anyway. When we'd emptied most of the Styrofoam containers, we retired to the couch instead of playing gin.

"I'm sorry," he yawned, "I've just got to… I'm just going to stretch…"

He extended the full length of the couch with his head in my lap. I gently ran my fingers through his hair and he was snoring within a few minutes. As he rested, I looked out the window at the starless night sky. The light pollution here was just enough to be an annoyance. My house was outside the city and there were quite a few stars to be seen from my yard, but nothing like Illinois. On a clear night, out in our meadow surrounded by woods, it was impossible to count all the lights in the purple heavens.

I thought about the meadow and the last time we had been there. It was when we had first spoken to Onoskelis through the spirit board. I didn't blame Aaron for thinking it was me. He shifted a little and I looked down at him. How could she want him dead?

Kids and Exes

Aaron and I were eating ice cream cones as we strolled past the park on the way to the edge of the lake. It was a little chilly out for ice cream but the sun was bright and the September sky was clear. Older children ran through the grass and tagged each other while younger ones played on the slides and tunnels. Moms and nannies rocked infants in the shade while vigilantly watching the games.

"You don't want any of those?" Aaron directed his cone towards the kids.

"I don't know. It's not really something I've ever given much thought to."

"Yeah. I never really saw you as a mom." He licked at the mint chocolate chip that was dribbling down his arm.

I stopped short. "You didn't?"

He smiled. "Nope. Too independent. Your mom may have sheltered you and thought you'd settle down, but I've always known there was more to you."

We walked a little further. "I didn't exactly have the best role model on how to be a mother anyway. Momma loves me but…"

He laughed. "There really wasn't much about growing up that was normal for you."

He didn't know the half of it.

"There's a father figure to consider too. My high school sweetheart and I got accepted to different schools on opposite sides of the country," I strategically neglected to mention his demise, "and I didn't really date very good men after that. I talked about kids with one guy I dated once but we didn't work out."

He nodded slightly. "So why are you single now?"

Because the homicidal succubus that lives in my plumbing wants to kill all of my boyfriends, I thought.

No. That wasn't it.

"I don't know. It just doesn't feel like a priority right now. Why aren't you seeing anyone?'

"Well, Amber, *my* high school sweetheart cheated on me. So did Kristen and Rachel. And Amanda just wasn't really in it. Then I met Hannah in college. She was the real deal. We were set to get married and everything but she was killed in a car crash before the wedding. I started traveling a lot more and never looked back. Been a long time since I've had feelings like that. I don't think I could live through anymore heartache."

He stuffed the rest of his ice cream cone in his mouth and put his arm around me. I had the feeling that was a memory he didn't want to surface and I respected that. He had always been sensitive when we were kids; like when we lost the fawn in the field. Even as an adult his heart seemed fragile.

Not a Weed

It was late on a cold November night. Hope and I had already settled in for the evening. We were lounging in the recliner with a cup of chamomile while I read a new fantasy novel I had picked up from the library. I had desperately wanted to escape into a completely different world after such a long day.

The knock was hard and rapid. I jumped and Hope leaped from my lap and tore down the hallway.

I opened the door a crack and peeked out.

"Chet?"

Chetna stood on my porch. Her eyes were red and puffy. Her normally perfectly painted face was streaked with tears. She may have even been holding her breath to keep from sobbing. I had never seen her in such a state.

"Jesus! What's wrong?" I asked.

I swung the door wide open for her to enter. I didn't even think to question why she hadn't just used her key to let herself in. Her lower lip quivered a little as she stepped in the door.

"It's over." She broke into tears.

"Here." I ran to the bathroom and grabbed a box of tissues. I shoved them into her hands as she sat on the couch. "Let me make you a cup of tea."

I hurried into the kitchen and threw together a quick cup of chamomile with the remaining water in the kettle. When I returned, Hope was cuddled up against my friend's thigh, trying to comfort her.

"Thank you." She said through choked-down tears as I handed her the mug of tea.

I sat down in my recliner so I could face her. "What's over?"

Her jaw started to shake again. "Kevin and I are done."

I sat upright. "What do you mean? You guys have fought plenty of times and you've always pulled through."

She took a careful sip of her tea. "Not this time."

"What happened?"

She had my full attention. I cannot stress enough, I never thought Kevin was good enough for her but I never expected her to realize that.

"Well, you know he still hasn't settled on a career path." That was a nice way of calling him a deadbeat. "And... I don't know... I guess I just realized that I'm thirty-one, he's thirty, and only one of us is actually an adult. He doesn't cook or clean or help around the house. He still thinks he can just spend all of his free time with his idiot friends. And today..." she started to tear up again but choked it back with a big gulp of tea. "Grace, I came home early and found him in his gaming chair in his underwear. He had left for – what he told me- was a ten-hour shift at seven this morning. When I asked what he was doing home, he confessed that he hasn't had a job in a month! He's been borrowing money from his family to put in our joint account so it would look like he was working!"

"Seriously?" I shrieked. "What was his plan?"

"I don't think he ever actually had one; for a job or for us." More tears started to roll down her cheeks.

"What happened after that?"

"I told him I couldn't keep living like this." She gulped more tea. "He tried to give me excuses but I said I wanted him gone by the time I got back. The condo is in my name only because his credit is so bad and even though all of the stuff in it is mine, I don't care if he takes all of the furniture and every dish towel. I can buy new things. I can't replace the time I wasted with him."

"Wow." That was all I could mutter.

She looked at me, pleading. "How could I have been so stupid? You tried to warn me. Ishwar tried to warn me."

"Love is blind."

"No." She shook her head slightly. "He was the exact opposite of everything my parents wanted me to marry. It wasn't all love. It was a lot of defiance."

"What are you going to do now?" I asked.

"I'm going to sleep here tonight and tomorrow, if he's still there, I'm going to call the police and have him removed."

I was proud of Chetna for standing up for herself. I was even happier that she had finally seen Kevin for the waste of a human he was. As I sat and watched tears roll down my best friend's face, I suddenly felt more than negative indifference towards Kevin. This was hatred. Maybe Onoskelis could help put Kevin in his place? I thought about her hiding in the well below and reading my thoughts. No. This was not a job for her. I watched my best friend cry into her tissues and sip her tea. I had told Shawn she was going to get hurt. I was both sad and glad I had been right.

The next morning we sat on my back porch with our coffee.

"Do you think someone will find me unlovable now? I am old," she said.

I laughed. "We aren't old, Chet. Not until we're dead."

She sighed. "I feel like I will be alone forever now."

"You have been alone for eight hours. I've been alone for... a lot longer. You are like a flower that blooms from a crack in the cement."

"Most people call that a weed," she pointed out.

"And those are people who can't see it for what it is. Can't see you for who you are. They don't see the beauty that has beaten the odds. This thing that has thrived where no one thought it ever would. You didn't just give up and keep working for your parents in California and marry a nice Indian man so you could make babies. You became a *doctor*, bought a home, and started a life of your own almost on the other side of the country."

She smiled. "You think so?"

"I know so. You are something special; not just a weed."

Not Again

Aaron and I had met to go bowling two nights after Chetna had stayed at my house. We were two games in and I had yet to score above a forty-seven. Aaron had had a few beers after a stressful day so I had agreed to drive. The bowling alley was crowded. There was a birthday party taking up six lanes and they were being exceptionally loud.

After throwing yet another gutter ball, I sat on the seat and stared at the screen. I was holding strong at thirty-two against his one-o-five. Aaron returned from the bar with a bottle of beer. He sat next to me.

"You're doing much better this game." He appointed at the screen.

"I'm not sure if you're being supportive or snarky." I narrowed my eyes at him.

"Maybe a little of both." He smiled and took a gulp of his beer. "Can I ask you something?"

"Of course." I turned to face him.

"You don't have to answer if I'm not supposed to know or if it's too personal. I won't push."

I looked at him in complete bewilderment. "Spit it out."

"Why did Kevin ask if he could sleep on my couch?"

I was a little shocked. "Is that where he is?"

A rush of relief came over me. I don't know what I expected him to ask me about, but Kevin wasn't even close to being on the list of possibilities.

"No. I told him 'no.' He still rubs me the wrong way."

I shrugged. "Chetna finally sent him packing. At least, she would have if he owned anything other than clothes."

"Really? Wow." His handsome maple eyes were watery from the alcohol, but they showed genuine surprise. "How long do you think it'll be before they make up?"

"Not this time." I shook my head. "She's had it. He can't keep a job. He refuses to grow up. She's tired of being more of his mother than his wife. He also told her a really big lie. The unforgivable kind. She's done."

"I can't imagine. How long have they been together?" He kept his eyes locked on mine.

"Ten years."

"Ten years." He repeated. "How do you just throw something like that away?"

I felt defensive. "Do you mean him or her?"

"Him. I don't see how you have the love of a great woman like that and don't do everything in your power to hold on to her."

I smiled. "She'll find someone who treats her right. So will you."

"I don't know about that. I told you before; I don't know if I could survive another heartbreak. Not again."

Home Sweet Home

In February of 2015, I received the worst news imaginable. Uncle James wasn't well at all. All of the years of bouncing between alcoholism and sobriety had taken their toll. Momma had called to say he didn't have very much time left. He was 'yellow as lemonade' and had asked to go home from the hospital to die in peace. When I hung up the phone, I sat on the edge of the bed and processed what she had said. My Uncle James was dying. The best father figure I could have ever asked for. I missed so many years with him just because I didn't want to go home and face my old life. He had taught me so much about life and the world. He had given me the courage to explore my humanity outside of the church. The only thing he asked in return was to give me away on my wedding day. I had failed him at that too. At the very least, I needed to go home and say goodbye.

I called Sonya and told her I was going home and I wasn't sure when I'd be back. She told me I had better return before my paid vacation was used up. I rolled my eyes and hung up in the middle of her lecture. I text messaged Chet and explained what was going on. She promised to take good care of Hope while I was away. I was halfway through packing when I heard my phone ring. It was Aaron.

"What are you doing for dinner?" His light-hearted tone felt out of place with my mood.

"Probably fast-food chicken nuggets while driving," I said as I stuffed a wad of socks in my suitcase.

"Huh? Where are you going?"

I felt my face get hot and my eyes started to sting. "Momma doesn't think Uncle James is going to make it too much longer. I'm going home to say goodbye."

He paused. "You okay?" he asked cautiously.

"No, but I will be." My voice cracked. "I've got to pack some more and get things set out for Hope. I'll call you from the road."

"Okay."

I clicked off the phone and threw it on the bed. After my smallest suitcase was stuffed with the clothing my mother was least likely to complain about, I wrote out specific instructions for Hope's food and medication. Chetna would follow it to the letter, I was sure. She loved that cat too. When I was satisfied that there was nothing left to prepare, I hugged Hope tight enough that she meowed in indignation.

"Hush. Mommy's going to miss you." I kissed the top of her head.

I opened the front door just in time to see the 4Runner park on the street. He hopped out of the driver's side and pulled a duffle bag out of the back seat.

"Don't think I'm going to let you go through this alone. Don't even argue," he said as he opened the back door of my car and tossed the duffle bag in before climbing into the passenger seat.

It felt strange to be going home. Not ominous or foreboding this time, but certainly not good. It was a long drive and, while I could have easily taken a plane, I was happy to have the extra time to think instead. My little Audi may not have been meant for distance driving but she got the job done. I hadn't been home in what I was pretty sure was close to a decade. Taking a plane would have meant I'd have been trapped there until the next flight back. With a car, I had the freedom to leave that my leisure in case anyone remembered me or if things became difficult with my mother.

February in the Midwest is a world of white. From Ohio, through Indiana, and into Illinois, the white-capped hills and frosted trees gave way to sprawling flatlands of winter white. The sky was clear and light from the moon, missing just a sliver, reflected off the ground and gave the world an eerie halo glow.

Aaron was snoozing peacefully in the seat next to me. I would have gladly made the almost ten-hour drive by myself. I don't know what made him decide to come with me but I was glad he had insisted. Returning home was something I was prepared to face alone, but the relief at not having to was immeasurable.

As we drove past the familiar shadows of the windmills in the fields of Illinois, that feeling of fear and excitement grew in my belly. I didn't know how many of my classmates had made it out. Ours was the kind of town that most people spent their entire lives in and those of us who managed to escape usually wound up returning at some point due to divorce or unemployment. Not me. No. I can honestly say that there was virtually nothing on this Earth that would make me move back home. I would be homeless in the tunnels of New York before I came back permanently.

As we drove closer, I realized just how much things had changed. Roads that had been virtually made of dirt in my childhood were well paved and even four lanes wide in some areas. Four-way stops now had traffic lights. There were strip malls everywhere with chain stores instead of local-owned businesses. It certainly didn't feel like home. It wasn't until I turned off of Fillmore Avenue and headed towards a familiar cluster of houses that the realization of where I was finally hit me.

The paint was peeling on the little yellow farmhouse. The flower bed was unkempt and a few of the shutters were missing, but it was the same house that I'd always known. As we pulled into the driveway, a couple of chickens ran to get out of the way of my car. At least some things don't change. Home sweet home. I gently shook Aaron's arm and woke him up.

He yawned and rubbed his face. "Are we there?"

I took a deep breath. "Yes."

"Are you ready to do this?"

"No. But I don't think I ever will be either."

"Okay then." He squeezed my hand and we got out of the car.

As we walked up the cement steps towards the door, it swung open and Jacob was standing on the other side. He looked old even though he wasn't. His hair was grey and thinning. His eyes had become far more watery. He looked like life had been brutal towards him and my heart hurt a little. We may have hated each other, but I still loved him. He almost seemed a shadow of the man who had shown up unexpectedly at my little apartment so many years ago.

"I'm surprised you showed up." His breath smelled heavily of beer and he crossed his arms in front of his chest.

"Don't do this. I love Uncle James."

"Whatever." He stepped to the side so we could come in. "Who are you?" He looked at Aaron.

"Aaron. Aaron Akakios."

Jacob's eyes got wide. "The fat kid from across the street?"

"Jacob. Really?" I scolded.

Aaron laughed. "I've changed a little."

Jacob looked at me and then back at Aaron.

"I'll tell you about it later. I promise. Where's Uncle James?" I set my purse on the floor next to the door.

"In your old room. He insisted."

I walked down the hall to the third door on the right. I put my hand on the knob and paused. Aaron put his hand on my shoulder and looked me in the eye.

"I'll wait here." He tried to reassure me.

I didn't know what I was going to see on the other side of that door and the possibilities terrified me. It was sadly of little comfort to know he was there for me. I turned the knob and walked in. It was as if nothing had changed. The ugly green carpet was still the same. My old dresser still sat in the corner. The curtains were the same. The floral border around the top of the room had faded with time but the familiar pattern was still the same. My eyes eventually fell on the bed. It was a small twin bed but my once plump uncle had lost so much weight that he fit on it perfectly. I knelt at the edge of the bed and took his frail hand in mine. His bony fingers wrapped around my hand and I looked at his sunken face for the first time. He was barely recognizable. His skin was yellow and ashy but the rims around his eyes were grey. His blue eyes held almost no light anymore.

"Grace. My beautiful girl. I knew you would come." His voice was weak and dry.

I tried hard not to cry. "How are you, Uncle James?"

He took a deep breath. "It hurts. Everything hurts. But it does me good to see you."

"I'm very glad I came."

His eyes moved over to the doorway. "I see he found you."

I looked over my shoulder and Aaron was standing in the doorway with a saddened look on his face. I didn't even realize that Uncle James had recognized him without trouble.

"He did."

My uncle grimaced a little. "Loving someone is easy. We are born to love. We have families and friends and even dogs to love and who love us. But being in love… that's something entirely different. Being in love is the most wonderful feeling in the world and you have to fight for it, but it comes with a price. Families and friends drift away and dogs die. But when someone you're in love with leaves, it'll kill you."

"I'm not sure what you mean Uncle James."

"You will." He winced with pain. "I hate to do this my darling, but I need to rest."

"Don't apologize." I kissed his hand. "I'm so happy I got to see you again."

I left the room and tried hard not to cry. Aaron wrapped his arms around my head and I wrapped mine around his waist and he held me tight. We went back into the kitchen. Jacob was sitting at the table with a bottle of beer.

"Does Momma know you have that?"

He huffed. "I'm an adult. "

"It's still her house."

He shrugged. "She won't kick me out."

I sat at the table across from him. "Where is she anyway?"

"She said she had to run to the store and stock up on some groceries for you."

"It's eleven o'clock at night."

"She's always been crazy." Jacob took a sip of beer. "You know that."

As if on cue, the kitchen door swung open and my mother walked in carrying two canvas bags of groceries.

"Grace! You made it!" She dropped the bags and embraced me.

"Yes, Momma."

At least she still looked the same. Her hair was longer and a little more grey and she looked like she may have shrunk about an inch, but she was still familiar.

She picked up the bags and set them on the counter. "I made sure I got plenty for you to eat. Did you pay your respects to James?"

"Yes, ma'am."

She glanced over at Jacob. "You know I don't like that stuff in my house."

He looked at the beer and looked at her. "Yeah. Yeah. I'm almost done with it."

He took a massive swig and finished up the bottle. He walked down to the mudroom and threw the glass bottle in the recycling container before he headed to bed. I was surprised he had enough respect for her to do that.

My mother turned to Aaron. She narrowed her eyes at him before her face lit up with recognition.

"I remember you," she said.

"Hello again, mis Nightingale," Aaron replied.

She squinted her eyes. "You two didn't go and elope or something behind God's back, did you?"

"Momma! No," I said exasperatedly and shook my head.

"Good. Now help me make some dinner. You had a long drive."

"Momma, it's almost midnight. Why don't we put the groceries away and head to bed and I'll help you make breakfast in the morning."

Surprisingly, she didn't argue. We put the groceries away and she made up a place for Aaron to sleep on the couch. Jacob was passed out back in his old bedroom. I had to share a bed with her. As I lay in that musty old house, I said the first prayer I had truly meant in a long time. I asked for God to take away Uncle James's pain. He passed in his sleep that night.

The loss of a loved one is always difficult and funerals are always sad. Uncle James' funeral, however, was truly dismal. Jacob, my mother, and I were the last of the family. We had invited everyone in the church, of course, and tried to reach out to Uncle James's old friends and Catherine's family, but he had alienated too many people with his drinking. Aaron held my hand as the four of us sat in an empty church and Father Anthony (Father Harold's replacement) went through the motions of a formal Catholic funeral. My mother stood up and said a few words. She tried to be kind but insinuated that his death and pain were punishment for turning his back on the church. I had expected nothing less from her. After the funeral, we went back to the house for supper. We ate in silence before Momma excused herself to go to bed early. I think she was more upset about the loss of her only brother than she wanted to let on.

Jacob looked at me across the table. "When you heading out?"

"First thing in the morning," I said.

He stood up and pushed in his chair. "So, see you at Aunt Janice's funeral?"

"Will you actually come?" I raised an eyebrow at him.

He shrugged his shoulders. "See you in another decade or so cousin," he called as he retreated back towards his bedroom.

I wish I could say I was sad to leave that place the next morning but I truthfully had hoped I would never have to return.

Coffee and Cardinals

It was April; two months after Uncle James's passing. It was difficult, but I moved on with my life and went back to my routine. That Friday, I was excited to be meeting with Aaron. I was going to surprise him at his office for dinner. I had escaped work behind Sonya's back and slipped away to the university. As I approached his classroom, I could see him erasing the whiteboard. He was laughing and it made me smile. There was an older, balding gentleman in a white polo shirt and jeans in the classroom with him. I assumed he was one of the other instructors.

"Come on, Aaron. What do you mean you're single?" the older gentleman asked.

"I mean I just haven't found the right one yet," Aaron replied, sounding uncomfortable.

"What about that cute little redhead? The little leprechaun girl?"

Aaron laughed. "She's short but don't you dare let her hear you call her a leprechaun. She's got a temper to match that hair. Grace is a wonderful woman and I've known her since we were children."

"Yeah, but you aren't children anymore."

"No. And I love her." I smiled when I heard him say that. "But I don't know what kind of love it is and I'm not going to risk doing anything stupid to ruin it now that she's back in my life. Not to mention, I don't know that I could really see us having a future together more than what we've got."

My heart sank into my stomach and I suddenly felt sick. I hadn't even considered a romantic relationship with Aaron until I heard him say that it wouldn't happen. In all of the evenings that we had spent together and all the conversations we had shared, I hadn't even noticed that my affection for him had grown into what it had. I loved him more than I had when we were children and in a different way than I had ever realized. In that moment, that plain and simple 'no' was one of the most painful things I've ever heard. He just couldn't see it going anywhere. I slipped away without him knowing that I had even been there and went home.

When I came in the door, Hope was nowhere to be seen. I looked in the closet and under the bed but didn't find her. It was unusual for her to not meet me at the door for dinner. I walked back into the living room. Onoskelis was reclining on the sofa. I rolled my eyes at her.

"Not now," I said through nearly gritted teeth.

"You see," she spat. "He does not love you."

"Yes, he does love me." A pang struck me again. "He just doesn't love me romantically."

"He does not know what love is." She stood. "He hurts you! He hurts you again and again! He should die!"

"Go back to the well and leave me alone." I turned my back to her.

"He will only keep hurting you."

"Go away!" I slammed my bedroom door and lay down on the bed to cry.

Hope crawled out from her hiding place and jumped up to join me. She curled up next to my face and purred gently as I wept into her fur.

I ignored Aaron's phone calls and text messages for the next few days. I knew he didn't understand why, but I didn't care. I needed to process and think about what had happened. I had suddenly found myself in a position where I didn't know how I felt about him and that wasn't fair to either of us.

It was an unusually warm, spring, Saturday morning following the incident at the university. I could hear the thunder from the oncoming storm in the distance. Over the horizon, the darker clouds made ominous threats. It was raining but bright out still in my backyard. I sat back in my comfortable porch chair with my morning coffee. It was incredibly peaceful to listen to the raindrops on the porch roof and the wildlife in the oaks and ash that outlined my property. I watched a rabbit in the back tree line near the fence for a few moments before my eyes were drawn to a group of birds.

A robin was happily plucking earthworms from the soggy soil. Nearby, a female cardinal was picking at something in the grass. A male flew down to her and started a little dance. She turned her beak up and looked away from him. He danced into her line of sight. She didn't waver. He eventually gave up and flew away. She went returned to pecking at the grass.

I realized that I envied her. She was so bland and boring. She didn't have all of the flash and pomp of the male's brilliant red. She was a drab, boring brown with a black mask. She was, dare I say, ugly. Yet she had the confidence to be discriminatory about her mate. She had the power to turn down a perfectly good-looking male because better genetic material MIGHT come along. She didn't have to jump at the opportunity for a potential mate or be a strumpet in exchange for multiple fleeting companionships. It was okay that she was ugly. Female birds don't have to paint themselves to appear attractive to the opposite sex or wear provocative clothing. They are allowed to be ugly.

I was only days away from my thirty-first birthday. I had become a stereotype; a single thirty-something alone with her cat and no prospects for love in sight. Every male that had ever wanted me had wanted me for some reason or another that wasn't really me. Chetna had taught me how to turn my canvas of a face into a work of art that attracted men. Brett had wanted my body. Christian had never wanted anything serious. Toby, maybe, had wanted me for me, but that was so long ago and even he had left me for something better. And Xander... Well, that was youthful stupidity, not love. It turned out that the only man I thought I might have been happy with, was someone I hadn't even considered and *he* didn't want *me*.

I took a long draw from my hot coffee. I was over thirty. There I sat in my pajamas with no makeup on. Every blemish was exposed and there was stubble on my legs. I would never find a suitable mate like that. Sure, I could find someone to *breed* with. But I wanted more than that. So, on Monday morning, I would shave my legs, paint my face, put on my high heels, and dress to impress because I am not a cardinal.

Those Who Help Themselves

Buzz. Buzz. Buzz.

It was late that Sunday morning. I had fed Hope hours earlier and returned to the sanctuary of my bed to continue to wallow in self-pity. I had only just realized my love for a man who did not love me and while I accepted that truth, the pain was still there. I hadn't left my house in more than a day.

Buzz. Buzz. Buzz.

It was late Sunday morning. There was only one person who would be calling. I pulled myself together enough to answer the phone.

"Good morning, Momma."

"Oh, Grace, you sound terrible. Are you all right?"

Thanks, I thought.

"I'm just not feeling very well," I replied.

"Well, I hope you aren't still in bed at this hour!" It was as if she had cameras in my house. "Make yourself some tea and go to church. Pray for good health. Then come home and have a nice bowl of soup. God helps those who help themselves and you aren't helping yourself by staying in bed all day."

I rolled onto my back and covered my eyes with my hand.

"Momma, all that means is to work hard and do it yourself but give God the credit."

"Grace Gertrude!" She yelled so loudly I had to pull the phone away from my ear.

I rolled my eyes.

"I'm sorry. I'm tired and I don't feel well," I repeated.

"That's no excuse." She snapped. "Listen to what Father Anthony said today. Hopefully, it'll give you the kick you need."

At that point, I stopped listening. Momma was right about one thing. Lying in bed wasn't going to fix the way I felt. Aaron didn't even know I had heard him. How could I be upset with him over something I wasn't even meant to hear? Was I even upset with him? Or was I mad at myself? Perhaps this feeling was chagrin. Maybe I was mad that I had fallen for him and hadn't realized it. Perhaps I was mad that I hadn't marched into his classroom and confronted him about it. No. I wasn't mad at all. It wasn't anger eating away inside me; it was heartache. I'd only felt it once before. And, just as when Xander and I had ended, I felt completely alone. Unlike Xander, however, Aaron wasn't leaving my life nor had our relationship changed. The only difference was the realization that I had feelings for him and that was something I could easily take to my grave.

God helps those who help themselves. I needed to do something for myself. I needed to pull myself out of this dark place and find a light. What was the one thing that always made me happy?

Momma finished her sermon. I told her I had to go if I was going to make it to noon mass. She promised to pray for me that night before hanging up the phone. In reality, I had no intention of going to church. I pulled myself out of bed and to my closet. Shoved in the back under a mound of forgotten clothes was a very old pair of sneakers. They had once been white with a blue tongue and blue rubber on the bottom. The once pristine white was now dingy and cracked. Chunks were missing from the bottom and the laces probably needed to be replaced. They had at one time been my favorite pair to wear to get lost in the woods when I was a teenager. It had been more than a decade since I'd worn them. I slipped them onto my feet. The lumps had changed a little from all the years of wearing heels, but they still fit. I pulled them back off my feet and looked at Hope on the bed.

I touched my necklace. "Should I do it?"

She meowed.

I put on a pair of old jeans and a t-shirt. I piled my hair into a tight knot on my head and put the sneakers back on. I could feel my despair lifting over the forty-minute drive to Cuyahoga. I hadn't gone into the woods since I was a teenager. Just remembering my boulder by the creek brought my spirit higher.

I spent four hours lost in those hills listening to the wind in the trees whispering secrets to my soul. Squirrels played tag in the branches above me while frogs soaked and swam in the waters in the valley. I sat in the dirt under a tree about fifty meters from the path. It was so peaceful. I just listened and let all of my emotions trickle into the earth. I don't know how long I sat there letting myself be absorbed before I finally felt well enough to make my way back down and to my car. I felt completely rejuvenated regardless of how much my thighs and calves were burning.

As I left the forest, my phone began to buzz in the seat next to me. I glanced at it. I had one missed call and two new text messages come through when my phone had found a signal. The phone call was from Aaron. We hadn't spoken in two days. The first text message was from Chetna asking if I wanted to get dinner that night. That sounded like a wonderful idea.

The second message was from Aaron. *I tried to call. Haven't heard from you in a bit. Just wanted to make sure you're all right.*

I was better than all right. I felt better than I had in a long time. I knew not all of the stress I had left in those hills was from Aaron, but I hadn't realized just how much I had been carrying around until that moment.

I replied to Aaron first. *I'm fine. Haven't been feeling myself lately and went hiking today. No cell reception.*

Oh, he replied. *Where'd you go?*

Cuyahoga, I answered.

Have fun?

Yup.

Want to tell me about it over dinner?

Normally I would have leaped at the opportunity to have dinner with him but not that day.

I replied, *No thanks. Having dinner with Chet.*

Oh, he responded. *Maybe another night.*

I messaged Chetna back. *The Cantina at six? I need a shower.*

When I arrived home, Onoskelis was standing in the living room waiting for me. She opened her mouth to speak.

"Nope." I held up my index finger at her. "Not today. I'm not doing it today."

I proceeded to the shower and left her to vanish in anger. I had just helped myself and I was not going to let her ruin that.

That night at dinner, Chetna asked me what would possess me to go wandering around in the woods alone.

I sipped my raspberry daiquiri. "I just needed some perspective."

"On?" she pressed.

"I don't know. Where I am in life. Where I am going. A little of everything," I said nonchalantly.

"That's awfully heavy thinking for a Sunday afternoon," she said.

"A little," I said as I stared at my drink.

She blew a straw wrapper at me. I looked up at her.

"There's something you aren't telling me, isn't there?" she asked.

"Yup," I answered.

"We tell each other everything!" she protested.

"I can't right now. Not this thing. Not yet," I said.

She nodded her head. "It's to do with Aaron, isn't it?"

I nodded in return.

"I won't ask what happened, then," she promised.

"I will tell you when I'm ready," I said.

"I know you will."

"And you can't talk to him about it." I looked her in the eye.

"You have my word," she swore.

Seemingly Absentmindedly

The first time I faced Aaron after my epiphany was difficult. We had dinner that following Wednesday night. He knew something was wrong but didn't know what. I wasn't going to tell my secret and he didn't push the issue. Over the coming weeks, I became more accepting of my feelings and was able to tuck them away. I had resolved myself to the conclusion that I was far happier with him in my life as a friend than nothing at all. Our relationship returned to what it had been and we thankfully moved forward.

The drama majors from the university were putting on a showing of A *Midsummer Night's Dream* at the park near the museum. For over a week, I would periodically wander to the end of the east wing and watch through the window as they set up the stage and practiced changing the set. I loved that play. Momma would have never allowed such a book in the house, so I had hidden it in my closet to read at night. I would dream of having Oberon's potion to sprinkle into a man's eyes so he would fall madly in love with me. Instead, I had Onoskelis, who would probably keep me single forever.

It was their big day. I watched as the cast and crew scrambled for last-minute preparations. I had only been in one play in my life and that was more than enough for me.

"We going?" Aaron's voice came from behind me.

I turned to face him.

"What are you doing here?" I asked.

"Playing hooky." He grinned. "Seriously, you want to go?"

I smiled. "Yes!"

He smiled back. "I will get us some dinner and meet you back here then."

I returned to my desk, excited for a simple night out.

At a little after two in the afternoon, I heard my cell phone buzz. I answered.

"Hello?"

"Is this Grace Nightingale?" an older, familiar voice came through.

"Yes."

"Hi, there. This is Dr. Watt over at Handschuh. How are you today?"

My heart leaped. I ran to the window separating my office from the seating area and tapped on the glass to call Shawn into the room.

"I'm great! How are you today?" I asked excitedly.

I set the phone on my desk and set it to speaker so Shawn could hear the conversation too.

"I'm good. I'm really good. Your artifact will be ready from the restoration office sometime in the next few weeks, but I wanted to talk to you about the sample we tested."

I felt myself sink a little. Maybe this wasn't the call I had hoped it would be.

I held my breath for a moment before I finally said, "oh?"

"Yes. It was terribly degraded so it took a lot longer to sequence than we'd hoped it would. The good news is, it is definitely a human female," he said.

I watched Shawn's face light up like magic.

"That's great!" I exclaimed.

"That's not all," he continued, "We got the report back from Miami. Carbon dating puts it around six hundred to eight hundred years old. That fits your time frame, doesn't it?"

I was overjoyed. Shawn was jumping up and down waving his arms silently.

"Yes, it does!" I cried.

"Well, I'm glad I could bring you some good news. I'll have the restoration office reach out to you when they're done putting everything back together. You have a good day, Miss Nightingale."

"You too! Thank you!" I pressed the off button on my phone and looked at Shawn.

"It's hers! I knew it! You knew it!" he yelled as he stopped jumping long enough to give me a hug and lifted me off the ground.

At that moment, nothing the bishop had said to me mattered. We had a story to tell the world. As long as I worded my story carefully, there was nothing he could do about it. I didn't see how that day could have gotten any better.

At five-thirty, Aaron appeared in my office doorway with a cardboard box.

"What's that? I pointed to it.

"I didn't have a picnic basket," he said sheepishly.

"What about the cooler we took fishing?" I asked.

His eyes widened as the realization set in. "I'm an idiot."

I laughed so hard I almost fell out of my chair.

The air was unseasonably hot for May but thankfully not humid as we walked together towards the park. I told him about the wonderful news we received from the lab and he seemed excited. In truth, I don't think he fully grasped how important this was to my career, the museum, or the Catholic story but I didn't care. I knew he was at least happy for me, and that was enough.

We set up a blanket on the lawn facing the center of the stage. I was happy to kick off my heels and feel the grass between my toes. He set out a feast of roasted turkey sandwiches, carrots, potato chips, strawberries, and chocolate chip cookies."

"You outdid yourself," I complimented as I looked over the spread.

"When I went to the grocery store, it occurred to me that I had never actually packed a picnic. Snacks, sure. But never anything like this."

"Who did you call?"

"Nicole," he said as he looked down at his plate.

I laughed.

We ate and settled in for the show. It seemed like half of University Circle had turned out for the evening. There was a clown, dressed as a fairy, making balloon animals for kids. Food carts sold hot dogs and elephant ears on the sidewalk. I looked at a pair of teenage lovers laying on their blanket and feeding each other grapes as they gazed into each other's eyes. To my left, an elderly couple sat in folding chairs, holding hands, and eating ice cream cones. I envied them all. Parents around us rounded up their children just before the play began.

It was easy to get lost in one of my favorite plays. The drama department in a park may not have been Broadway, but they were talented nonetheless.

"The course of true love never did run smooth," Lysander called from the stage.

Tell me about it, I thought.

I thought of Toby, Christian, and Xander. They had all ended in heartache. Now the one my heart wanted most did not reciprocate. I glanced over at Aaron. He was leaning back on his forearms with his legs splayed out in front of him. I wanted to tell him how I felt and I wanted to tell him I knew what he said to his coworker. But those were my secrets to bear.

"Better as a friend," I whispered to myself.

After the play, we gave a standing ovation before Aaron walked me back to the museum parking garage to my car. We laughed and critiqued the play in lighthearted fun. We gave our customary hug goodbye but this time was a little different. When we released our embrace, he seemingly absentmindedly gave me a kiss on the cheek before walking away. I stood stunned for a moment. Did he realize what he had just done? Had I imagined it? I touched my cheek where I could still feel the impression from his soft lips. I had not imagined it.

As I drove home, my mind reeled. Maybe he did have feelings for me too. Maybe it was just a kiss as friends. He had never kissed me like that before, though. He had kissed the top of my head in friendly affection before. This was just a dash on my cheek. It wasn't passionate. It wasn't heartfelt. It couldn't have meant anything.

When I opened my front door, Hope hissed at me and ran for the bedroom. That usually meant one thing. I looked to the left and Onoskelis was standing in the kitchen doorway.

"I really don't want to deal with you right now." I was instantly exacerbated at the sight of her and put my keys in a bowl by the door. "I had a nice evening and I'd like to end on a high note."

"'A high note!'" she repeated in disbelief. "He kissed you! He toys with your emotions!"

"I seriously doubt he did it on purpose."

I slipped my shoes off and carried them towards the bedroom. Onoskelis followed.

"He acts like he does not love you. He says he does not love you. Then he does *this!*" She was shrieking. "You are a fly in his web! He toys with you before he devours you!"

"You're being a bit dramatic."

"You may mock me, but in your heart you know I am right; else I would not be here." Her voice became lower.

"You are here because *you* want to be here. I've told you to leave a thousand times."

"I could not be here if you did not want me here," she reminded me.

"That's obviously not true. You've been skulking under my house and whispering lies in my ear for two years now."

"I cannot be here if you do not want me here," she repeated. "And I will not leave until I've had what I want."

"You're giving me a headache and ruining my day," I said as I rubbed my temples.

"He does not love you."

"You think I don't know that?!" I hadn't realized I could yell that loud before. "You think I don't know that he doesn't want me? I know it! I heard him say it! He doesn't have a reason to lie. It hurts enough without you sinking your claws into my wounds. Now go away!"

She bared her teeth at me before disappearing.

I crawled into bed, still half-dressed, and buried my head under a pillow. I touched my cheek again. I promised myself I would not read more into it than there was. We were friends and he absentmindedly kissed me on the cheek. That was all there was to it.

Figure it Out

My third-floor office at the museum had a glass welcome area that overlooked the mezzanine. In the welcome room, there were a couch and a few comfy-looking chairs (that were terribly uncomfortable) around a coffee table. Along the wall were artifacts from my private collection, a few potted plants, and photos of me on my travels such as my obligatory picture with Pope Benedict the XVI, shaking hands with celebrities who had hired me to authenticate their collections, etc. I hated that room. One glass wall looked into the hallway, one glass wall overlooked the mezzanine, one windowed wall looked into my actual office, and the only solid actual *wall* was a bland color of taupe. The carpet was a drab shade of brown and the furniture was white. Nothing about it was my taste at all but I had an impression to make on people who came to me professionally and the interior decorator the museum had hired assured me that forcing people's attention to the artifacts and photos was the way to do it.

That day my focus wasn't on the drab walls or the painting of St. Jerome. I stood in my office smiling at the tall, thin man in wire-rimmed glasses who sat on one of those awful chairs. He had his hands behind his head, his legs crossed, and he was grinning at me.

I walked out of my office and into the welcome room.

"I'm sorry, sir. I don't have any visitors scheduled today." I crossed my arms and smiled back at him.

"You might want to pencil me in." He grinned wide. "I talked Chef into making a little something special for us."

"Hmm. I might be able to work you in after all."

The door to the hall suddenly swung open and Shawn stepped in. He looked between the two of us like a dear in headlights.

"I'm sorry. I can come back later" he apologized and tried to exit.

"It's okay. We can talk in my office." He was radiating distress and I felt like I shouldn't make him wait. I turned to Aaron. "Give me a moment?"

Without waiting for Aaron to respond, Shawn and I stepped into the smaller room that housed my desk, current projects, paperwork, and what-have-you. Through the windowed wall, I could see Aaron still in the chair but I didn't think I needed to close the privacy curtains.

I leaned against my desk and faced Shawn. "What's up?"

He took a deep breath. I'd never known him to be so unglued.

"It's- it's my sister, Ashley." His chin started to quiver. "My mom was crying and it was hard to understand her. She was hurt bad in some accident at Kingsley Field."

"Good, God. I'm so sorry. Why are you here and not on a plane to Oregon?"

"I didn't want to just up and leave you. We still have a lot of work on that reliquary exhibit and-"

"Don't be ridiculous." I threw my hands in the air. "That hunk of junk is four hundred years old and it's not going anywhere. You need to be with your family."

His lower lip quivered. "Thank you," he whispered.

I smiled and pushed myself off the desk. I stood on my tiptoes and wrapped my arms around his neck. He hugged me back and tried not to cry. I escorted him back through the sitting area, past Aaron, and to the hall door.

I squeezed his hand. "Let me know when your plane lands safely."

"I will. Thank you." He turned and left.

I turned back to Aaron. His entire body language had changed. He was stiff and seemed upset. His eyes were wide and he had a strange look on his face.

"So, about that lunch." I smiled.

"I'm not hungry." He stood up.

"What?" I was genuinely confused.

"I'm just going to head out." He started for the door.

"Whoa. What the fuck?" I got in between him and the door.

"I just want to leave. Okay?"

"No!" I yelled. "Not okay! What the Hell, Aaron?"

He stepped back and pursed his lips. "Maybe I don't like seeing you hugging all over some other guy."

I stared at him in total disbelief. "You cannot possibly be telling me you're jealous."

He exhaled loudly through his nose.

I stepped towards him. "No. You don't get to do that. You're the one that said YOU don't want ME, remember?"

"Yeah, but- Wait…when…?"

"No! No buts! First of all, Shawn is a great friend and colleague. There is nothing romantic there. I have told you that before. It's *your* problem if you refuse to believe it. Don't you *dare* make it mine! Second, you don't get a say in my romantic life when you're not a part of it. I am not going to stay single forever just because you don't want me but you don't want anyone else to either!" I suddenly became aware of the people in the hall who could hear and see me through the glass. "You need to take some time and figure out what exactly it is you want and then tell me." I opened the door. "NOW you can leave."

I am A Spirit Wrought

It was late in the afternoon on a Saturday. There was a steady, light rain outside. I'd opened the windows to let the cool, fresh breeze through the house. I'd spent the entire day in fuzzy socks, flannel pajama bottoms, and a hooded sweatshirt while cleaning almost everything except the ceiling. The floors shined, the sink in the kitchen was empty and the toilet was clean enough to eat out of.

When I had awakened that morning I'd had an impending feeling of dread. Something horrible was just going to happen. I just didn't know what. I decided the safest place to be was at home. The only horrible thing in my house lived in the well beneath me. Aaron and I hadn't spoken in three days. I decided it meant he was taking my advice and thinking about what he honestly wanted. I didn't want to just sit around and wait for his decision but I didn't want to go anywhere either. My attempts to spend a lazy day on the couch with Hope proved futile, so I cleaned. The theory was that giving myself something to focus on would subdue the horrible feeling in the pit of my stomach. I didn't work.

I was standing in the living room with my hands on my hips and staring up at the fan blades. I was trying to decide how best to wash them when there was a knock at the door. I shoved a lock of hair up and out of my face and back into the pile on top of my head on the way to answer it. I didn't need to open it or guess who was on the other side. Hope's eager pawing and loud purrs told me exactly who it was.

Dark circles under his eyes told me he hadn't slept in quite some time. He was unusually fidgety and seemed excited but upset.

"We need to talk," he said flatly.

I stepped aside and let him into the entryway without thinking about the succubus below us.

"Is this a 'cup of tea and conversation' talk or a 'get something off your chest and I end up crying' talk?" I half-joked.

He looked straight into my eyes. I felt my stomach flip.

"What's going on?" I asked.

All light-heartedness had left the room.

"I got a call the day before yesterday at work. I've been invited to help at a new site that was found in Turkey."

"That's good, isn't it? How long until you come back?"

"A couple of years. Maybe. At least."

I felt my heart stop and I stumbled backward. Hope hissed and ran towards the bedroom. I looked past Aaron to the corner behind the front door. Onoskelis stood in the shadow, grinning viciously. I looked back at Aaron. The edges of my vision began to go black. I knew this feeling. I squeezed my eyes shut tight and shook my head. My hair fell out of its pile and cascaded around me. I pushed it back out of my face and looked back at the door. She was gone. I looked back into his beautiful maple eyes. They were flooding with suppressed tears. I tried to catch my breath.

"What do you mean 'a couple of years'?"

"It depends on what we find and how much I'm needed. And funding, of course," he answered.

"You just got here! You just started *this* job a few years ago! You told him 'no', right?"

Aaron broke our gaze and looked at the floor.

"No. No." I shook my head. "You said you were here because you were ready to settle down!"

"Maybe I'm not as ready as I thought I was. Besides, this is *Turkey*. This is my dream!" "You told me not to worry. You said you weren't going anywhere!" I yelled.

"I think you were right. I need to figure some things out. I need to take this job."

My mind was reeling.

"I think you need to go," I said in the calmest, steadiest voice I could muster.

He stepped towards me.

"Gracie-" He sounded pleading; almost apologetic.

"Now," I insisted.

He dropped his arms, turned, and saw himself out the front door.

I collapsed on the floor in tears. I couldn't breathe. My heart had stopped. My stomach felt like a stone.

"You see. He chooses to sacrifice your happiness to save himself. You should have let me-" Onoskelis began.

I looked at her and screamed. I screamed as if someone had been trying to murder me. I felt like I was dying. I screamed out every ounce of rage I held for her and for Aaron. I screamed in anguish for my broken heart. I screamed until my lungs were empty and I lost consciousness.

When I awoke, it was nearly dark. My devoted black cat was lying next to my face on the floor, waiting for me to rouse. I sat upright. My body didn't feel like it was mine. It responded to my commands, but nothing felt real. I went to the bathroom and washed my face with cold water. As I replayed the interaction with Aaron in my mind, I heard the words Uncle James had spoken on his death bed. Being in love would kill you. I looked at my reflection and touched the stone around my neck. I had to talk to Aaron before he flew halfway around the world and I never saw him again. I changed into jeans and a sweatshirt before rushing out the door.

I had a twenty-minute drive to rehearse what I was going to say. I kept vaulting from enraged confrontation to desperate pleading. Nothing sounded right. I kept running it over and over in my mind right up until I knocked on his apartment door.

He opened it.

"I'm in love with you," I blurted out.

That wasn't any part of anything I had rehearsed. It should have been alleviating to admit it to him. Instead, I still felt hollow and hurt.

"Gracie..."

He closed the door and pulled me to him... and kissed me. It was a true, passionate, sincere kiss. Nothing else existed in that moment. My anger and pain disintegrated for one fleeting minute. He pulled back and looked into my eyes.

"I know how you feel about me. It's the same way I feel about you," he admitted.

"Then why are you leaving?" I felt the pain return.

"Because I love you, Gracie. I always have. More than anyone else alive in this world. I would die if you hurt me."

"Why would I hurt you?" I protested.

"I don't know." He threw his arms in the air. "What if you find someone else? What if—" he paused. "What if you die like Hannah?"

"Aaron." I stepped towards him. "I'm not Hannah or any of the other women in your past."

I saw tears in his eyes as he said, "I can't take that chance."

It was a thousand arrows straight through my heart.

"I guess this is 'goodbye' then," I choked.

"I'm sorry, Gracie."

He pulled me in for another kiss. It was much longer, as a goodbye kiss should be. When we separated, the corners of my eyes started to go dark. I frantically looked out his apartment window. It had stopped raining hours ago and the full moon was encircled with a halo. I looked past his arm and saw Onoskelis smirking in the corner of the living room

"No. No. No! You can't!" I yelled at her.

Aaron looked over his shoulder. "Who are you talking to?"

Everything went black.

When I opened my eyes, Aaron was sprawled on the floor next to me.

"No," I whispered.

His eyes were bloodshot and glassy. His face was purpled. Around his neck was a quartz stone, worn from years of fidgeting, on a silver chain that cut into his skin.

"No," I whispered again.

I heard Onoskelis cackle and I looked up.

"Why?!" I screamed.

"I am a spirit wrought. I only come when I am called," she said. "I told you you needed me."

www.ingramcontent.com/pod-product-compliance
Lightning Source LLC
Chambersburg PA
CBHW010448010526
44118CB00019B/2506